IMAGES
of America

GREEN RIDGE

On the Cover: St. Joseph's Foundling Home. Since 1888, St. Joseph's Center has provided much-needed services for the community with an overabundance of care and compassion. (Courtesy of St. Joseph's Center.)

IMAGES
of America

GREEN RIDGE

Margo L. Azzarelli

ARCADIA
PUBLISHING

ISBN 978-0-7385-9231-2

Published by Arcadia Publishing
Charleston, South Carolina

Printed in the United States of America

Library of Congress Control Number: 2011940554

For all general information, please contact Arcadia Publishing:
Telephone 843-853-2070
Fax 843-853-0044
E-mail sales@arcadiapublishing.com
For customer service and orders:
Toll-Free 1-888-313-2665

Visit us on the Internet at www.arcadiapublishing.com

This book is dedicated to Mark Boock; his wonderful collection will keep Scranton's history alive for generations to come.

Contents

ACKNOWLEDGMENTS

First and foremost, I wish to send out a big thank you to my brilliant daughter, Marnie—this is her book as much as mine—to my husband, Dominick, for being my guy Friday, and to Dr. Ta-Ta's and Gram and Gramp for all their love and support.

This book would not have come to fruition without the help and contributions of the following people: Greg and Mark Boock, Robert J. Walker, Erin Vosgien and my editor Abby Henry, Frank McDonald, Sr. Maryalice Jacquinot, the Brunetti family, Ryan and Yore Antiques, Kathy Norton, the Lackawanna Historical Society, Jesse Hinkley, Irwin Adler, the Sinkaus family, Constance Denchy, Kristine Pocius, Christine and Jack Schaefer, Joanne and Bill Hector, Virginia McGregor, Marywood archivist Jim Sullivan, and "Determinate" by Lemonade Mouth.

And a very heartfelt thank you goes to the following sisters of the Immaculate Heart of Mary (IHM): Sr. Eleanor Desaulniers, MBA, IHM consultant archivist; Sr. Francine Fasolka, MA, IHM director of communications; Sr. Michel Keenan, PhD, IHM congregation historian; and Sr. Anitra Nemotko, PhD, IHM congregation archivist, for their generous contribution of Chapter Seven's pictures and text and for the wonderful services the IHM sisters have given to our community for over 100 years.

INTRODUCTION

Long before the Honorable George Sanderson started laying out streets and developing buildings, the Indians of the Capoose Village followed the Minisink Trail, which crossed the Lackawanna River, in order to join their Monsey family members. *Monsey*, as in Monsey Avenue, is a derivative of *Minisi* (Minisank Trail). While most of the credit should go to the Sanderson family for the development of Green Ridge, some must be reserved for the Griffins, a Quaker family who resided in the area in the early 1800s, when it was still a wilderness. Their home was located in what is now Green Ridge Corners. In 1815, it was called Griffin's Corners. Later, in 1826, the Griffin family clearing was connected to the outside world with the construction of the Philadelphia and Great Bend Turnpike. Only a few houses and a one-room schoolhouse stood along what is now East Market Street, and there was a covered bridge where the street crossed the Lackawanna River.

The Griffins, along with other Quaker families in the area, attempted to raft lumber down the Lackawanna River, but unfortunately, their rafts were destroyed somewhere near Old Forge. In an attempt to solve the problem, they blasted out a channel but with no success. However, a section of the river is named Quaker Falls in honor of their efforts.

Among the area's first settlers were John Dings, Henry Whaling, and Michael Lutz. At the time, the land was bountiful with plants and animals. Hank Whaling's farm did not have a house on it, only an orchard, a barn, and a rail fence. Envisioning the possibilities, George Sanderson purchased it and proceeded to transform a wilderness into a village. He also purchased a tract of land from Vine Street to the Lackawanna River. The two areas of land that Sanderson owned were separated by a knoll that was two square blocks long, one-half square block wide, and 30 to 40 feet high.

Due to a shortage of work, Sanderson was able to initiate the help of the Lackawanna Iron and Coal Company employees to strip down the knoll until it was flat, thereby connecting the two tracts of land. The ridge that ran between the two pieces of Sanderson's property is what gave Green Ridge its name. Sanderson Avenue, appropriately named for its founder, was where he built his palatial mansion in 1865. Today, it is the site of the Green Ridge Nursing Home. George was an early entrepreneur; he was also one of the organizers of the Scranton & Providence Passenger Railroad Company. The company built a horsecar line through Green Ridge to entice new residents to the area, which succeeded in its goal.

The new residential section grew quickly; with a growing population, schools and churches were built out of necessity. The earliest church services were held in the old Delaware & Hudson depot on East Market Street. The Episcopalians were the first to organize a church in Green Ridge in 1868. The Presbyterians followed in 1875, and the third congregation was composed of Methodists in 1876. The first public school, built in 1870, was located on the corner of Dickson Avenue and Electric Street. The two-story building was called the "Breaker" school. The Delaware & Hudson Railroad opened the first mines in Green Ridge and built the Von Storch Breaker in 1859 on the Green Ridge Flats. It later opened the Manville Breaker on Glen Street and the

Dickson Breaker on Meylert Avenue. These mines remained opened until the 1950s. The original business district was located at the corner of Green Ridge Street and Dickson Avenue; around the beginning of the 20th century, it transferred to Sanderson Avenue and East Market Street, also known as Green Ridge Corners. Many businesses have come and gone over the years, such as the Roosevelt Theatre, Burke's Pharmacy, and the Green Ridge Bank. However, the Howard M. Snowdon Funeral Home has remained a part of Green Ridge since 1907. Industries such as the Green Ridge Iron Works, the Scranton Glass Company, the Paragon Plaster and Supply Company, and the Scranton Pump Works, which manufactured mining pumps, all lined Green Ridge Street. The Scranton Lace Company was a major source of employment for the city up until its closing in 2002. The company was the largest producer of Nottingham lace in the world.

As the historic neighborhood grew, its serene beauty attracted many and became home to some of Scranton's prominent citizens, like Mayors J. Benjamin Dimmick and Howard Snowdon; architect Edward H. Davis; publisher E.J. Lynett; contractors James Sweeney and Conrad Schroader; and attorneys F.L. Hitchcock and E.B. Sturges, who organized the Scranton Suburban Electric Railway Company in order to build the first electric trolley that ran from downtown Scranton to Green Ridge. Among the more recent notable residents are Vice Pres. Joseph Biden and the late governor of Pennsylvania Robert P. Casey.

Even though times have changed, Green Ridge has managed to remain a delightful neighborhood with a rich history that oddly enough has rarely been written about . . . until now.

One

Early Prominent Residents

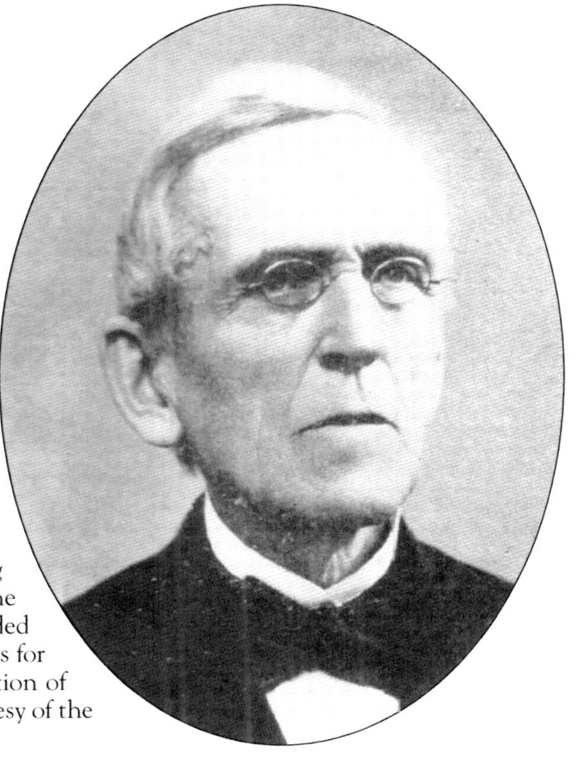

Hon. George Sanderson. He is the founder and developer of Green Ridge. Originally a native of Boston, he moved to Towanda, Pennsylvania, where he practiced law for a time. He came to Scranton in 1855 and organized one of the first banking firms in the city. In 1865, he purchased the Whaling farm and proceeded to have wooded the area surveyed into wide streets and lots for building homes. This new residential section of Scranton was named Green Ridge. (Courtesy of the Lackawanna Historical Society.)

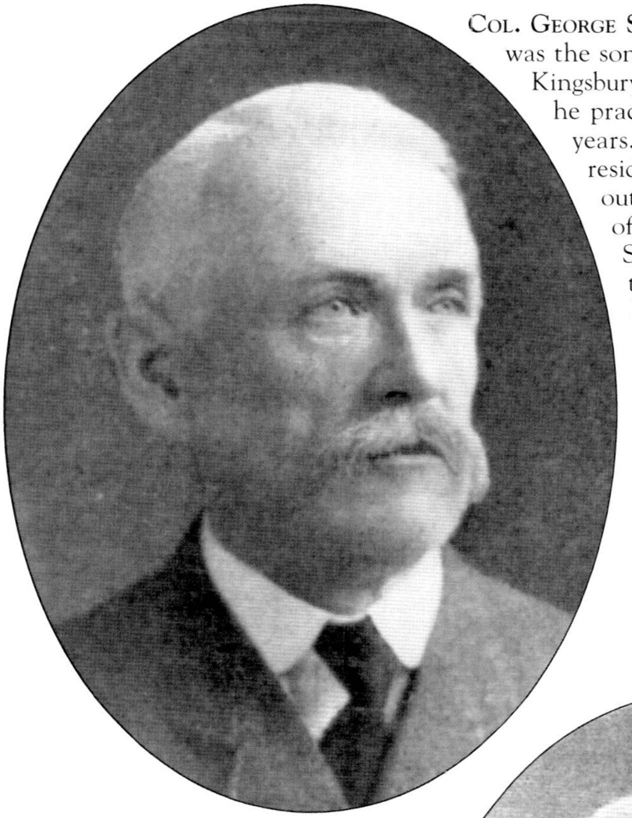

Col. George Sanderson. Col. George Sanderson was the son of George Sanderson and Marion Kingsbury. Following in his father's footsteps, he practiced law in Philadelphia for two years. In 1873, he became a permanent resident of Green Ridge and gained an outstanding reputation for being one of the leading attorneys in the city. Sanderson succeeded his father in the management of the family's Green Ridge property following his father's death in 1886. (Courtesy of the Lackawanna Historical Society.)

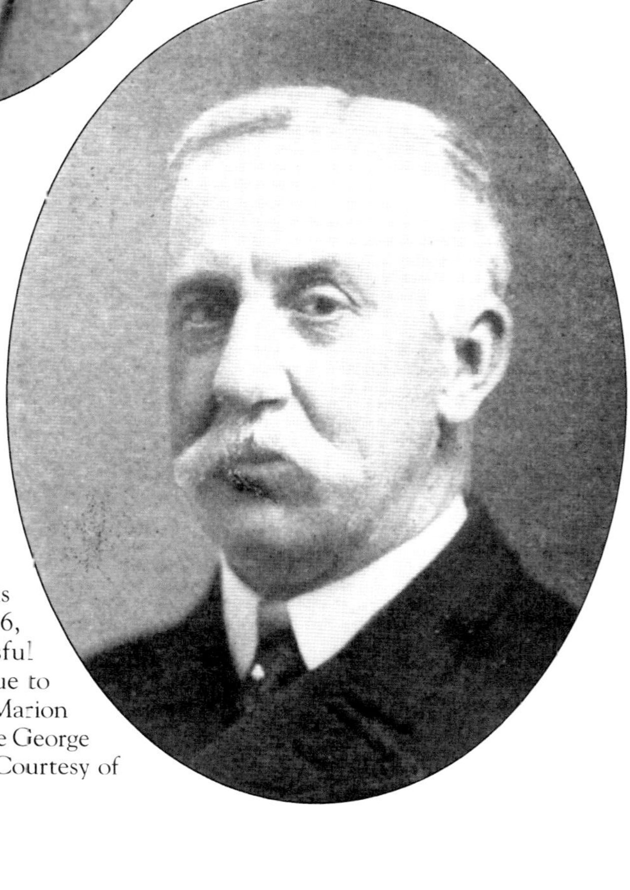

Edward Baker Sturges. E.B. Sturges settled in Scranton in the late 1860s and immediately began to practice law. In 1886, he organized the Suburban Street Passenger Railway, the first electric trolley system on this continent. On November 30, 1886, the trolley made its first successful trip from North Washington Avenue to Green Ridge Street. Sturges married Marion Sanderson, daughter of the Honorable George Sanderson, on September 2, 1873. (Courtesy of the Lackawanna Historical Society.)

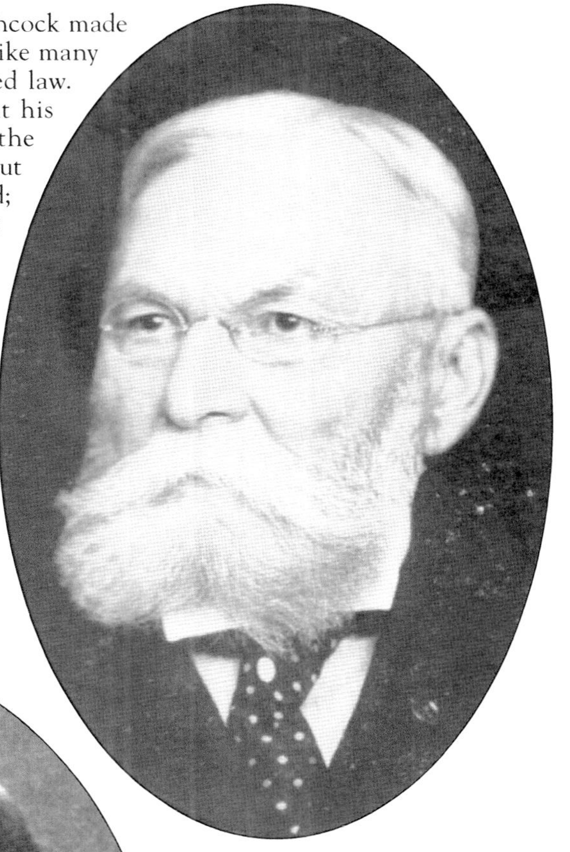

FREDERICK LYMAN HITCHCOCK. F.L. Hitchcock made Scranton his home at a very young age. Like many of his Green Ridge neighbors, he studied law. He was admitted to the bar in 1860, but his successful practice was interrupted by the Civil War. When President Lincoln sent out the call, Hitchcock immediately answered; he was mustered into the 132nd Regiment of Pennsylvania Volunteers and bravely fought in the bloody battles of Antietam, Fredericksburg, and Chancellorsville. In December 1863, he became lieutenant colonel of the 25th Regiment US Colored Troop. Upon his return to the city, he was elected the first clerk of the Mayor's Court of Scranton and, in 1878, was appointed the first prothonotary of Lackawanna County. Colonel Hitchcock became a resident of Green Ridge in 1881 and was very involved in the development of the community. (Courtesy of the Lackawanna Historical Society.)

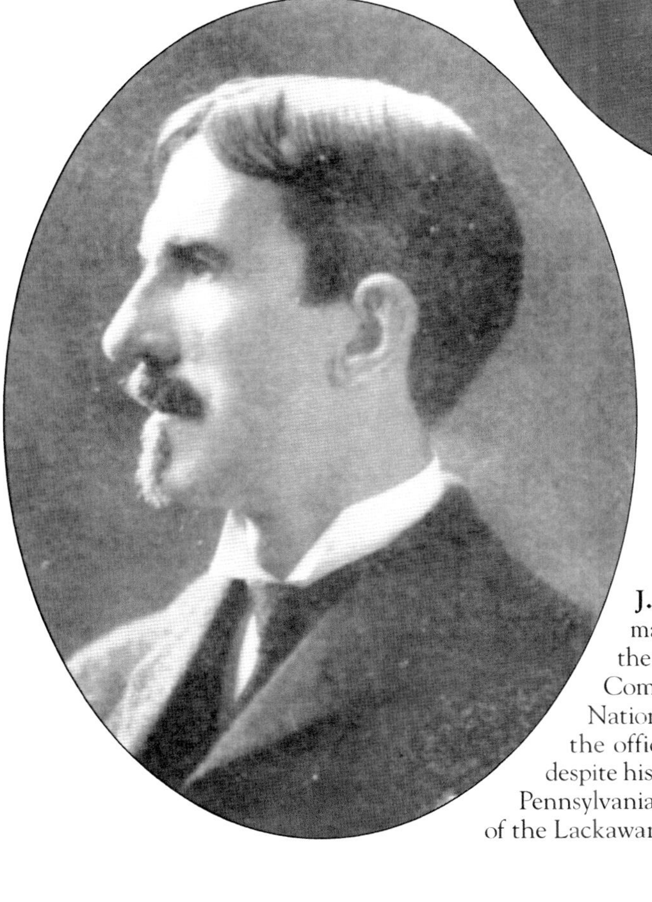

J. BENJAMIN DIMMICK. The 13th mayor of Scranton, Dimmick served as the first president of the Scranton Lace Company and vice president of the First National Bank. In 1914, he made a run for the office of US senator but was defeated despite his efforts. He was also a trustee for the Pennsylvania Oral School for the Deaf. (Courtesy of the Lackawanna Historical Society.)

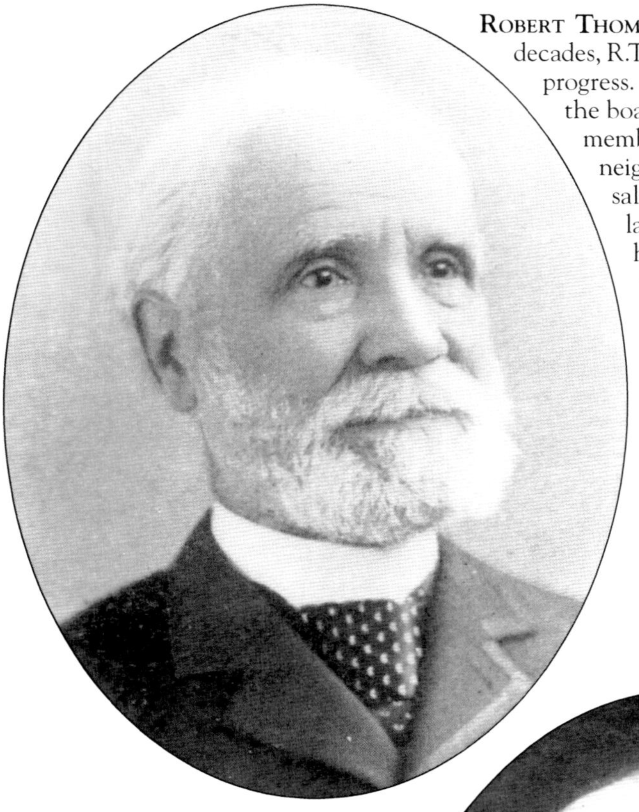

ROBERT THOMPSON BLACK. For more than three decades, R.T. Black was instrumental in the city's progress. He represented the Eighth Ward on the board of control and was also an active member of the poor board. He joined his neighbor E.B. Sturges in the fight against saloon keepers for violation of the liquor laws in the 1870s. During his later years, he withdrew from the public eye due to declining health. (Courtesy of the Lackawanna Historical Society.)

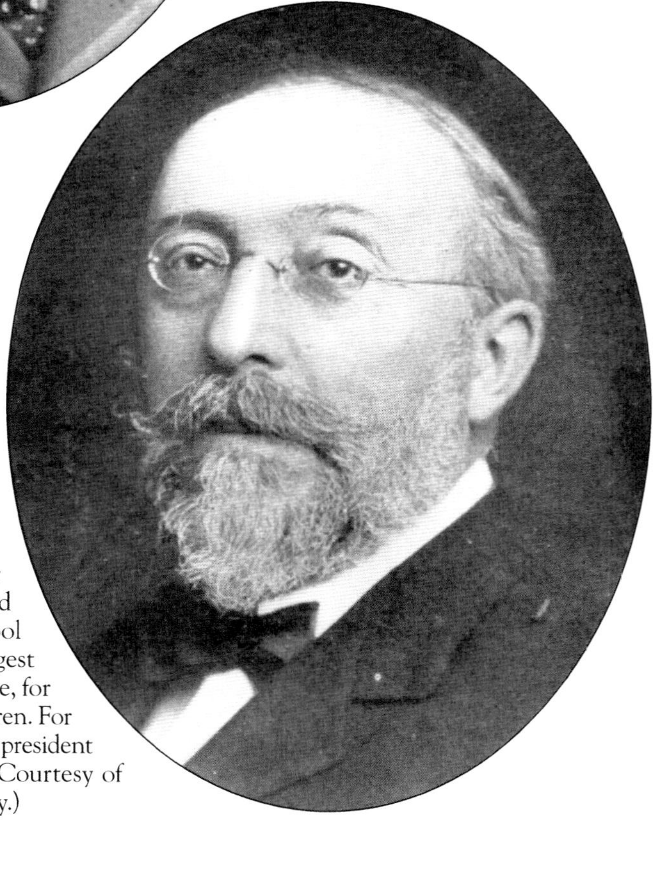

HENRY BELIN JR. Henry began his business life with E.I. DuPont de Nemours and Company, powder manufacturers, as president. In 1870, he became best identified with the establishment of the Pennsylvania Oral School for the Deaf. He was one of the charter founders and served on the board of trustees as treasurer. The school recognized him as one of its strongest supporters, which was not a surprise, for he was the father of three deaf children. For a time, he served as director and vice president of the Scranton Lace Company. (Courtesy of the Lackawanna Historical Society.)

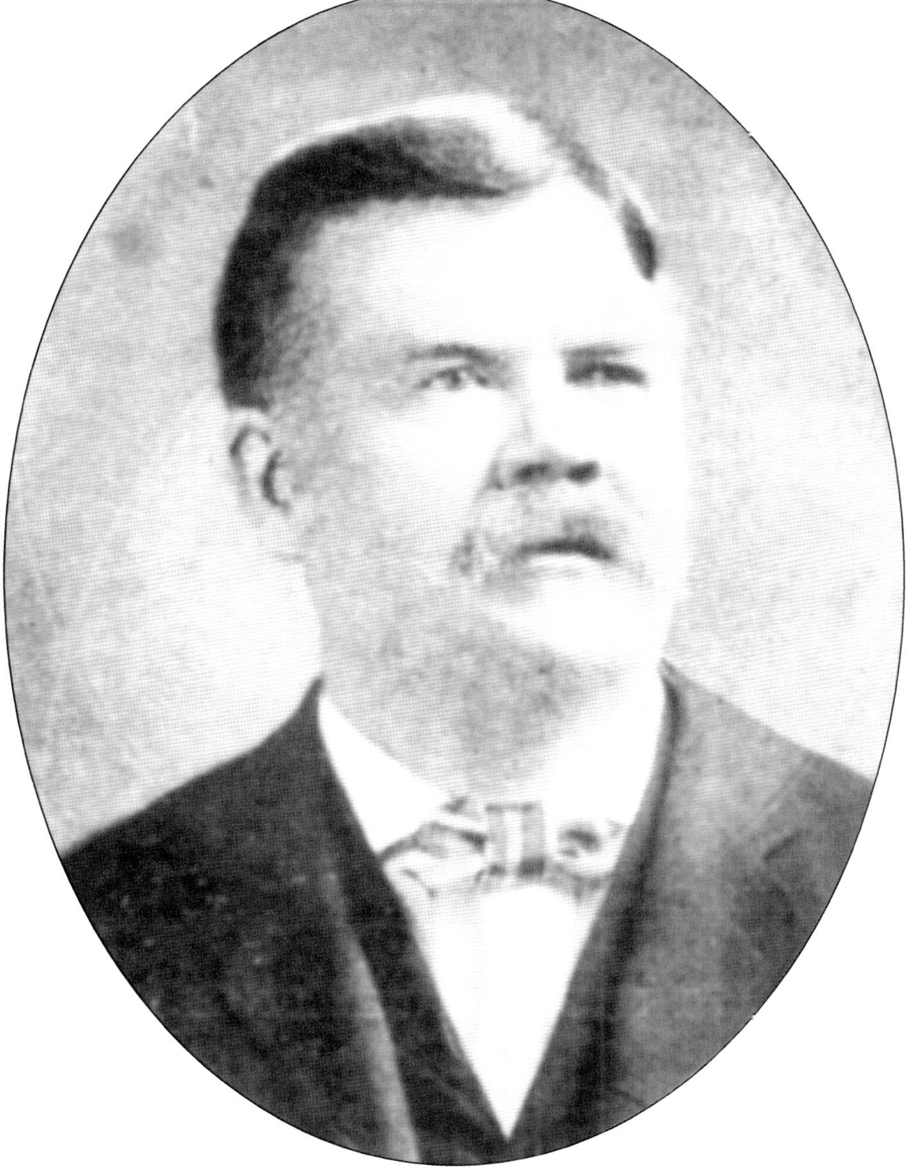

EDWARD J. LYNETT. Editor and proprietor of the *Scranton Times*, E.J. Lynett's first job was not at a newspaper but in a coal breaker. When he reached the age of 16, he became a deputy clerk in the mayor's office for three years. He then decided to try his hand at the law, but his decision to become a lawyer was soon overshadowed by his passion for the written word. Lynett took a job as a reporter for the *Scranton Free Press*. He stayed with the publication until October 10, 1895, when he purchased the *Scranton Times*. While the newspaper always remained his first priority, he donated much of his time to the community. He served as secretary for Scranton's poor district for 13 years, as a member of the mine cave commission from 1911 to 1913, and, for several years, as director of the Associated Charities of Scranton. He also held the office of president for the Paragon Plaster and Supply Company on Green Ridge Street. (Courtesy of the Lackawanna Historical Society.)

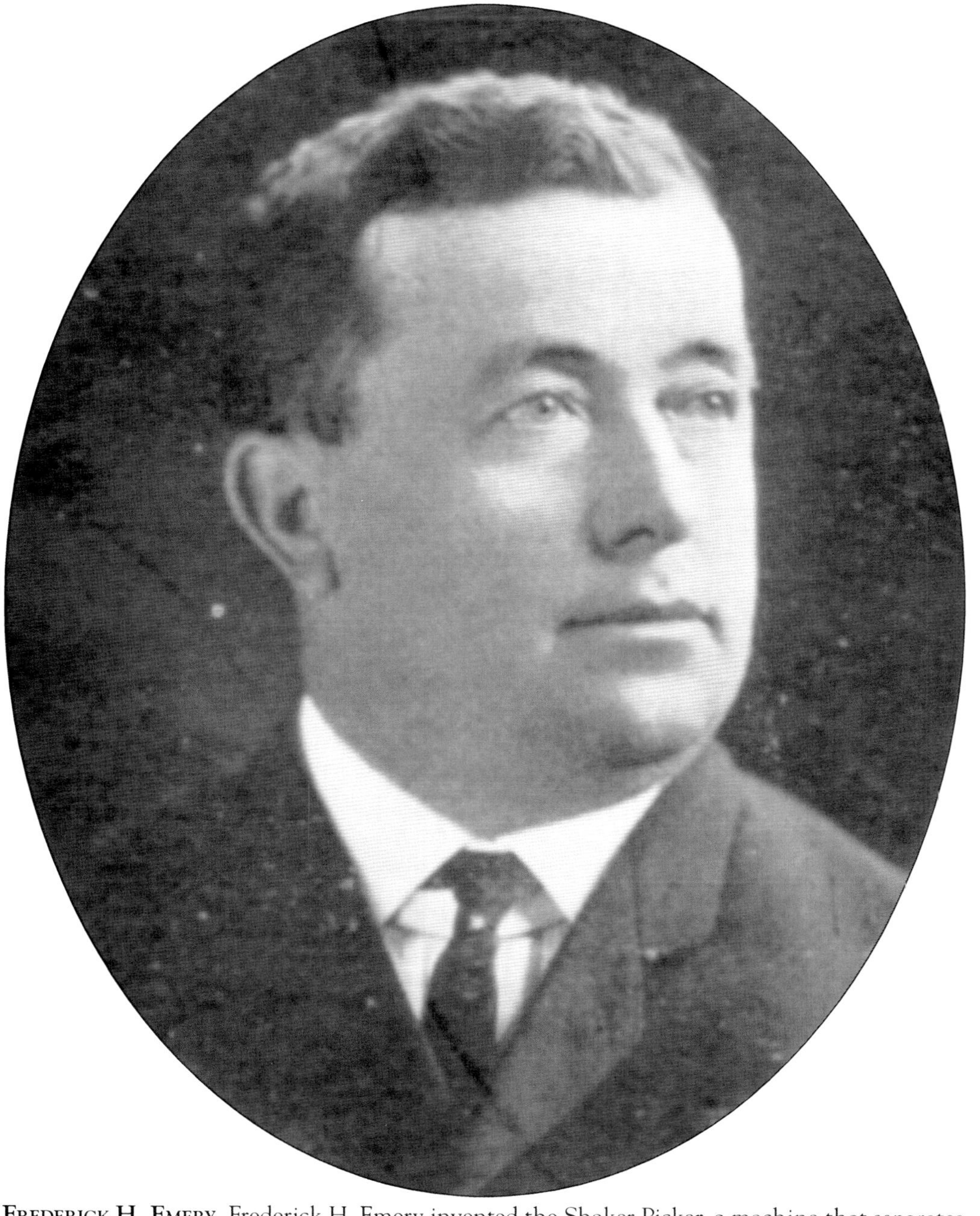

Frederick H. Emery. Frederick H. Emery invented the Shaker Picker, a machine that separates slate from coal. Emery was not the first to design this type of machine in order to replace breaker boys in this dangerous work, but his invention lost less coal than the others. The Shaker Picker was used by many of the leading coal companies in the anthracite region. The idea stemmed from not a dream but from years of hard work as a breaker boy in local mines. For 14 years, he worked on perfecting the machine, and in 1907, the firm of F.H. Emery and Company was formed. It is gratifying to note that he was able to quit his day job at the post office and live off the profits of his brainchild. (Courtesy of the Lackawanna Historical Society.)

Conrad Schroeder. Some refer to Conrad Schroeder as the man who built Scranton. He served as master builder and president of the Carlucci Stone Company and director of the Lackawanna Hospital, Scranton Lace Company, and the Paragon Plaster and Supply Company. Schroeder constructed hundreds of private residences and public buildings in the city. A few of them are the Watres Armory, Hotel Jermyn, Albright Memorial Library, and Scranton City Hall. (Courtesy of the Lackawanna Historical Society.)

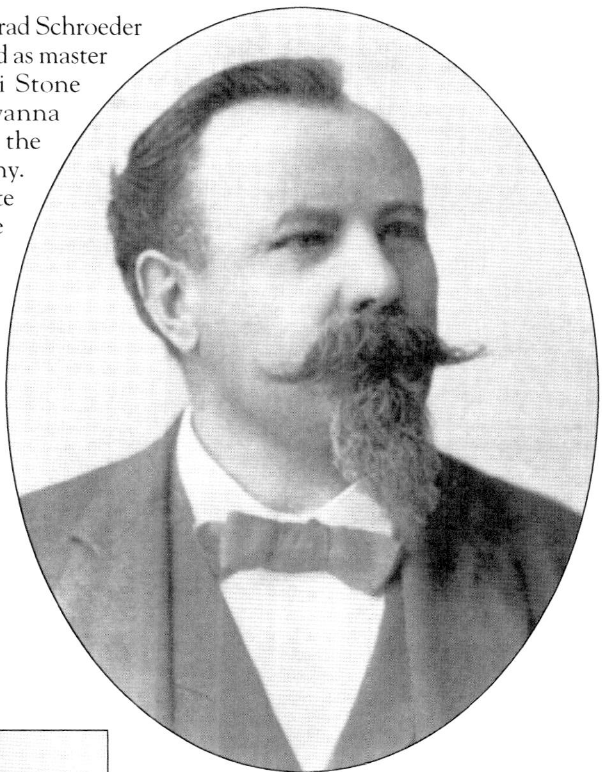

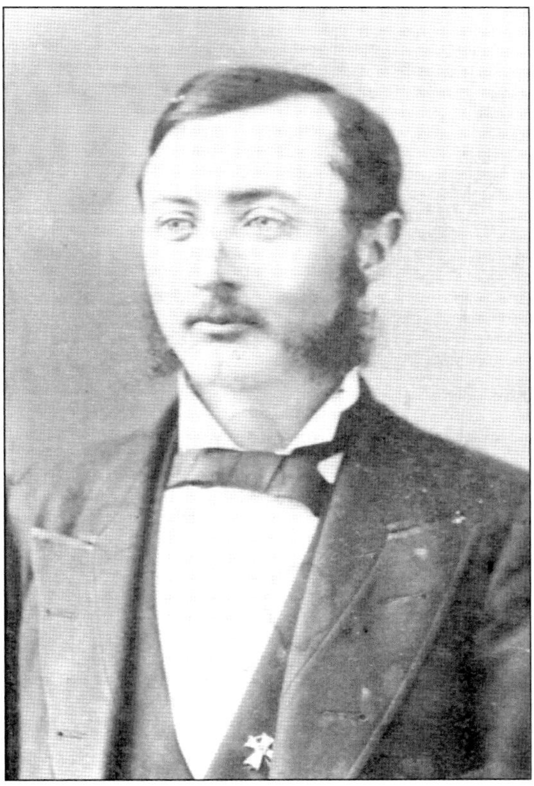

James Hall Rittenhouse. The Rittenhouse family can be traced back to Mathias Rittenhouse of Holland; the surname originated in 1591 when he was knighted. J.H. established himself in Scranton as a civil and mining engineer. His office was located downtown in the Connell Building. In 1892, he was hired as chief engineer for the construction of the Winton Dam. Many companies engaged his services, and he enjoyed a long, prosperous career until his death in 1925. (Courtesy of the Lackawanna Historical Society.)

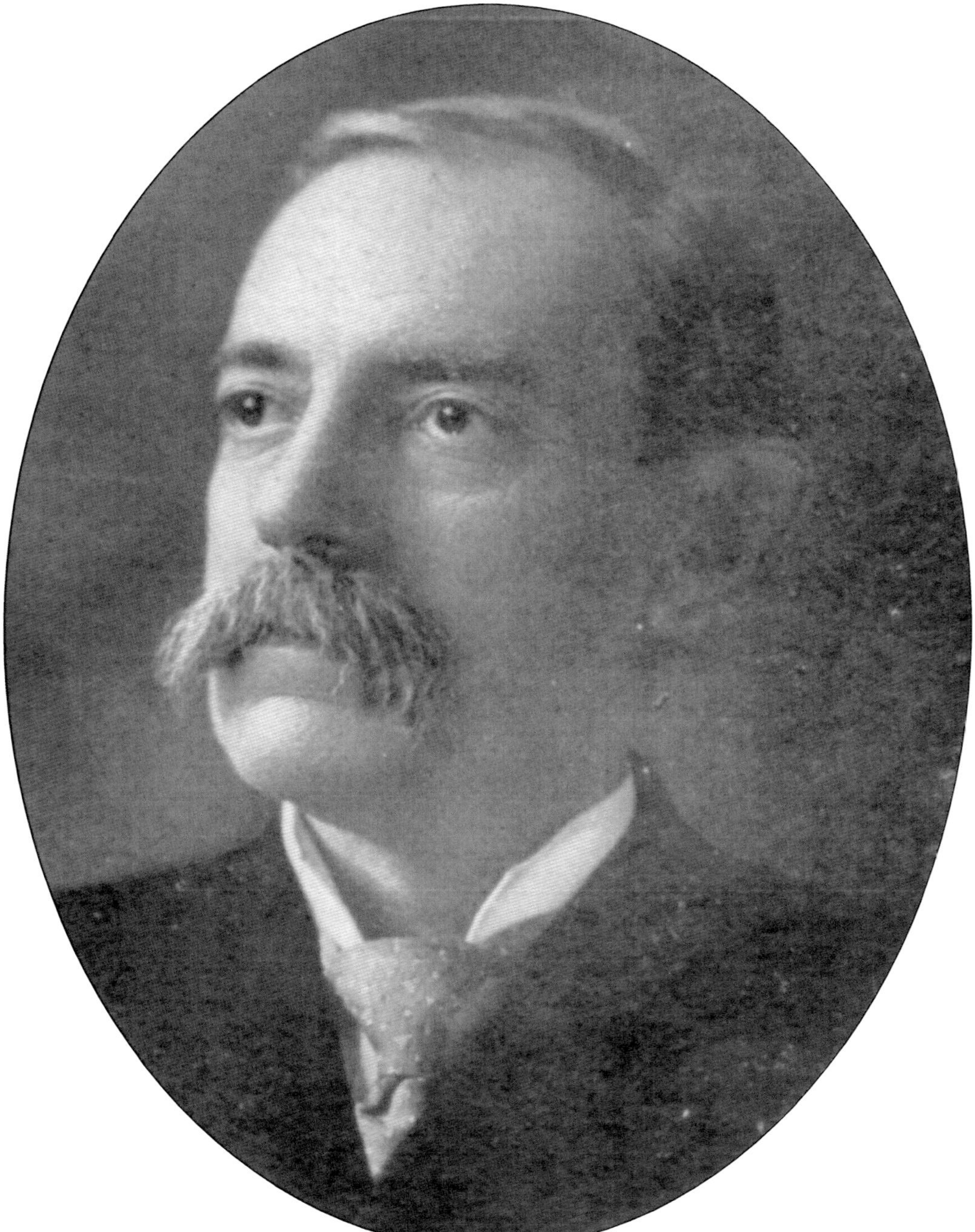

Charles Henry Lindsey. When Lindsey arrived in Scranton in 1870, he found employment with Hunt Brothers and Company. In addition, he was the manager of the Academy of Music from 1877 to 1891. He married Annie Mitchell in 1886, and the couple resided at their Green Ridge home on North Washington Avenue. (Courtesy of the Lackawanna Historical Society.)

Two

Charity Hill

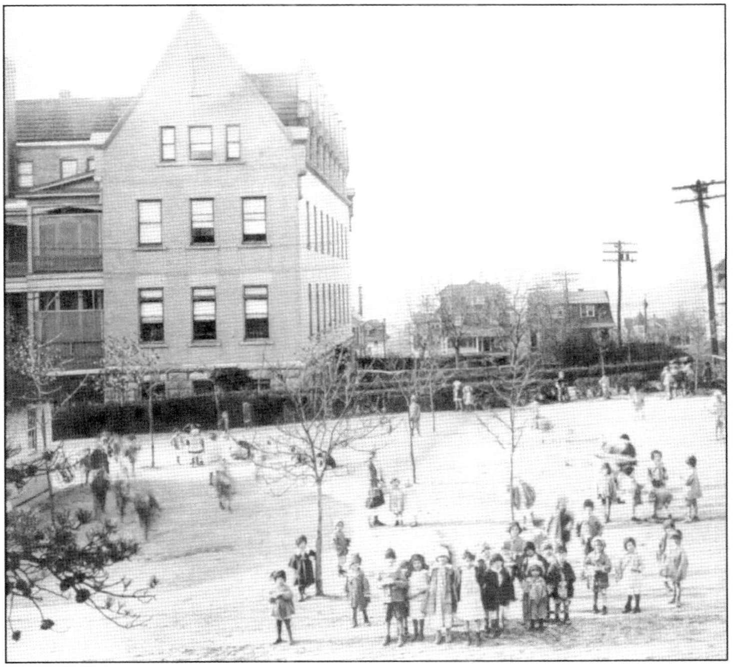

St. Joseph's Foundling Home. St. Joseph's began in 1890 with the help of a small group of women and the Sisters, Servants of the Immaculate Heart of Mary, in order to address the problem of deserted orphans in the city of Scranton. Babies and children arrived daily, and the organization quickly outgrew three different buildings before settling in its present location on Adams Avenue. In this photograph, the children are enjoying themselves on the playground. (Courtesy of St. Joseph's Center.)

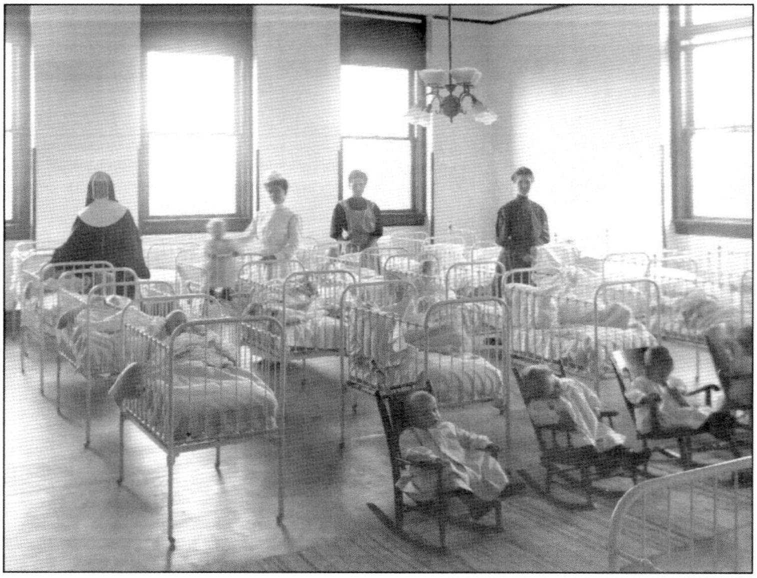

Maternity Ward. Eventually, St. Joseph's expanded its services to include helping unwed mothers, and the facility's name was changed to St. Joseph's Children and Maternity Hospital. In 1927, St. Joseph's housed 40 young women and 166 children and babies. (Courtesy of St. Joseph's Center.)

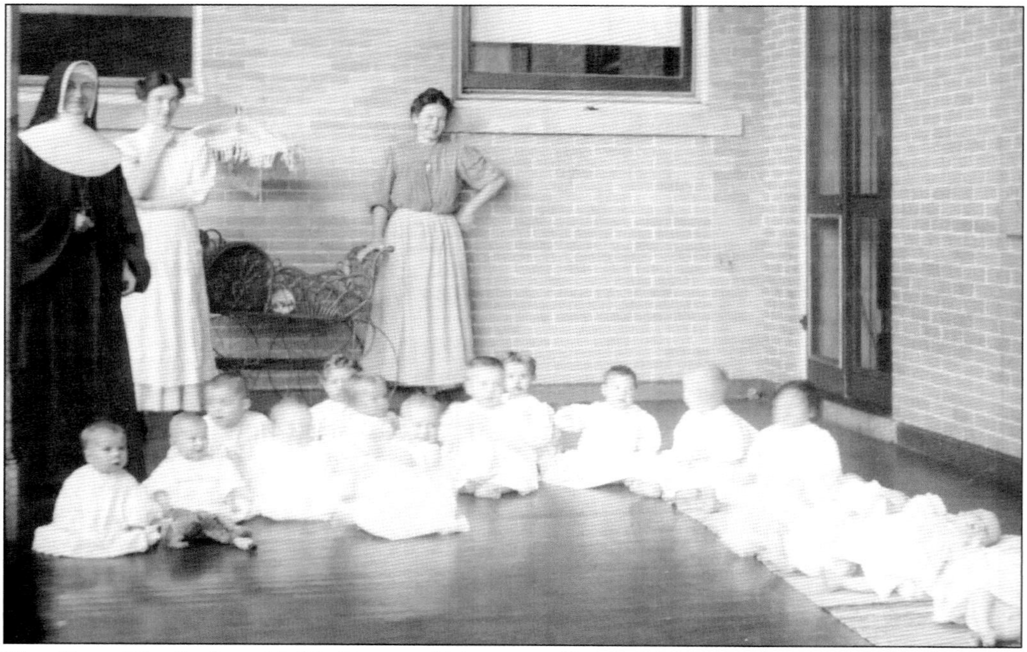

Nap Time. The St. Joseph's Children and Maternity Hospital became a licensed child placement center. Pictured are some of the babies enjoying the fresh air on the back porch with the IHM sisters watching over them. (Courtesy of St. Joseph's Center.)

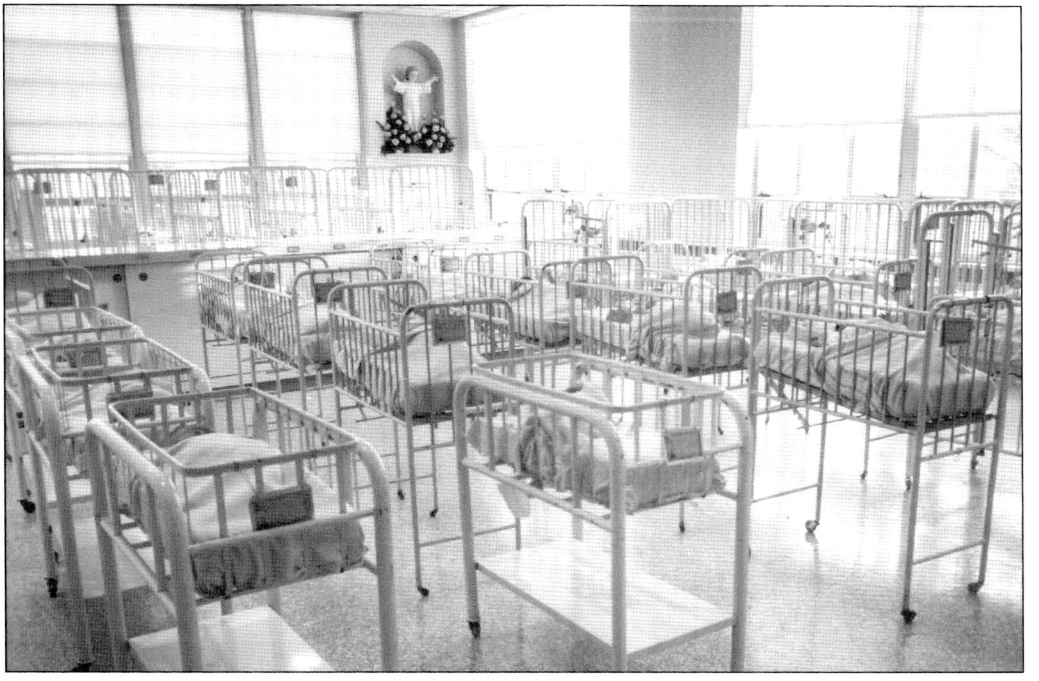

Newborns and Toddlers. The cribs for the toddlers were located in ward No. 1. About 110 babies were born in total at St. Joseph's. After the Second World War, the number of women and children needing St. Joseph's services lessened, and a decision was made to phase out the orphanage. In the early 1950s came another change; St. Joseph's began accepting as residents children diagnosed with mental and physical disabilities. In the years that followed, the program grew in size, and St. Joseph's community outreach was and still is respected by one and all. (Both, courtesy of St. Joseph's Center.)

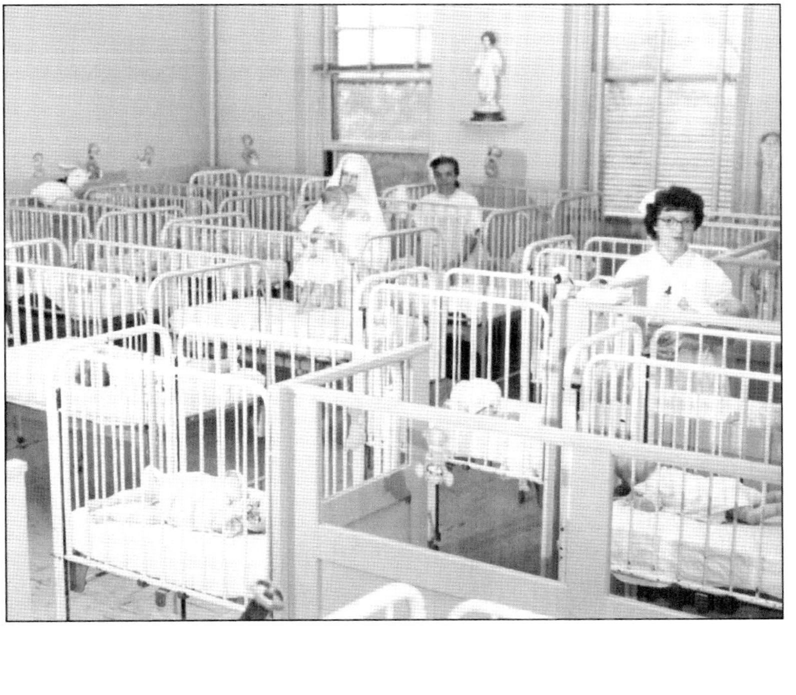

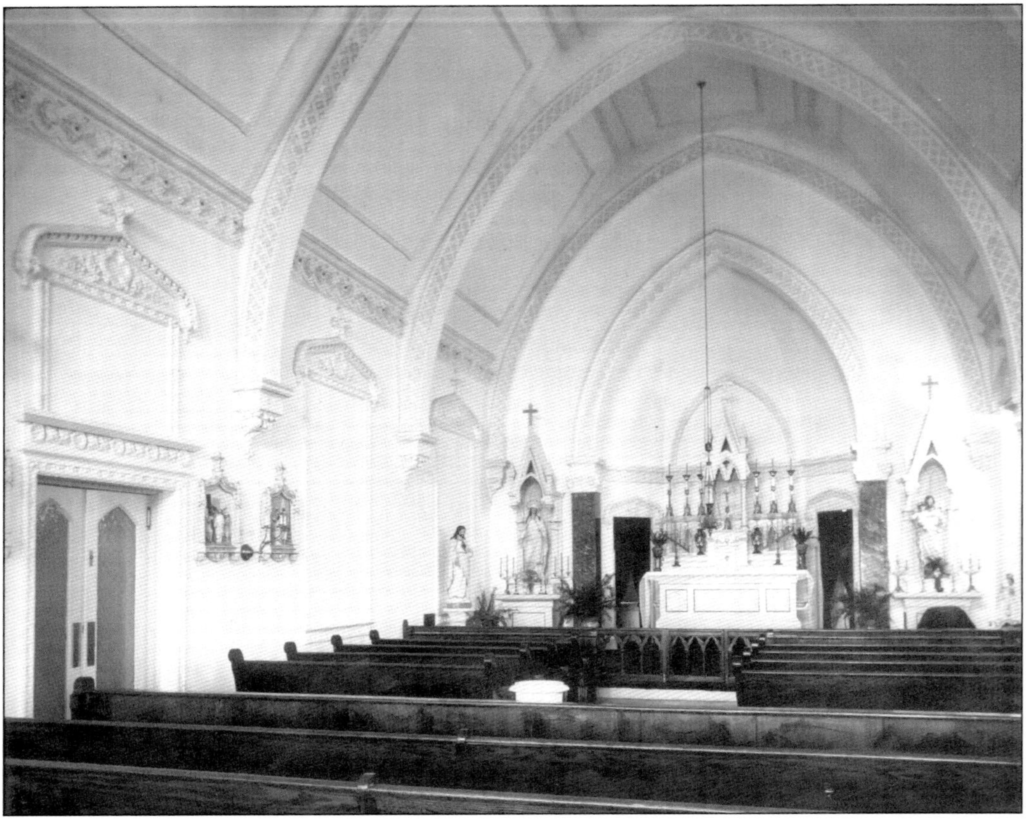

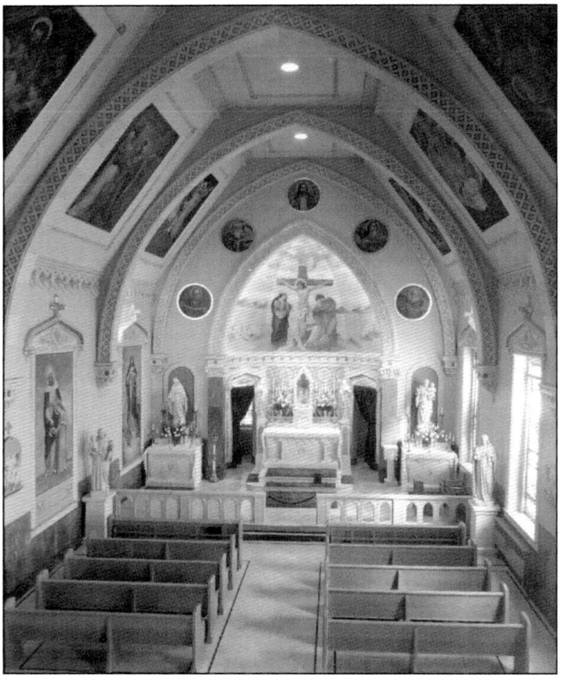

Original Chapel and Artwork. Above, St. Joseph's Chapel is seen in its original state. At left, take note of the addition of the beautiful artwork adorning the ceiling and walls. The current chapel was renovated in 1985. (Both, courtesy of St. Joseph's Center.)

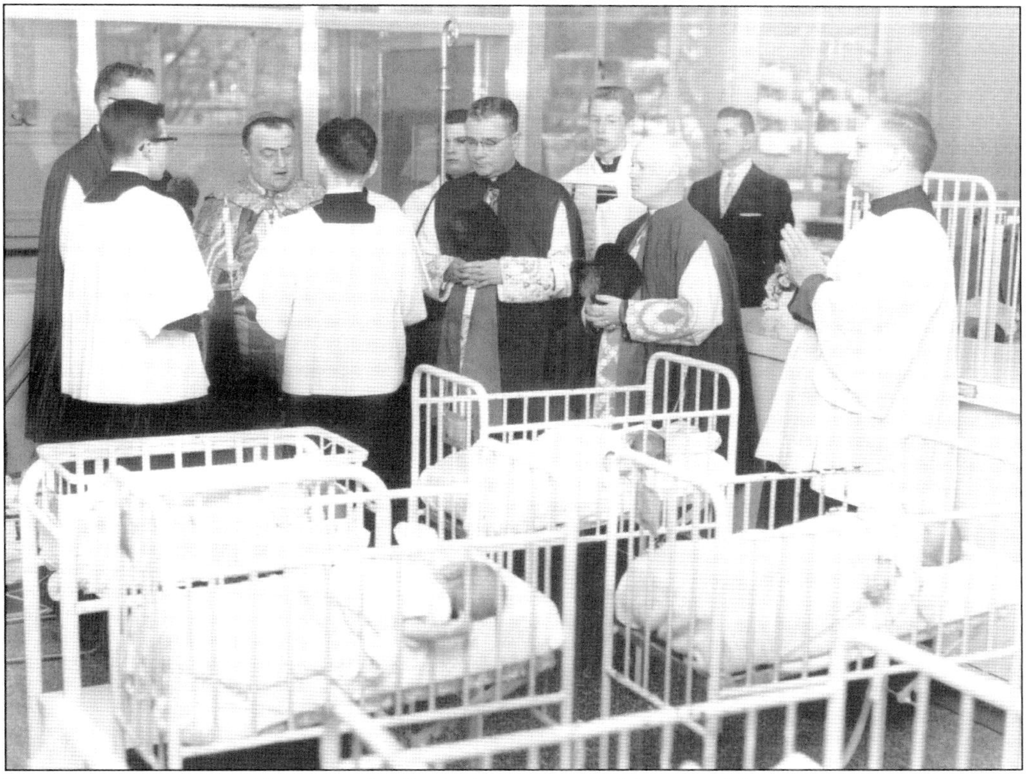

BLESSING OF THE LITTLE CHILDREN, 1950S. Bishop Jerome D. Hannan of Scranton is pictured blessing the children. Though no more births occur at St. Joseph's, the adoption program remained active for numerous years, resulting in over hundreds of adoptions. The newest addition to St. Joseph's Center is the Weinberg Therapy Building, where patients can enjoy the soothing waters of the therapeutic pool and a fully equipped treatment facility. (Both, courtesy of St. Joseph's Center.)

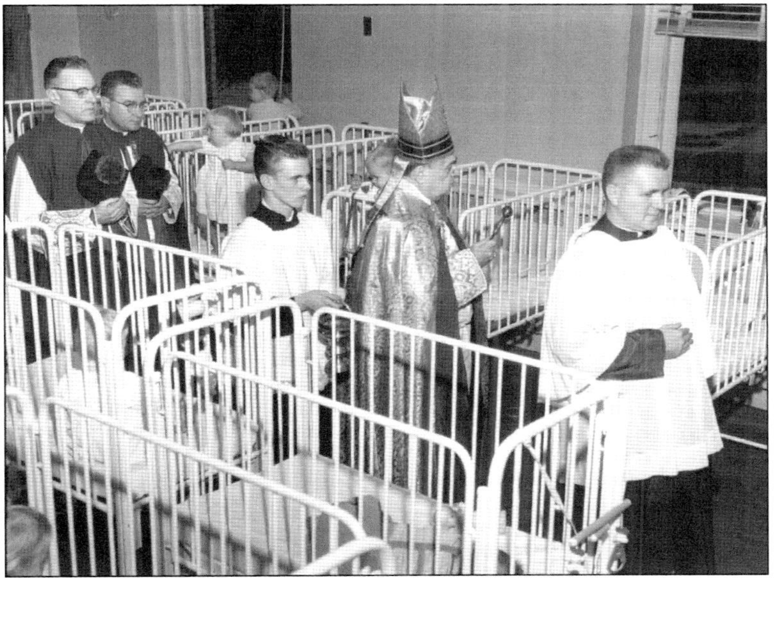

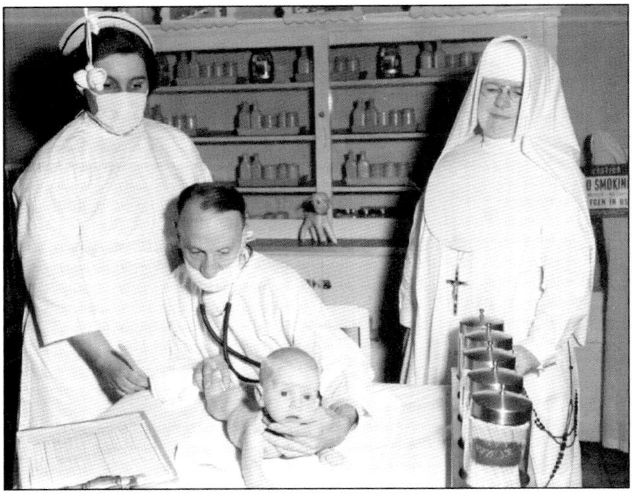

"OPEN UP AND SAY, 'AHH,' " c. 1958. Dr. Vincent Curtin became a welcomed addition to St. Joseph's staff in 1932. The doctor is examining a child in ward No. 1. (Courtesy of St. Joseph's Center.)

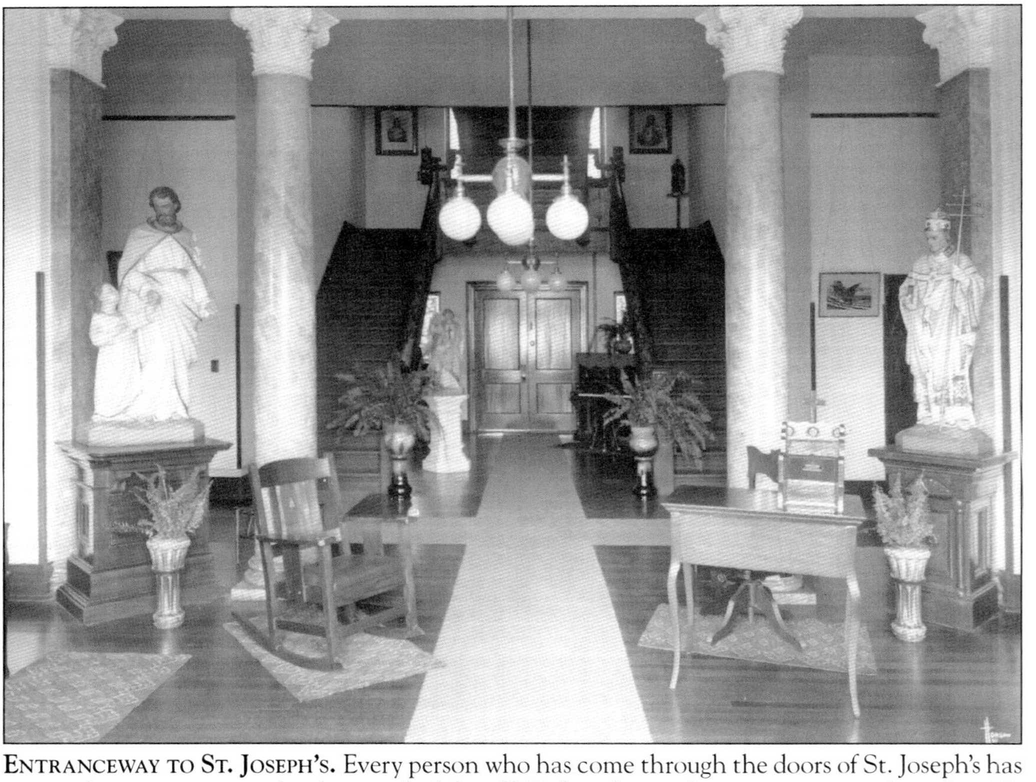

ENTRANCEWAY TO ST. JOSEPH'S. Every person who has come through the doors of St. Joseph's has received a warm greeting by the wonderful staff. Today, the residents range in age from 2 to 52. Every year during the last full weekend in July, St. Joseph's has its festival, which is often referred to as the "biggest picnic in Northeastern Pennsylvania." Local television station WNEP plays host to St. Joseph's Telethon, where people call in donations to help fund the many programs St. Joe's provides, and to "Go Joe," the annual bike ride by meteorologist Joe Snedeker. Thousands of people attend the festival each year; some even schedule their vacation around the dates. In 1996, the festival outgrew the center's property and moved to the nearby Marywood University. In July 2011, the festival celebrated its 50th anniversary. (Courtesy of St. Joseph's Center.)

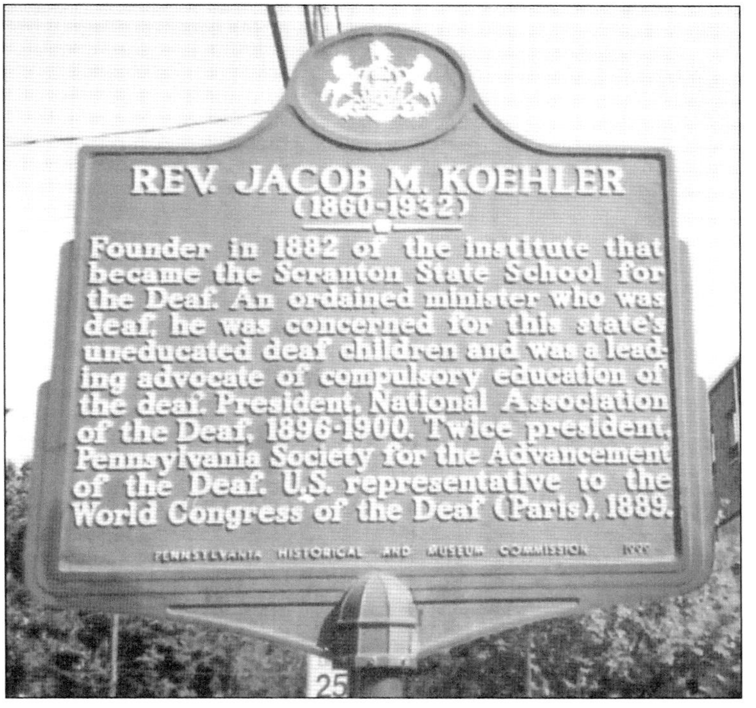

HISTORICAL MARKER. In 1941, the Pennsylvania Historical and Museum Commission dedicated this marker to the founder of the Pennsylvania Oral School for the Deaf, Rev. Jacob M. Koehler. (Courtesy of the author.)

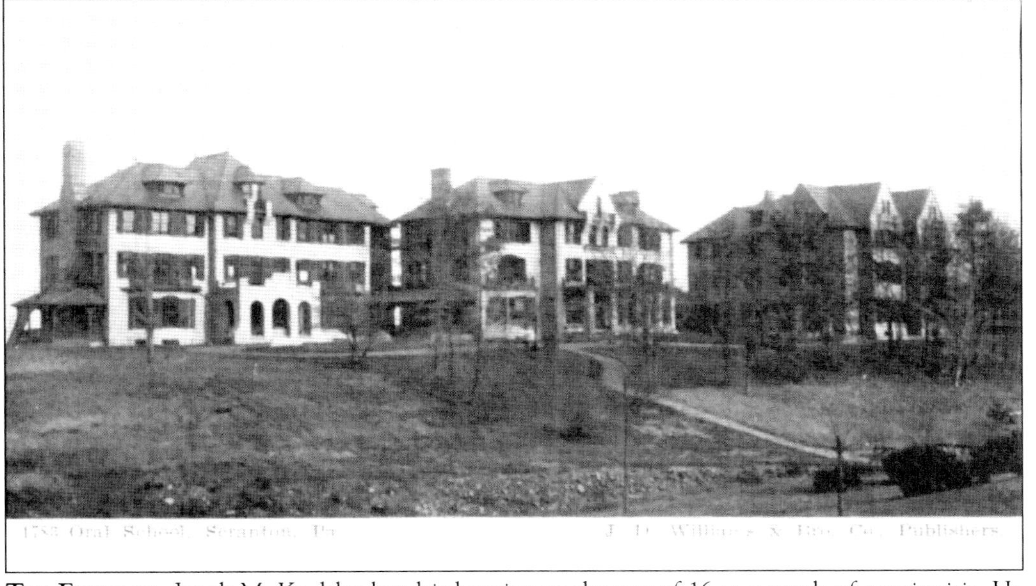

THE FOUNDER. Jacob M. Koehler lost his hearing at the age of 16 as a result of meningitis. He attended Gallaudet College, the famous college for the deaf, but quit in his sophomore year in order to return to Scranton to teach deaf children. His first class consisted of eight students, and classes were held in the basement of a Baptist church located at the corner of Adams Avenue and Mulberry Street. When the number of students kept growing, it was decided to start a state school for the deaf in Scranton. (Courtesy of Mark Boock.)

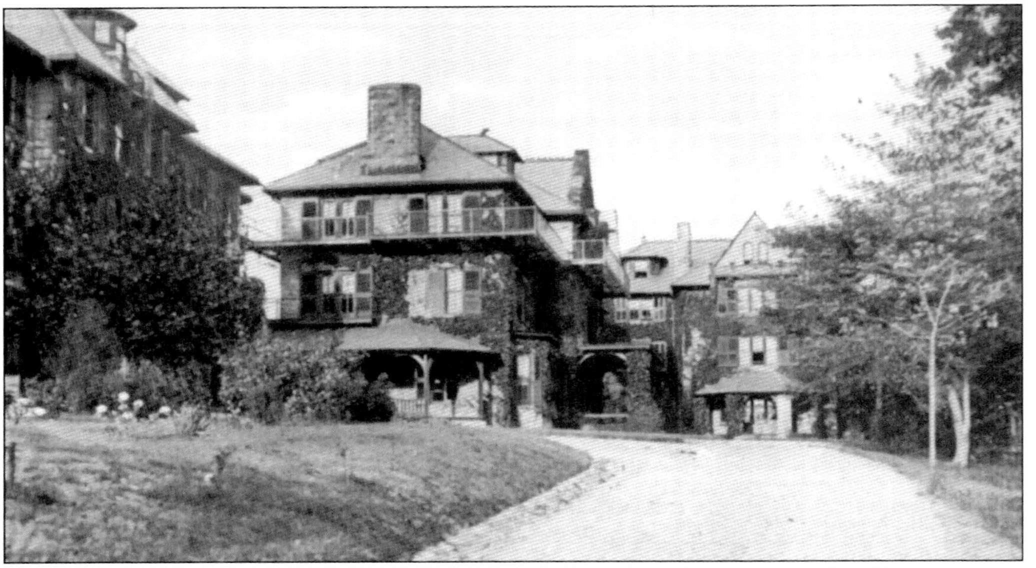

Early Days. The original plan was to use the sign method of teaching. But teacher Emma Garrett from Philadelphia was hired, and it was then decided to teach the oral method. Some accounts report Jacob Koehler lost his job due to the change of teaching methods, but no one is certain of the reason for his departure. (Courtesy of the author.)

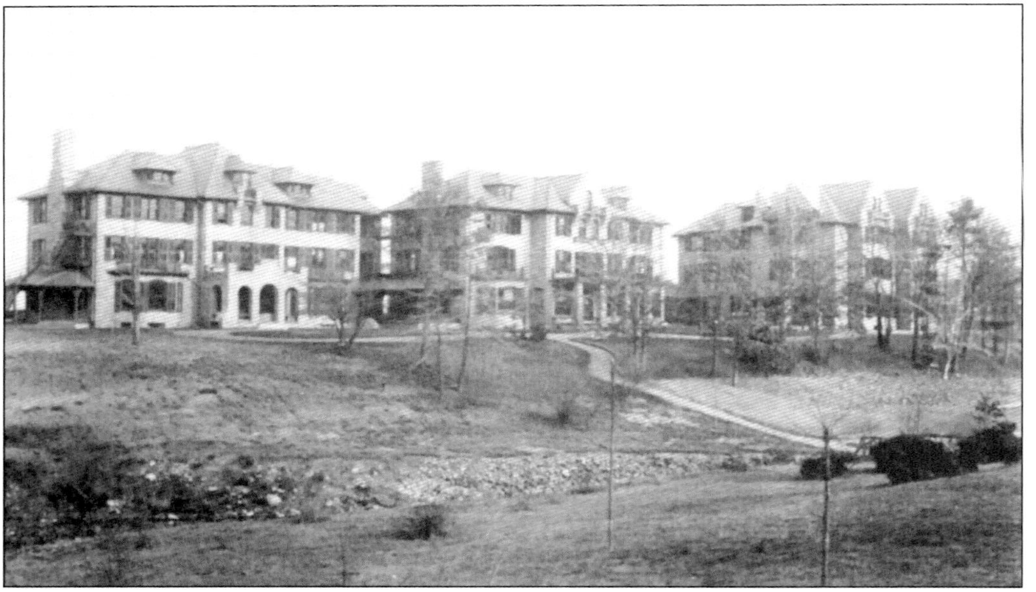

The Pennsylvania Oral School for the Deaf. The school opened on September 10, 1883, and was incorporated on November 11, 1884. Thirteen students were in attendance, with 11 residents of Scranton, one of Minooka, and one of Pleasant Valley. The name was officially changed to the Pennsylvania Oral School for the Deaf in 1889. The school purchased a plot of land then called North Park from Robert E. Hurley and Edward B. Sturges. Jefferson and Washington Avenues and Electric Street bound it on three sides. This site would become the school's permanent home for the next 129 years. In 1913, the commonwealth took control of the school and renamed it the Pennsylvania State Oral School for the Deaf. (Courtesy of the author.)

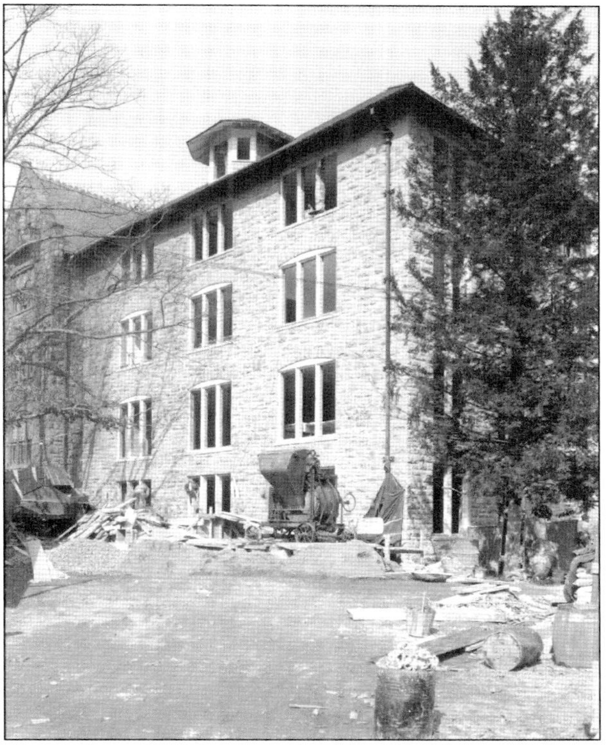

Construction Begins. In April 1938, major construction began on the school. Among other additions, a new gymnasium was built in which the students could participate in sports, such as volleyball, basketball, and archery. In the early days of the school, students had classes in articulation, language, geography, arithmetic, letter writing, and incidental writing. More advanced students studied US history and physiology. (Both, courtesy of the author.)

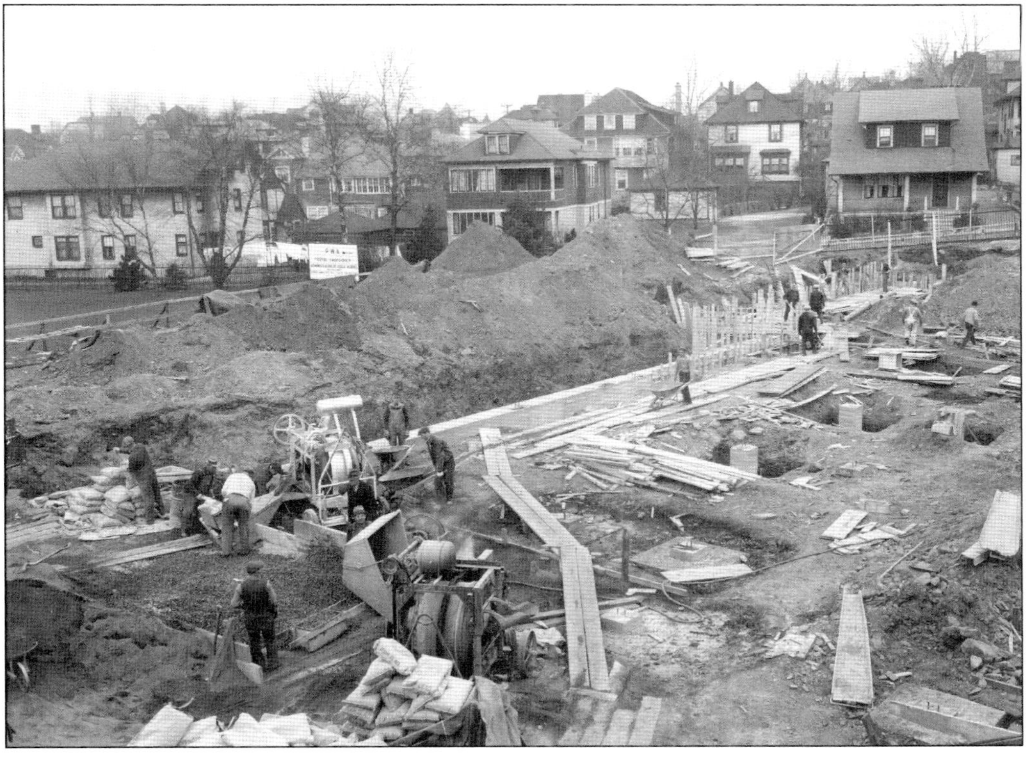

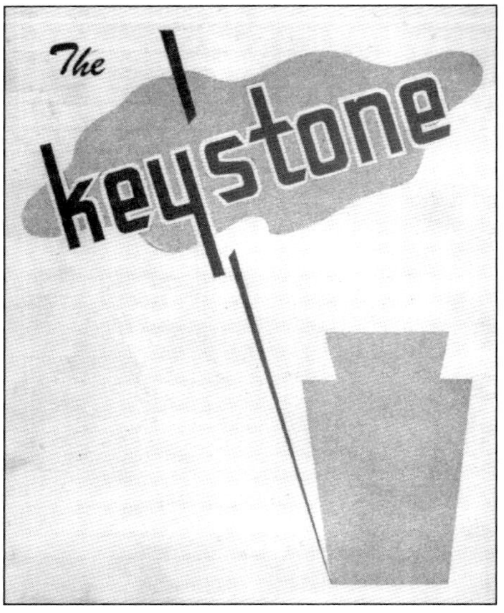

The Keystone. Here is the Pennsylvania State Oral School's yearbook. The school's motto was "Be Doers, Not Dreamers." Class colors were green and white, and the class flower was the red rose. (Courtesy of the author.)

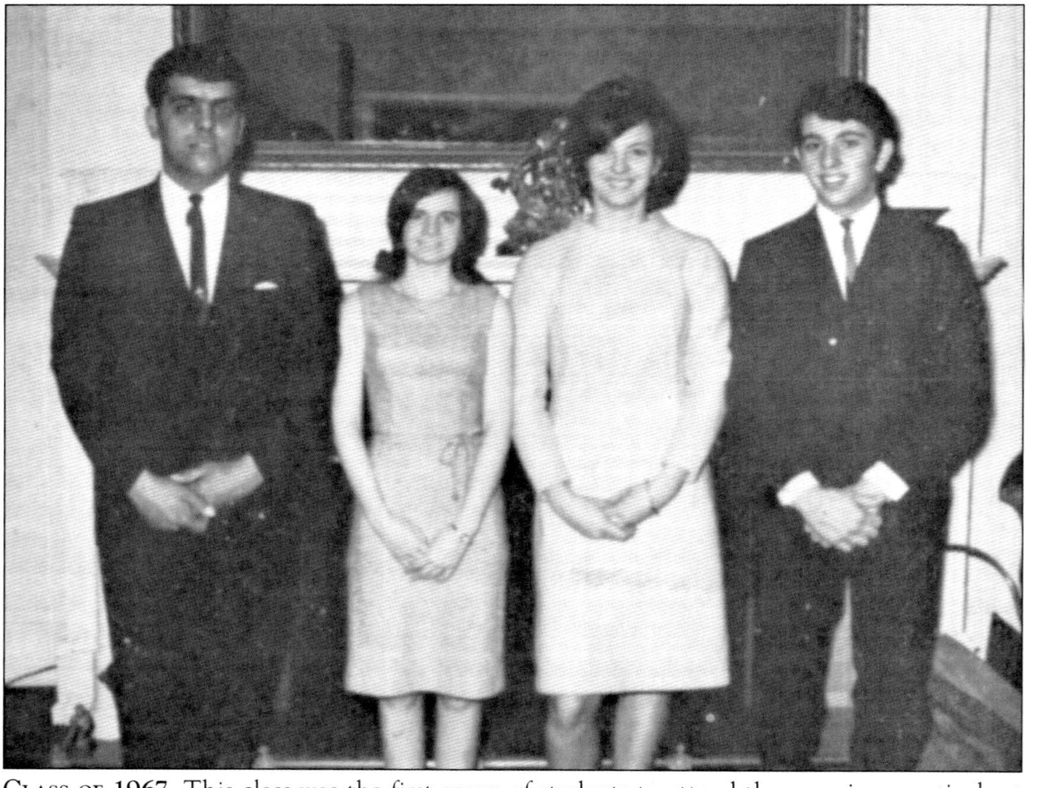

Class of 1967. This class was the first group of students to attend the morning practical art classes at Technical High School. Members of the graduating class are, from left to right, Al Giovenelli, Sharon Fox, MaryAnn Smith, and Jerry Sabatini. In 1976, the name was changed to the Scranton State School for the Deaf. Sadly, due to state budget problems, the school was closed in 2009. Marywood University purchased the property, which includes nine buildings, in 2011. (Courtesy of the author.)

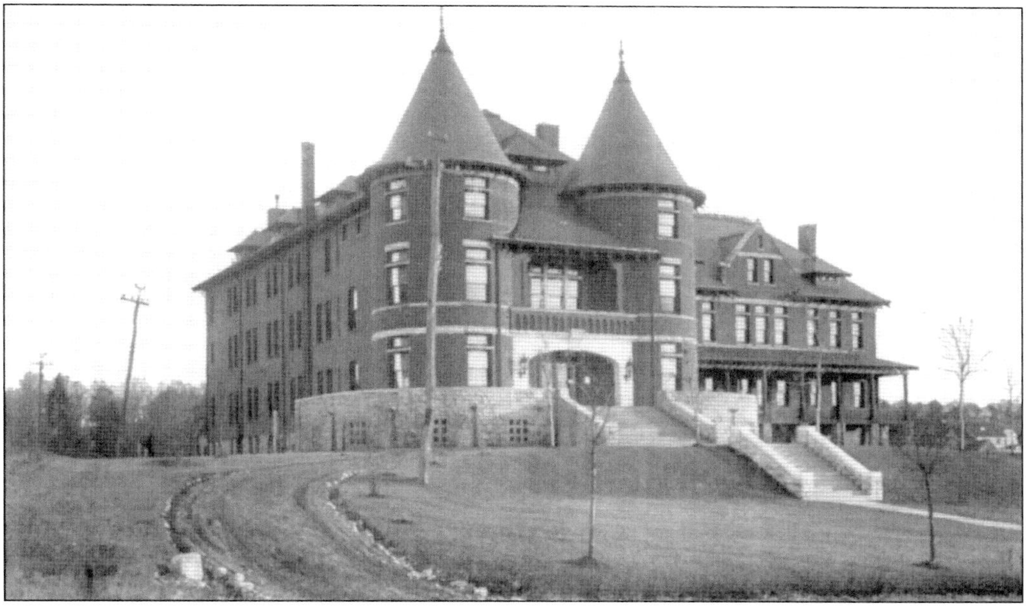

Home for the Friendless. William D. Mossman, the city missionary, found a sick and helpless woman wondering the streets of Scranton at night; he immediately realized the need for a facility to care for the destitute women and children of the city. The Young Men's Christian Association put out the call, and the women of the city answered. In 1871, a committee of 10 was formed in order to draft a constitution and make arrangements for such an organization. In October of the same year, 50 ladies became members. At their first meeting, Mrs. C.H. Dowd was elected president and the name "Home for the Friendless" was given to the newly formed institution. Today, the organization exists as the Friendship House. (Both, courtesy of the author.)

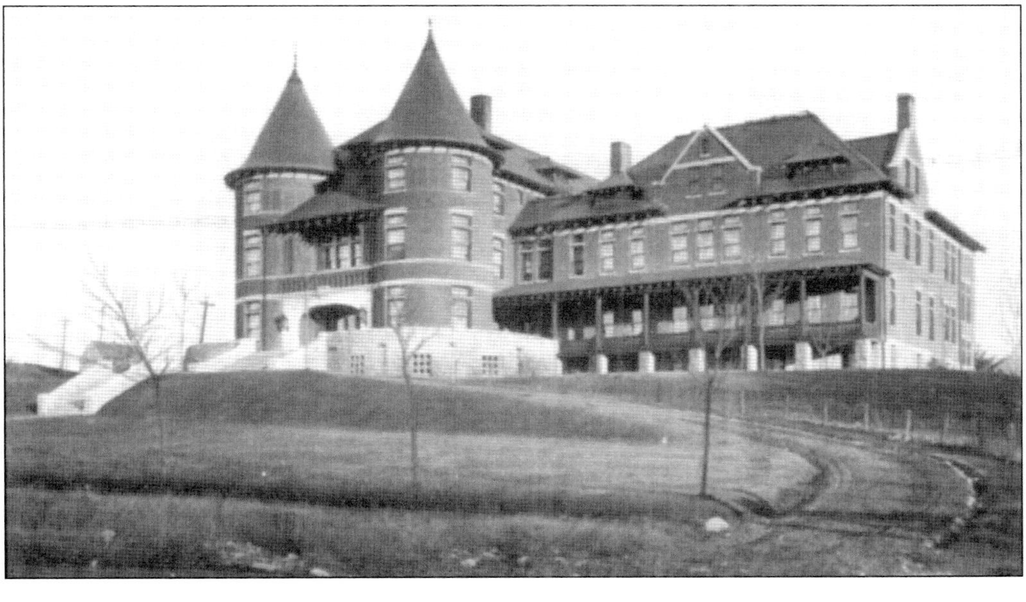

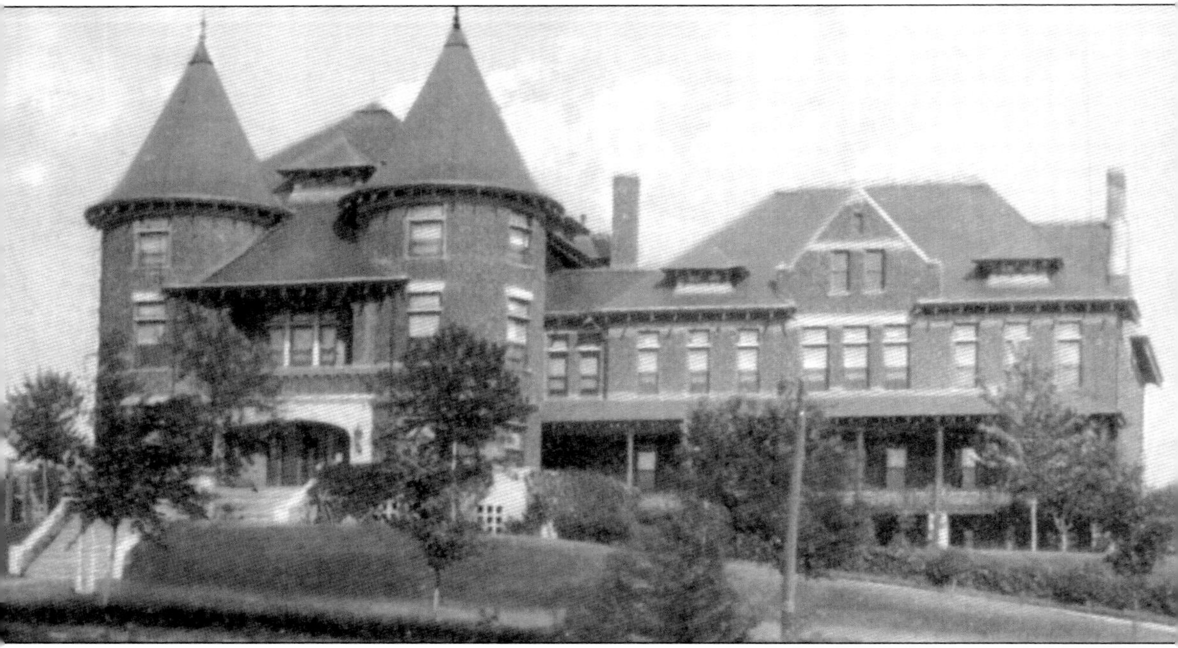

A Part of Green Ridge. The first residence for the Home for the Friendless was located on Franklin Avenue and Linden Street. However, the facility moved several times; according to the 1919 Scranton directory, the address for the Home of the Friendless was 1830 Adams Avenue, near Electric Street. Because of its nearness to St. Joseph's Foundling Home and the Pennsylvania Oral School for the Deaf, this area was often referred to as "Charity Hill." (Courtesy of the author.)

Three

Faith and Religion

Green Ridge Presbyterian Church. The church was founded in 1875 by a committee with the following men: Revs. S.C. Logan, J.B. Fisher, D.K. Freeman, Joseph Corey, and J.W. Partridge. A stone octagonal church was built on Green Ridge Street and Monsey Avenue that same year, and people worshipped there until 1893. Having one of the biggest congregations in Green Ridge at the time, a much larger church on the corner of Green Ridge Street and Wyoming Avenue was built. In 1982, the Scranton Revival Baptist Church purchased the building for the sum of $90,000. Today, the beautiful Gothic building stands empty. (Courtesy of Mark Boock.)

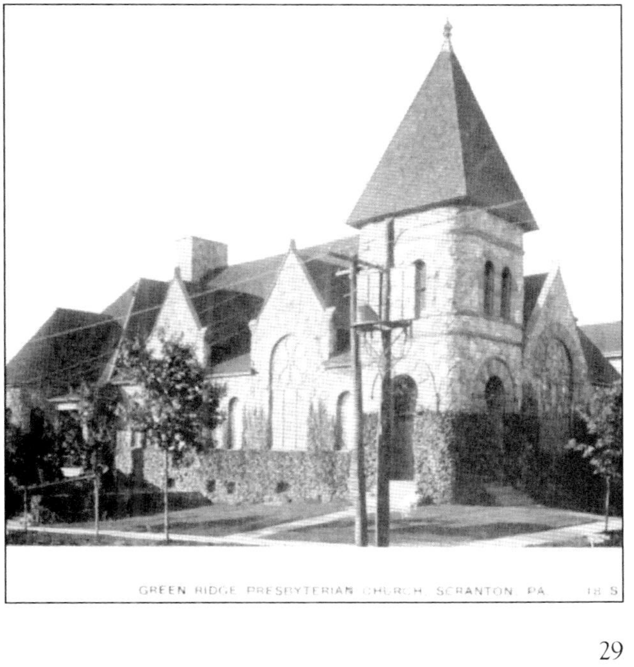

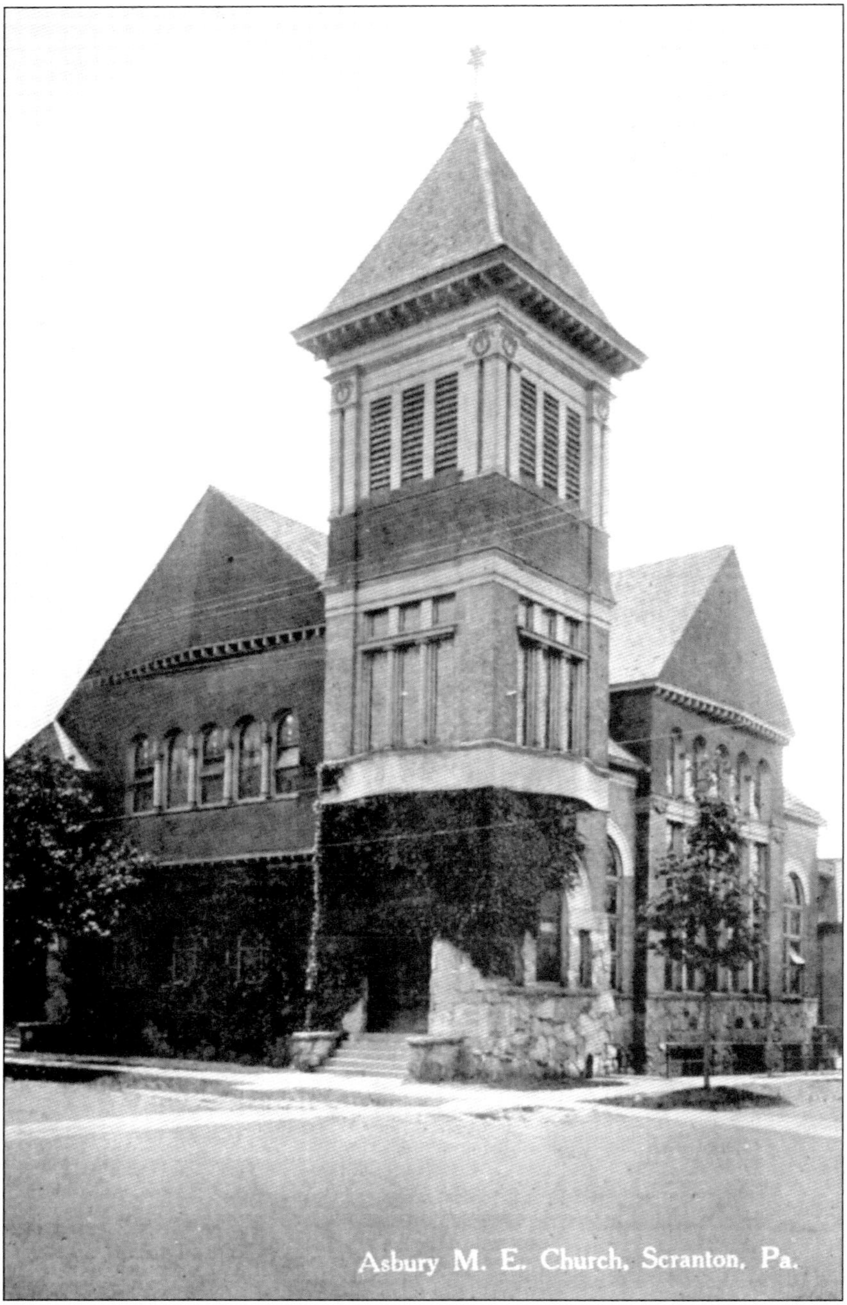

Asbury Methodist Episcopal Church. The third congregation to be established in Green Ridge was the Asbury Methodist Episcopal Church in 1876. The beautiful church on Delaware Street was dedicated in 1893. In 1938, a scandal rocked the church when one of its parishioners, Russel McGarrah, murdered his young wife, Dorothy, after Sunday mass. It was reported that several hours after the gruesome homicide took place McGarrah sought out Reverend Nicholson and confessed to the crime. McGarrah was committed to an institution for the criminally insane, which was where he remained until his death. (Courtesy of Mark Boock.)

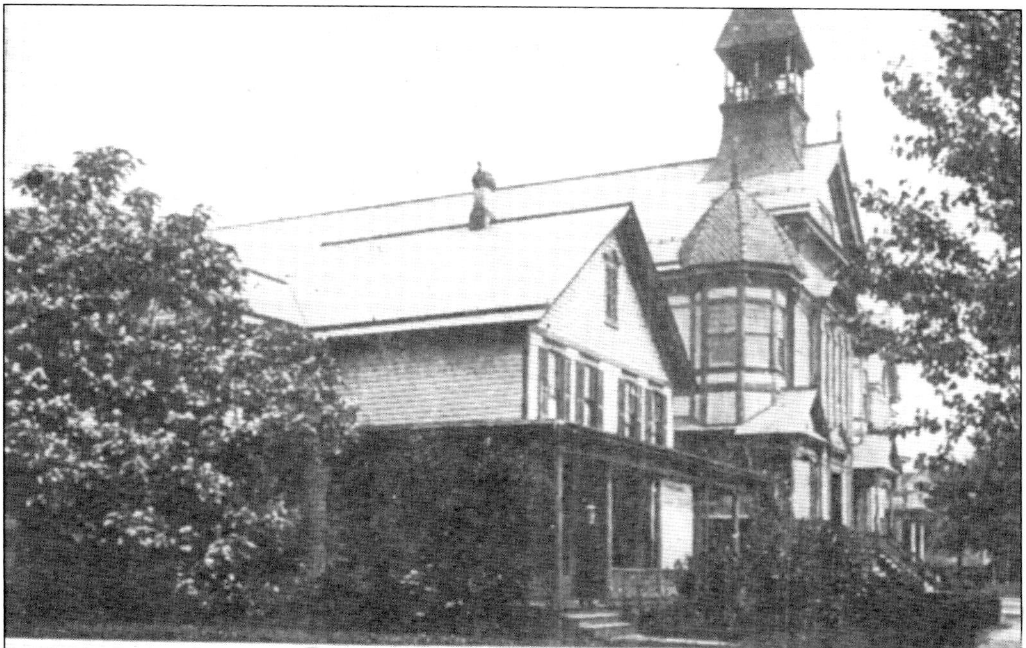

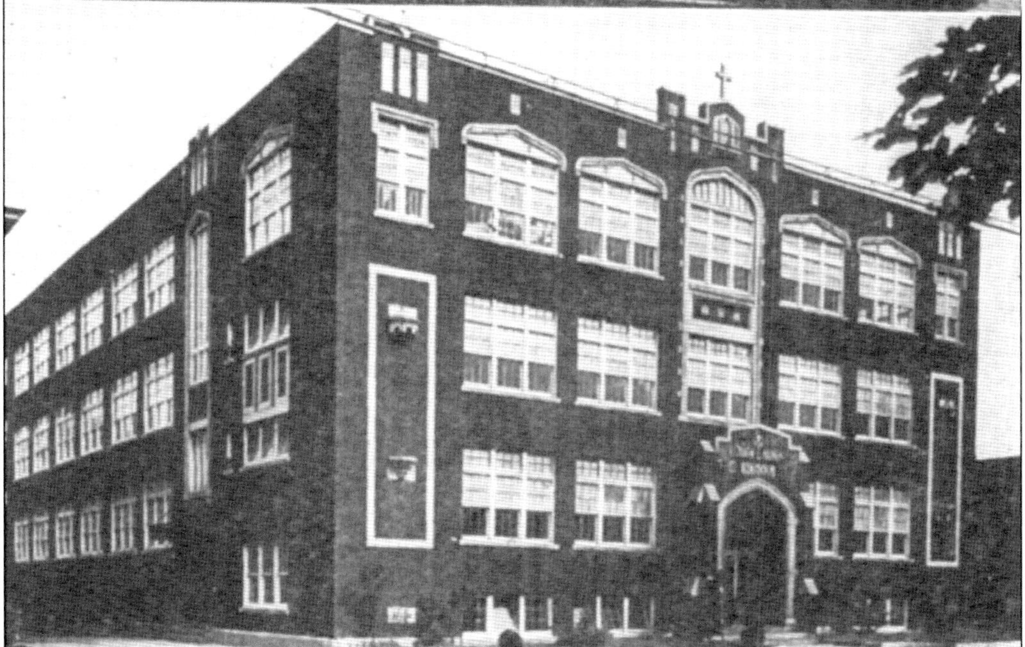

ST. PAUL'S ROMAN CATHOLIC CHURCH. The first rectory, shown above, was a combination church, school, and parish hall. It replaced the little log cabin building made of hemlock, which was known as the "Wigwam." In the 1880s, Green Ridge was sparsely populated, and there were only four houses on the same block as the parish. The side opposite the church was called "Sanderson's Park" and was used as a picnic grove and baseball field. The new church-and-school combination, shown below, was opened and blessed on June 5, 1928. (Courtesy of Kristine Pocius, St. Paul's Archives.)

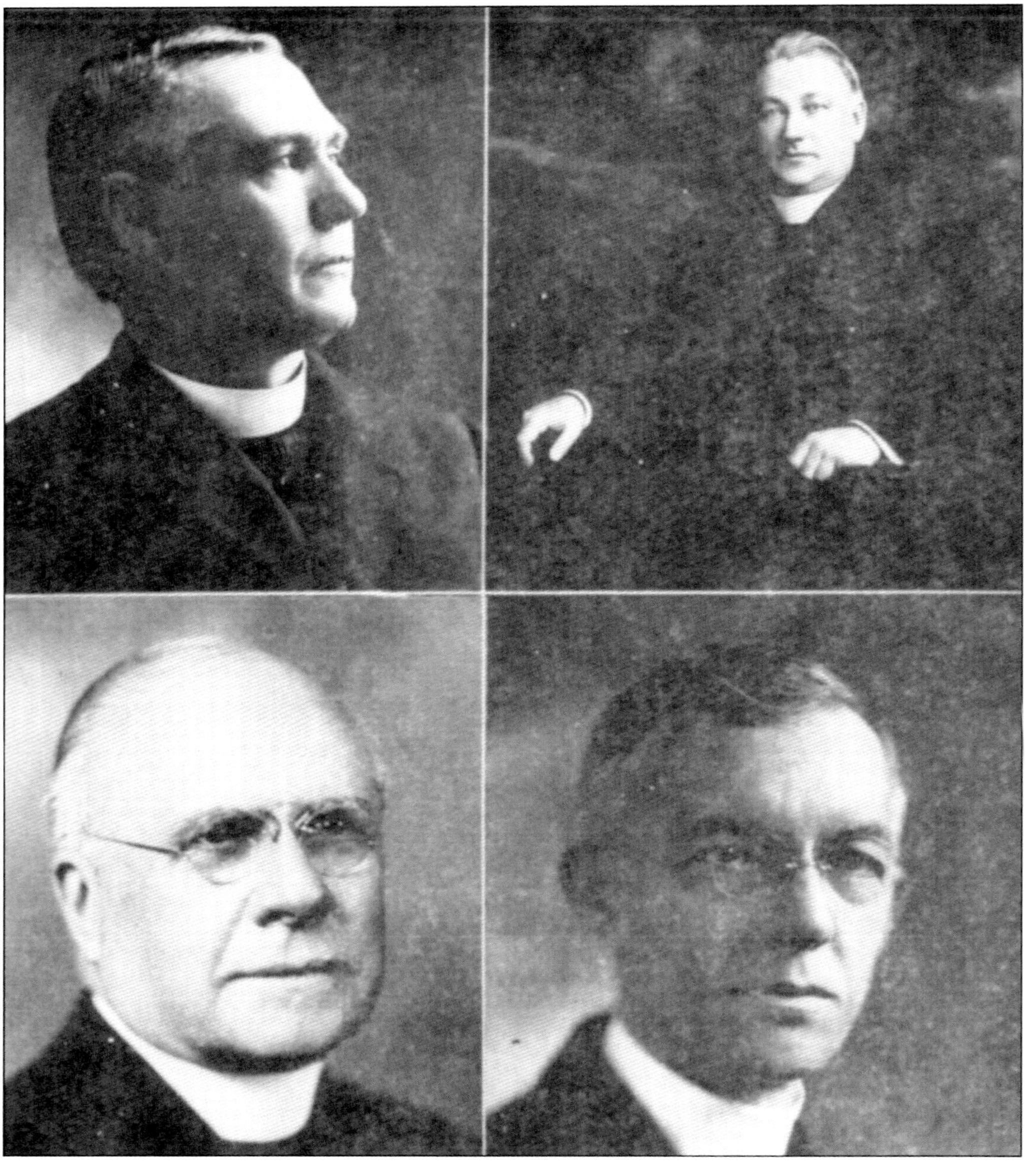

First Four Pastors of St. Paul's. Those pictured are, from left to right, (top row) Revs. P.J. McManus (1887–1910) and P.C. Winters (1910–1921); (bottom row) Revs. M.F. O'Rourke (1921–1925) and D.J. Connor (1925–1927). (Courtesy of Kristine Pocius, St. Paul's Archives.)

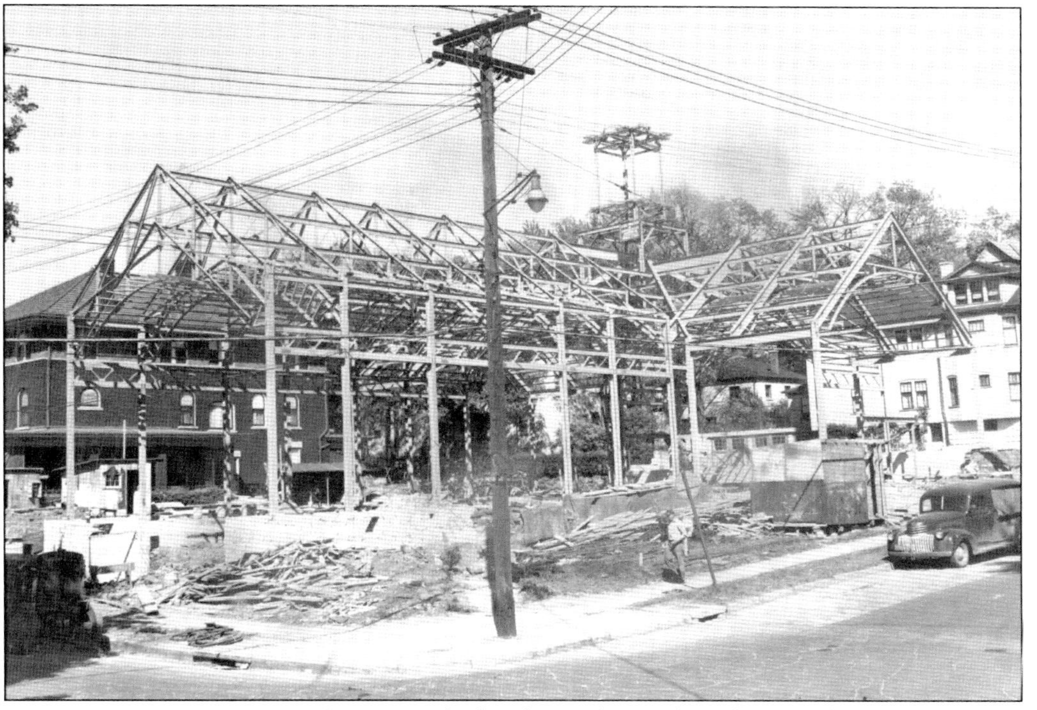

Construction of the New Church. The breaking of ground on the new church of St. Paul's took place on January 10, 1951. Work progressed rapidly on the steel structure that served as the framework for the $300,000 edifice. Msgr. John J. Vaughon was the pastor at the time. (Courtesy of Kristine Pocius, St. Paul's Archives.)

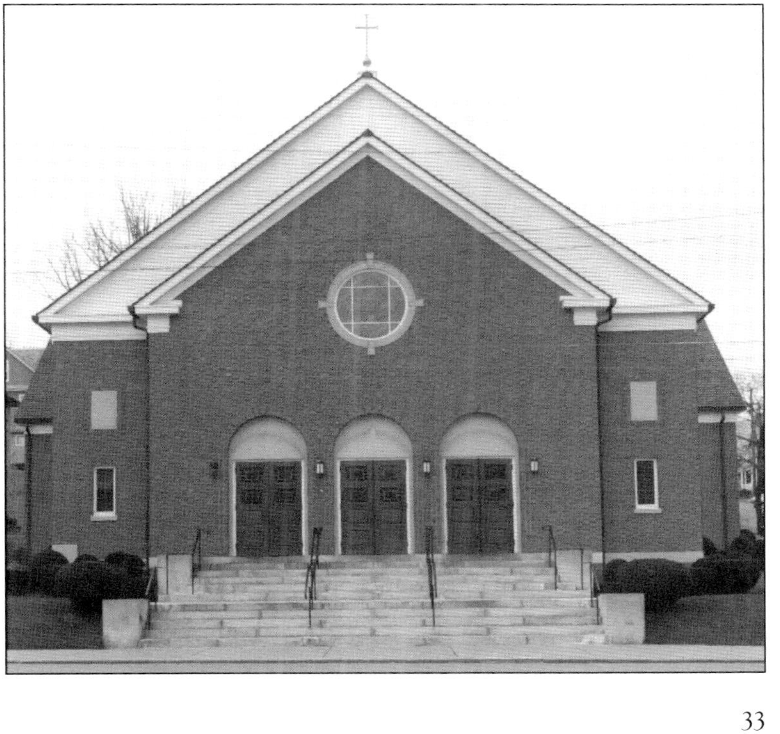

The Dedication. The dedication of the new church took place on March 23, 1952. The Most Reverend William J. Hafey, DD, bishop of the Diocese of Scranton, blessed the church and was the celebrant of the Pontifical High Mass. (Courtesy of Kristine Pocius, St. Paul's Archives.)

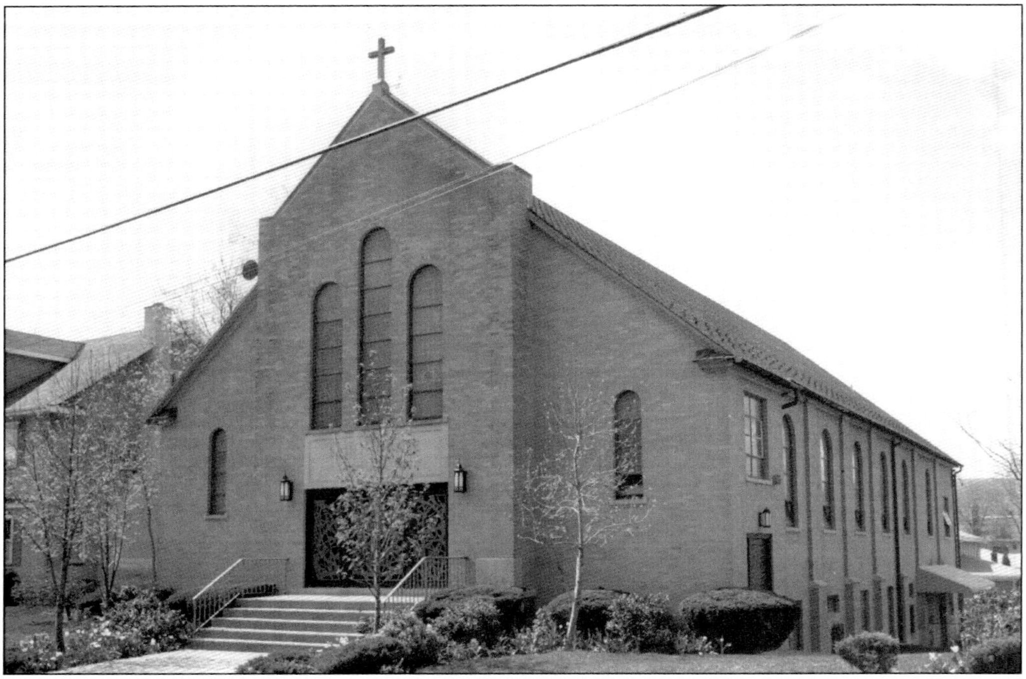

St. Clare Church. In December 1953, ground was broken for St. Clare Church and School. It was built on the corner of Park Street and North Washington Avenue. At the time, the school was a one-story building with eight classrooms, a health room, and a principal's office. The Sisters, Servants of the Immaculate Heart of Mary, staffed it. The church and school were completed in 1954 and officially dedicated on March 20, 1955. Bishop Jerome D. Hannan officiated at the ceremonies, and Msgr. John J. Vaughan, pastor of St. Paul's and St. Clare, offered the solemn High Mass. It would not be until June 16, 1967, that St. Clare Church would become an independent parish from St. Paul's with its own pastor and rectory. (Courtesy of Kristine Pocius, St. Paul's Archives.)

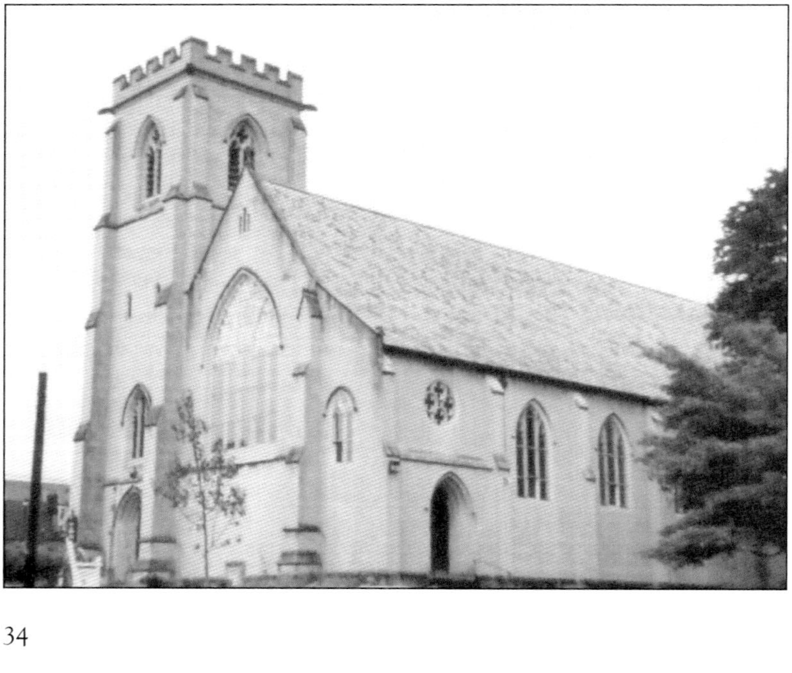

Church of the Good Shepherd. Originated in 1860, people of the Church of the Good Shepherd first worshipped in a hall on Monsey Avenue. The beautiful Gothic stone church on the corner of North Washington Avenue and Electric Street was built in 1912. (Courtesy of the author.)

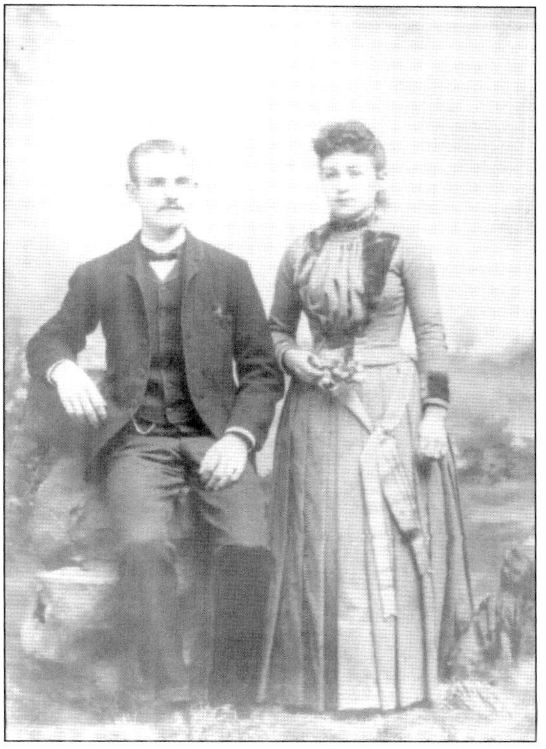

NOVEMBER 1889 TO NOVEMBER 1939. On November 7, 1889, the Reverend G. Jeffries united George J.M. Dicker and Mary Ann Gwyther of Scranton in holy matrimony at the Primitive Methodist Church of Green Ridge. The couple poses below for a photograph in honor of their golden wedding anniversary 50 years later. The church in which they were wed was built on East Market Street in 1883 and organized in 1890. (Both, courtesy of the author.)

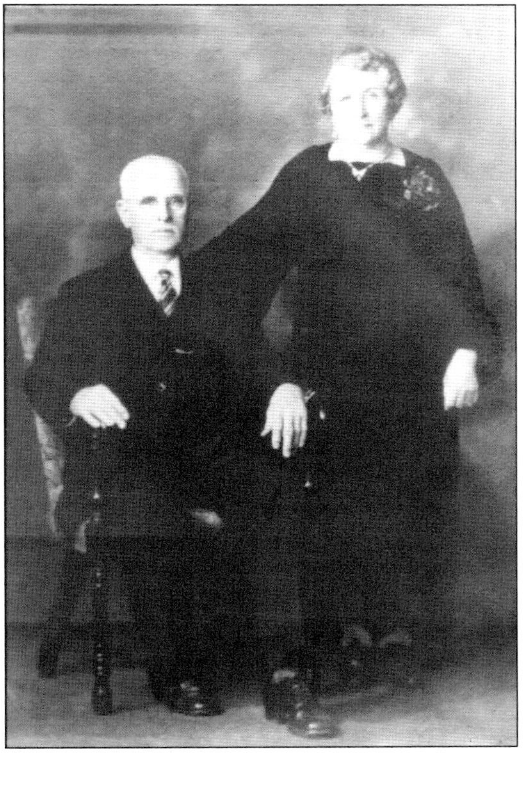

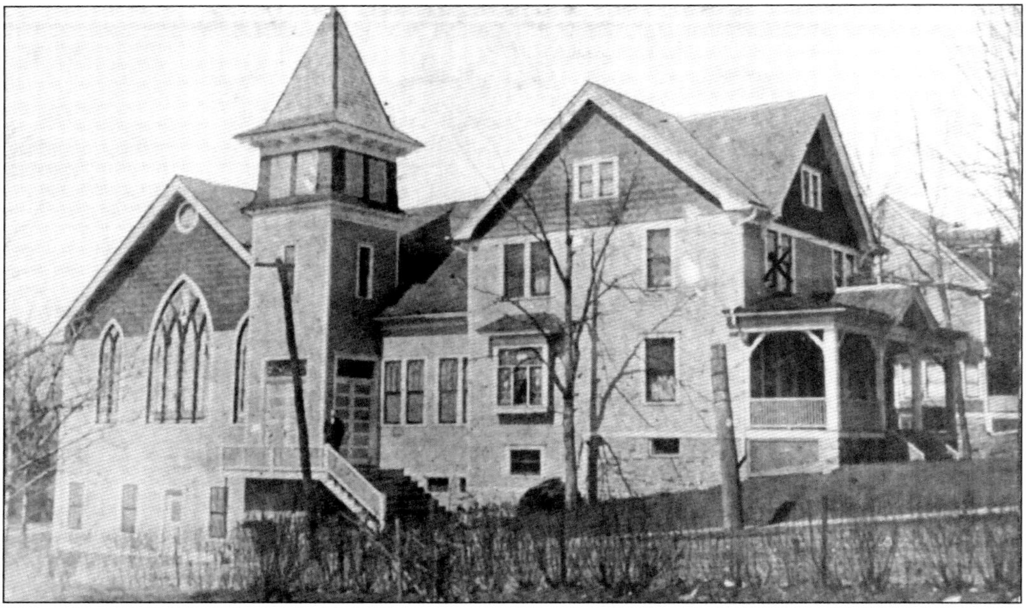

GOSPEL TABERNACLE OF THE CHRISTIAN MISSIONARY ALLIANCE, C. 1909. Once located at 1501 Wyoming Avenue, the Gospel Tabernacle is now the site of Linn McDonald's Dance School. (Courtesy of Mark Boock.)

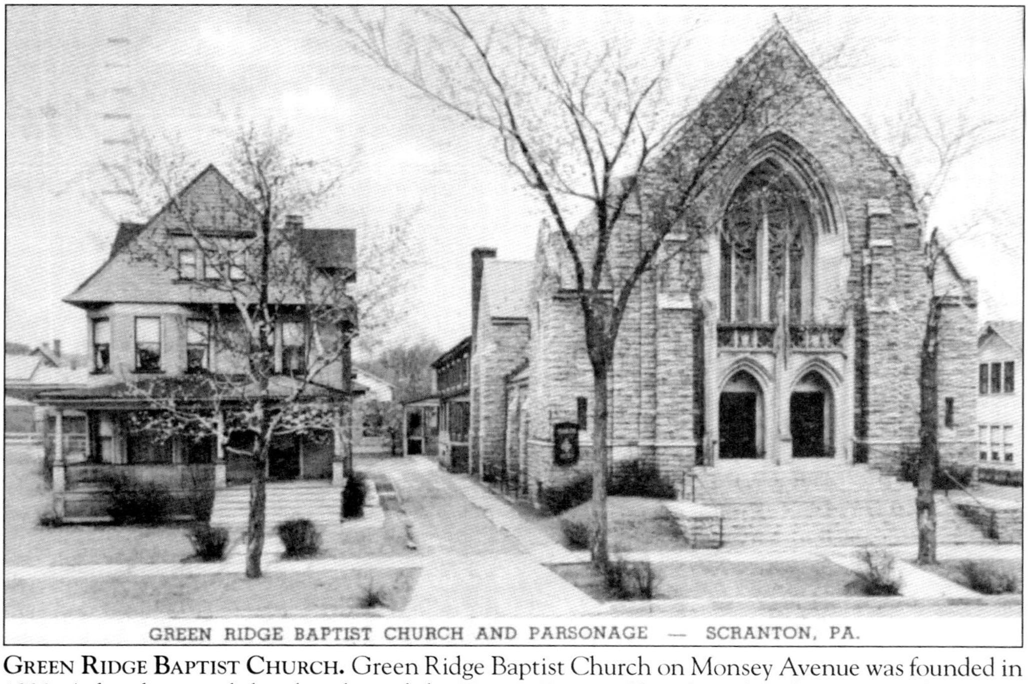

GREEN RIDGE BAPTIST CHURCH. Green Ridge Baptist Church on Monsey Avenue was founded in 1892. A fire destroyed the church, and the Trinity Baptist Church replaced it in 1932. (Courtesy of the author.)

Four

Industry and Business

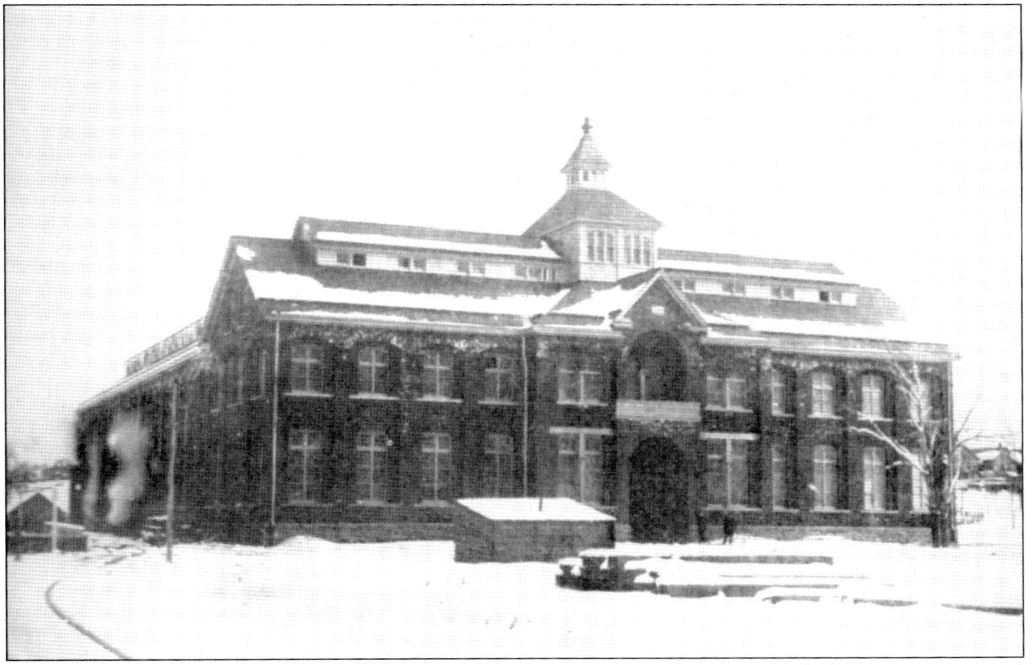

The Scranton Lace Curtain Company, c. 1897. The company made lace curtains and tablecloths that were eventually sold all over the world. The early days were a bit of a struggle; a supply of trained lace workers was nonexistent. The company reorganized and worked out the problems, and a charter was granted on June 15, 1897, by the State of Pennsylvania in the name of the Scranton Lace Curtain Company. J. Benjamin Dimmick was appointed the company's first president. (Courtesy of the author.)

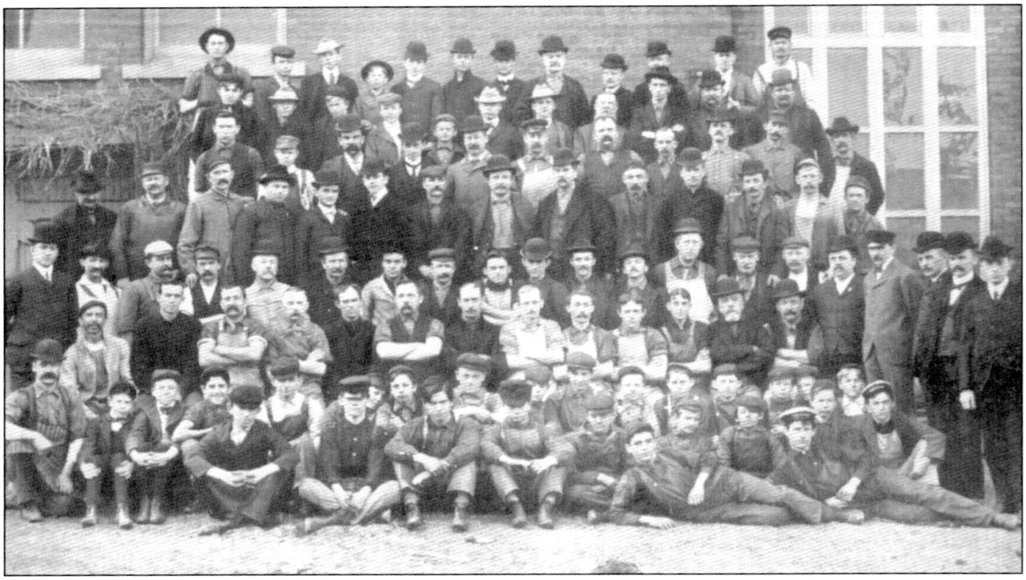

Scranton Lace Employees. The new company had many valuable assets, such as a plant of 54,762 square feet, 16 of the finest lace machines, looms imported from Nottingham, England, and a staff of skilled employees. During its heyday, the company employed over 1,400 people. (Courtesy of the author.)

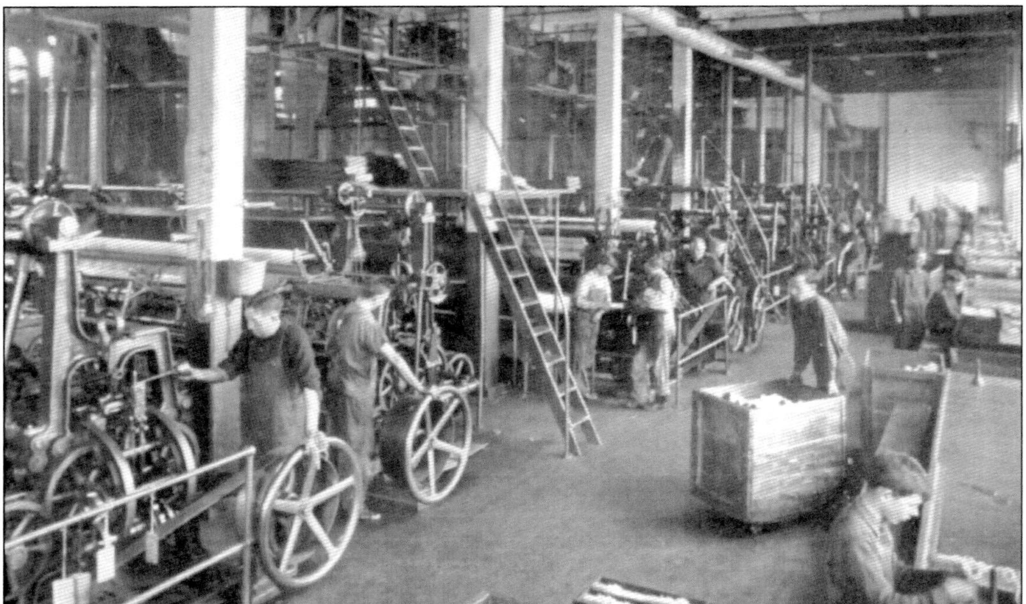

Weaving Room. The new lace company was soon operating on a substantial scale. In the first year, its sales totaled $236,000. President Dimmick was ably supported in company operations by his vice president Henry Belin Jr., both outstanding businessmen of the community, which lent to the company's success. It is said that Babe Ruth would often visit Scranton Lace when he came to town because the looms fascinated him. (Courtesy of the author.)

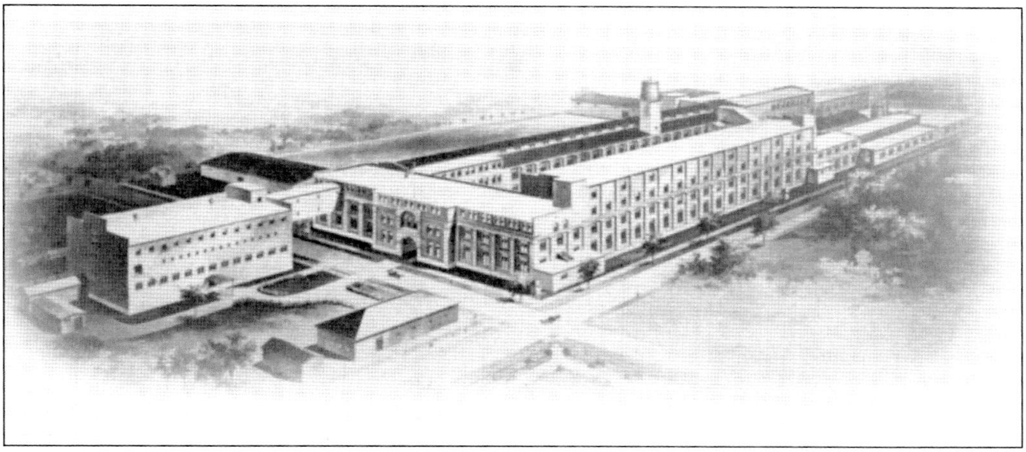

THE PLANT IN 1914. Until 1916, operations continued under the name of the Scranton Lace Curtain Company, and sales were under the name the Scranton Lace Company. In that year, President Dimmick consolidated the two, using the name the Scranton Lace Company, under which the company operated until its closing in 2002. (Courtesy of the author.)

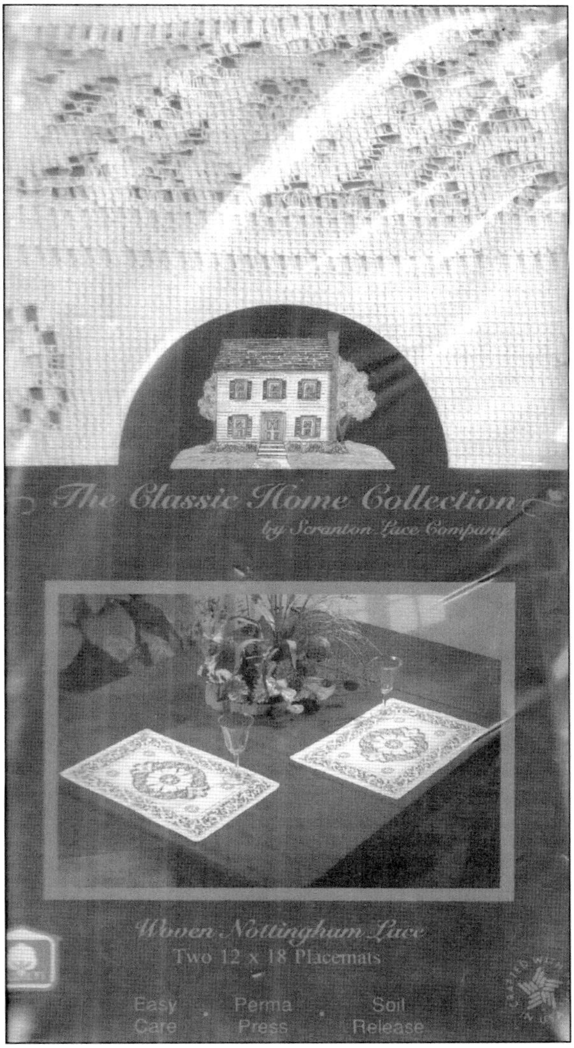

NOTTINGHAM LACE. Nottingham lace was made with pride by the Scranton Lace Company. The company will always be known as the largest manufacturer of Nottingham lace in the United States. (Courtesy of the author.)

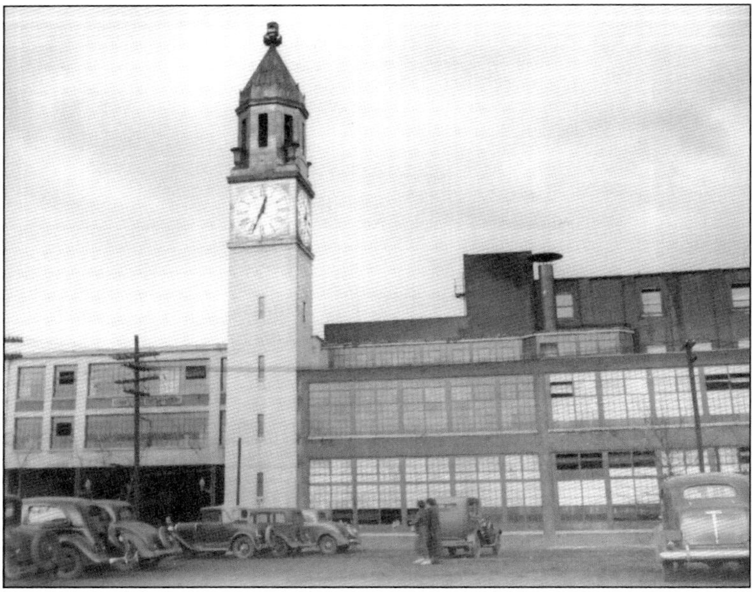

SCRANTON LACE CLOCK TOWER. To this day, the clock is a familiar landmark in the Green Ridge area; some say it was built for the employees who lived nearby so that they would not be late for work. (Courtesy of Mark Boock.)

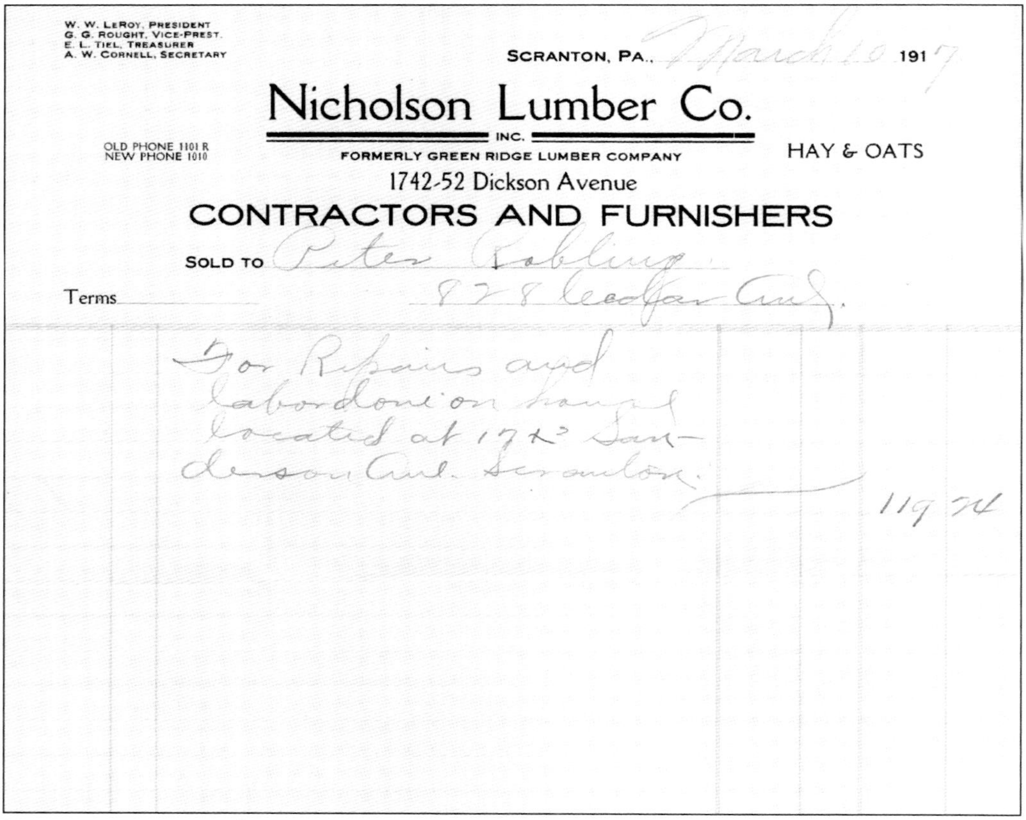

W. W. LEROY, PRESIDENT
G. G. ROUGHT, VICE-PREST.
E. L. TIEL, TREASURER
A. W. CORNELL, SECRETARY

SCRANTON, PA., ______ 191__

Nicholson Lumber Co.
INC.

OLD PHONE 1101 R
NEW PHONE 1010

FORMERLY GREEN RIDGE LUMBER COMPANY

HAY & OATS

1742-52 Dickson Avenue

CONTRACTORS AND FURNISHERS

SOLD TO

Terms

NICHOLSON LUMBER COMPANY, C. 1914. Located on Dickson Avenue, the Nicholson Lumber Company was formerly the Green Ridge Lumber Company. This bill totaling $119.24 was for repairs and labor done on a house on the 1700 block of Sanderson Avenue. (Courtesy of Mark Boock.)

Joseph F. Hangi. As a "dealer in staple and fancy groceries," Joseph F. Hangi's store was located on Dickson Street. He was known for selling Alden Fruit Vinegar, with "it is a pure, wholesome vinegar produced by natural fermentation from fruits." (Courtesy of Mark Boock.)

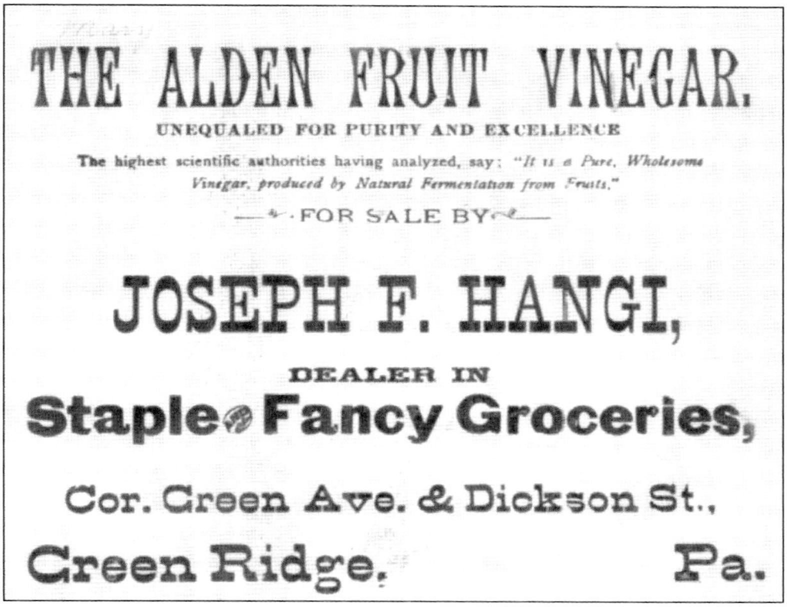

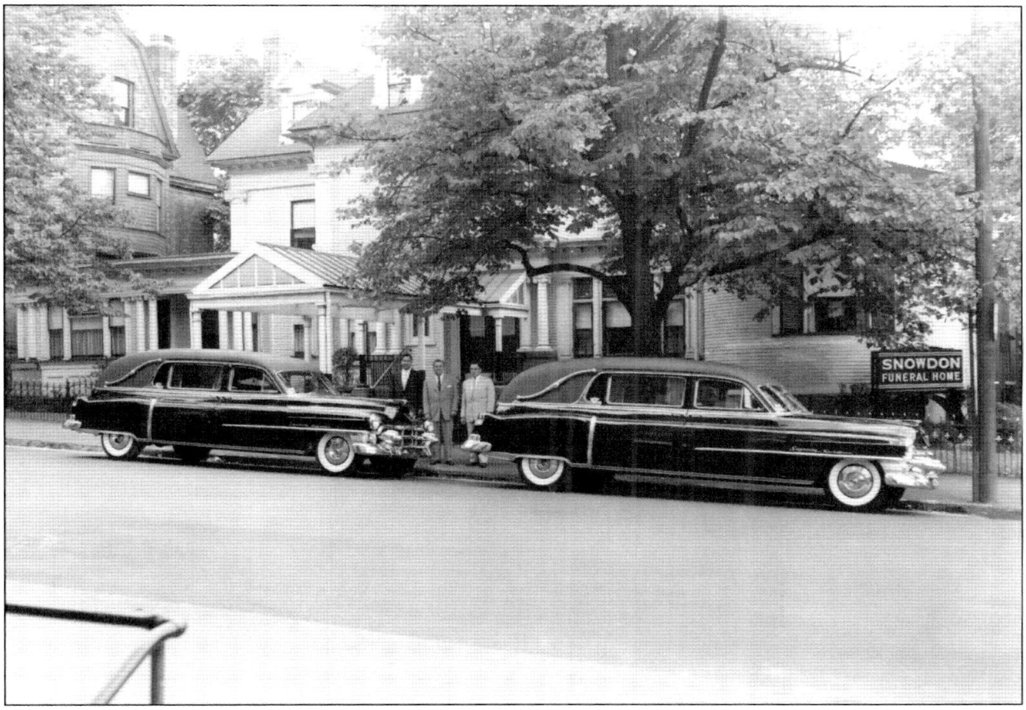

Snowdon Funeral Home. The family-owned funeral business has been a prominent landmark in Green Ridge since 1907. It is located at 1810 Sanderson Avenue. The first proprietor, Howard M. Snowdon, was mayor of Scranton from 1942 to 1946. (Courtesy of Mark Boock.)

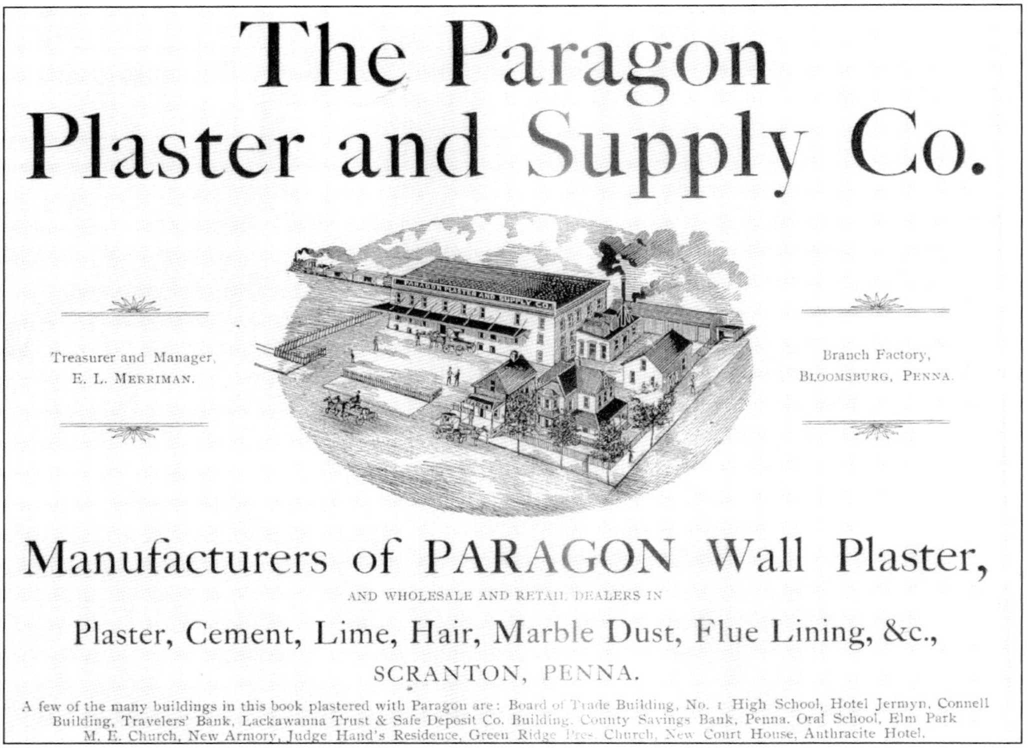

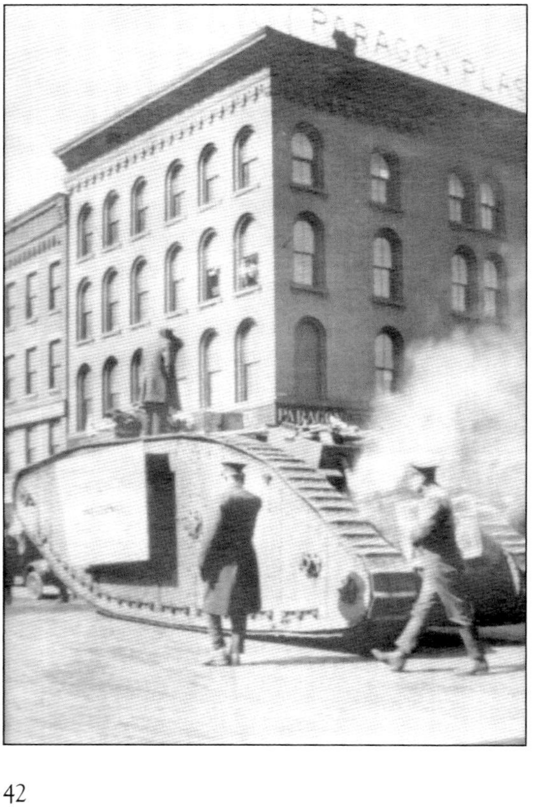

The Paragon Plaster and Supply Company, c. 1910. The Paragon Plaster and Supply Company manufactured Paragon wall plaster, cement, lime, hair, marble dust, and flue lining, among other items. The Paragon occupied two blocks, from 101 to 121 Green Ridge Street. Eurie L. Merriman was president of the company. His son Richard took over for Eurie and remained president until the Paragon closed its doors in the late 1950s. (Courtesy of Yore Antiques.)

Paragon Supporting the Red Cross. A US Army tank was in town advertising thrifty stamps and a show to benefit the Red Cross. The tank was equipped with a knight motor similar to a car. The Paragon is in background. (Courtesy of the author.)

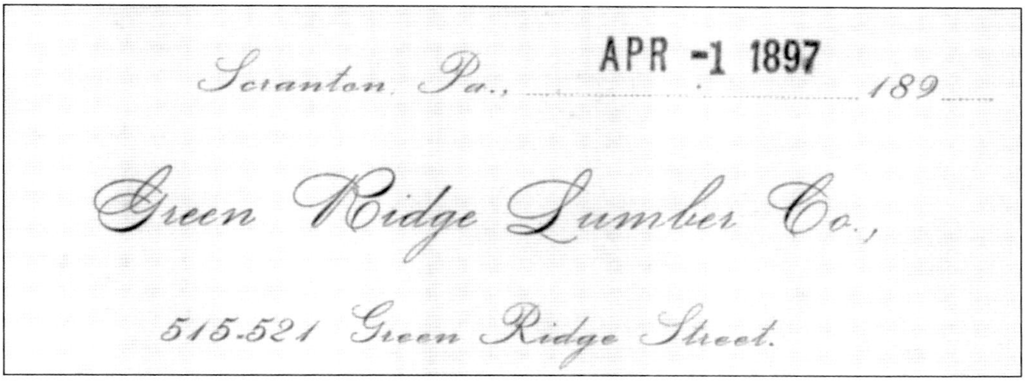

Scranton, Pa., APR -1 1897 189

Green Ridge Lumber Co.,

515-521 Green Ridge Street.

GREEN RIDGE LUMBER COMPANY. M.D. Brown, who at the time owned half-lots on Green Ridge Street near the Delaware & Hudson Railroad Depot, established the lumber business in May 1885. In 1888, the firm became incorporated under the name Green Ridge Lumber Company with W.L. Scott as president. The company was located at 515–521 Green Ridge Street. (Courtesy of the author.)

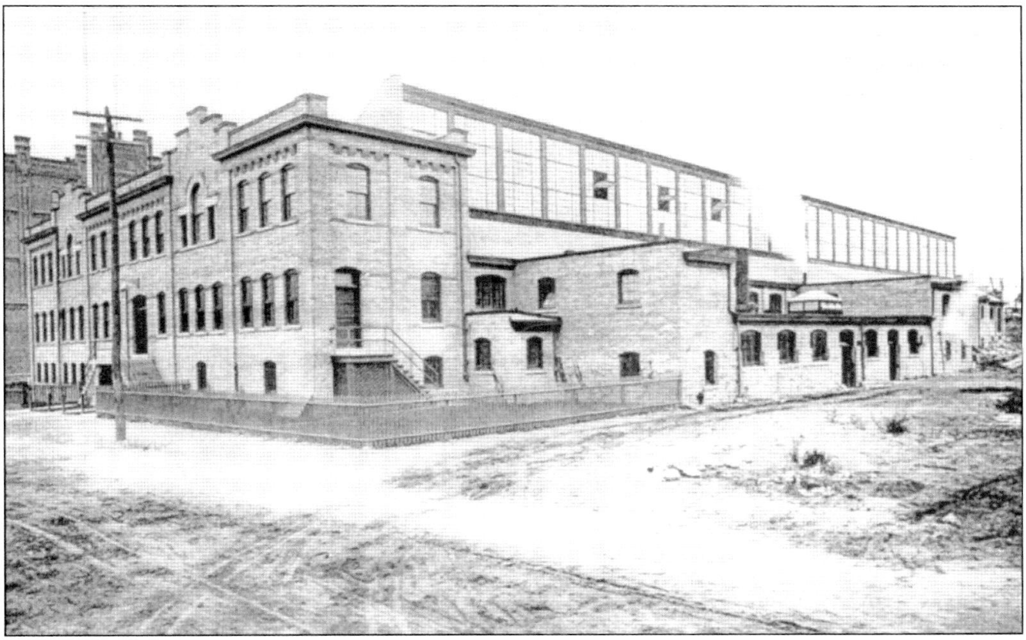

KLOT'S THROWING COMPANY. This silk manufacturer, located in Carbondale from 1894 until 1918, had a mill in the Green Ridge section of the city. The majority of its employees were women. Members of the Belin family, natives of Green Ridge, were investors and officers in the company. (Courtesy of Yore Antiques.)

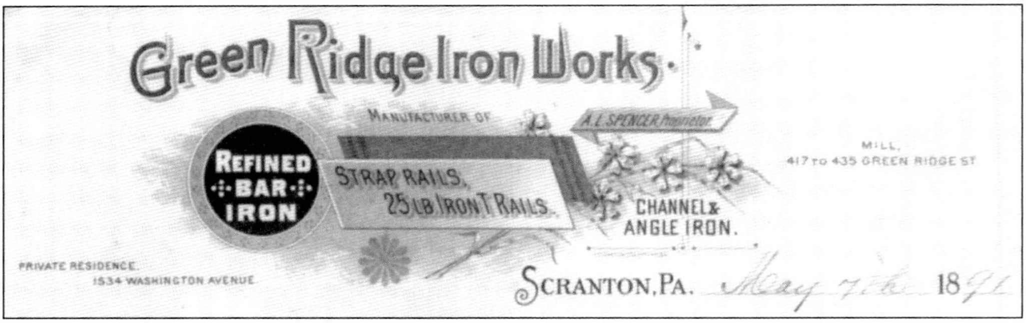

Green Ridge Iron Works. Green Ridge Iron Works was established in 1876 on Capouse Avenue. The iron works consisted of one furnace with the capacity to make three tons of iron per day. A.L. Spencer was proprietor. The firm eventually became Spencer and Price. The partnership between the two men lasted until 1878, when Price retired. (Courtesy of the author.)

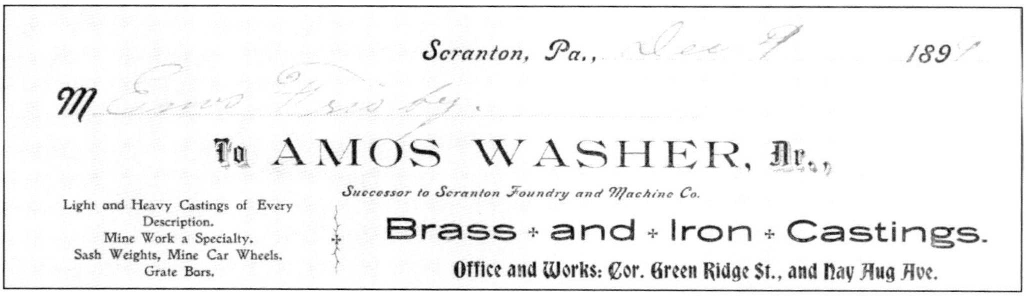

Amos Washer, c. 1899. Amos Washer was the successor to Scranton Foundry and Machine Company. The business was located on Green Ridge Street and Nay Aug Avenue. Mine work was its specialty. (Courtesy of the author.)

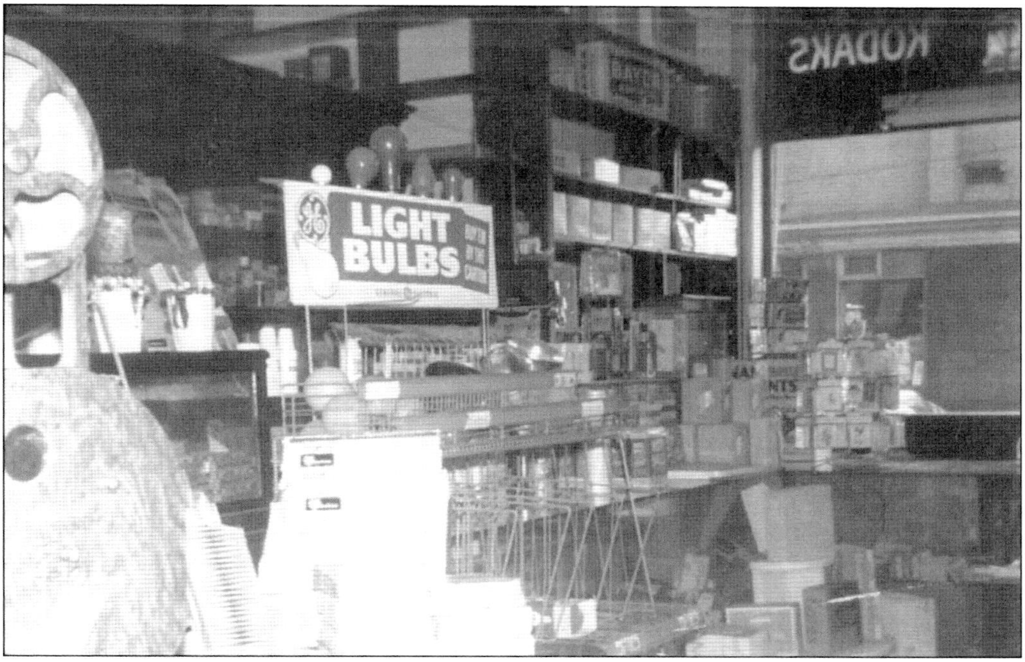

THOMPSON'S PHARMACY, c. 1965. Before Burke's, there was Thompson's Pharmacy on Green Ridge Corners. People shopped there for all their health and beauty needs. And like the sign says, "G.E. Light Bulbs, Buy them by the Carton." (Both, courtesy of Joanne Hector.)

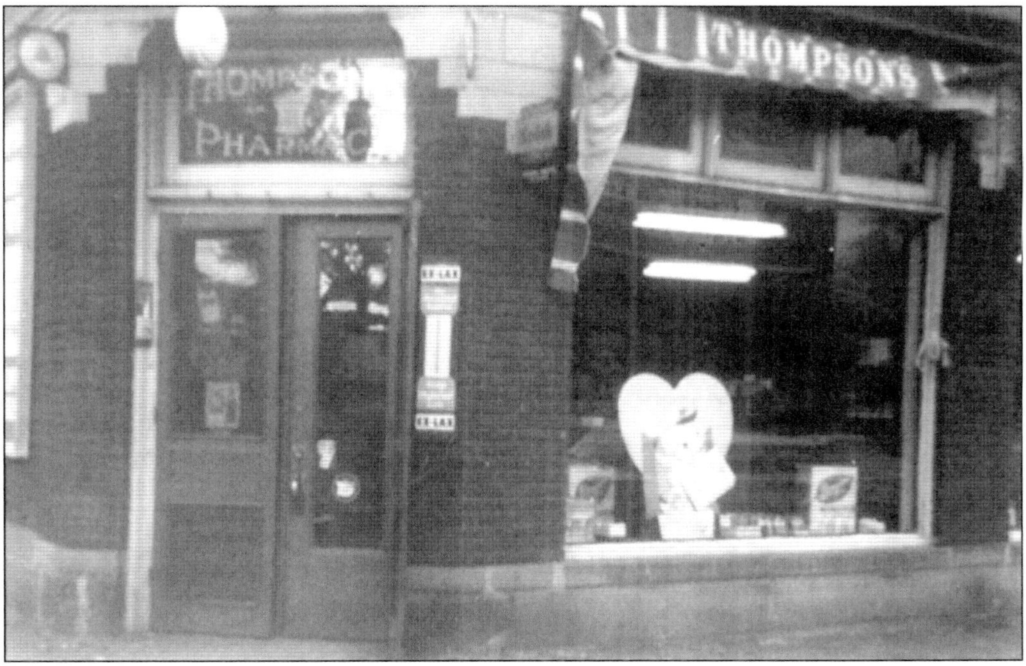

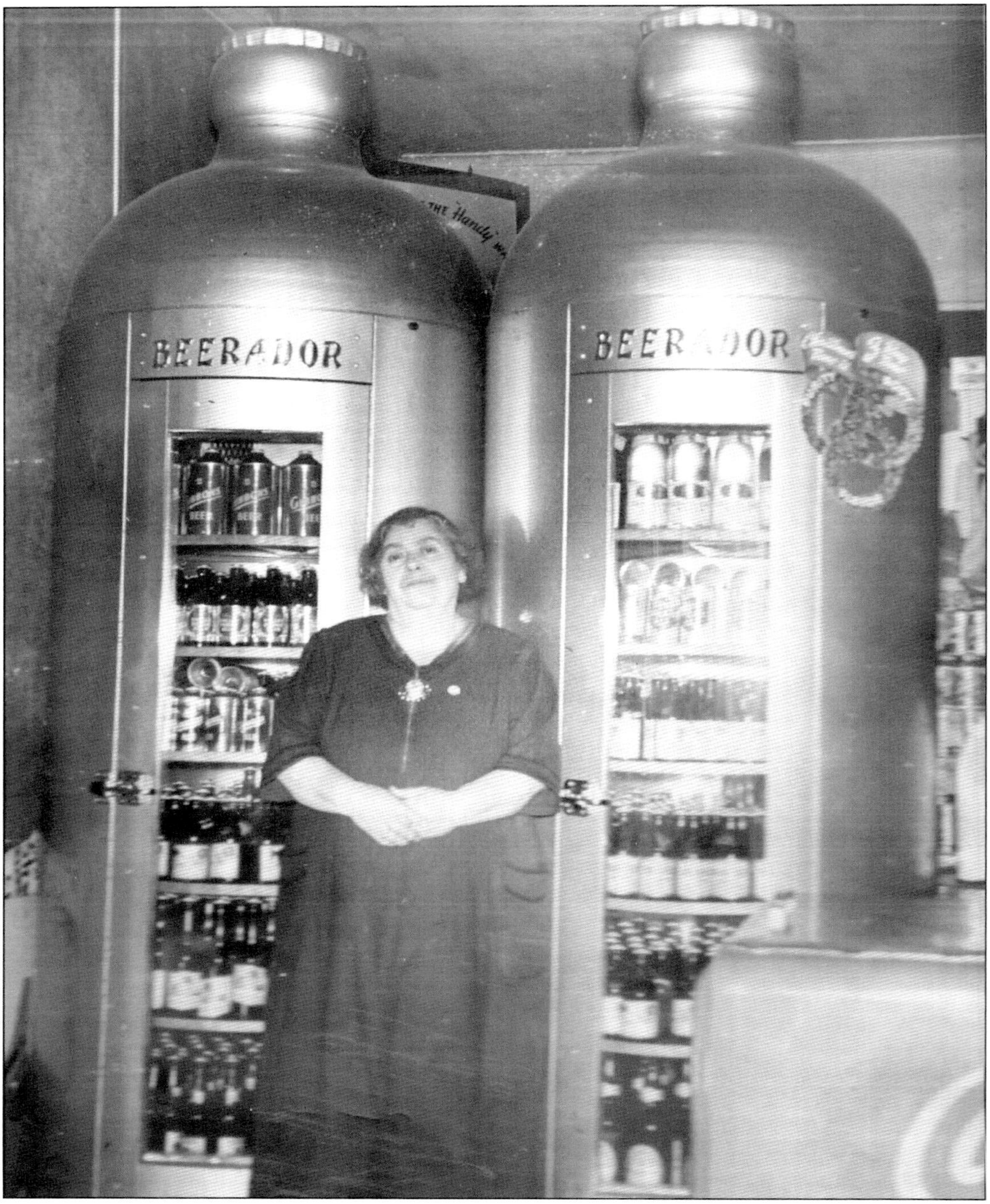

DIRTY MARY'S TAVERN. Mary Ricardo, affectionately known as "Dirty Mary," owned a drinking establishment in Green Ridge for many years. She is pictured standing in front of two huge beer coolers called "Beeradors." Mary was the first saloon keeper in the city to obtain a liquor license when Prohibition ended. There was more to Mary than just beer; she was awarded a medal and citation from the American Red Cross in 1918 for "Service faithfully performed on behalf of the Nation and her Men in Arms" during World War I. She had knitted tons of socks, sweaters, and other articles that were sent to the boys in the American camps and on the frontline in France. Mary had no relatives in World War I, "she just loved the boys who were in the service," as she said, and everyone who knew Mary loved her too. (Courtesy of the Brunetti family.)

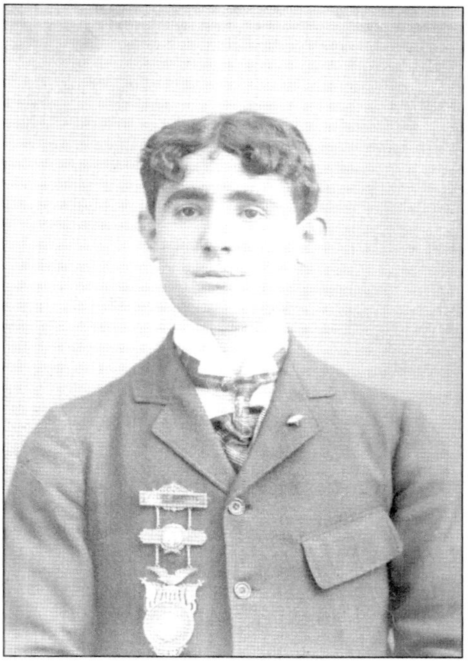

Most Popular Barber, c. 1899. Joseph Vola owned and operated a barbershop on Boulevard Avenue in the late 1800s. He was the son of Scranton policeman Teddy Vola. The *New York Police Gazette* awarded Joseph the title of "the Most Popular Barber in the United States." (Courtesy of the Brunetti family.)

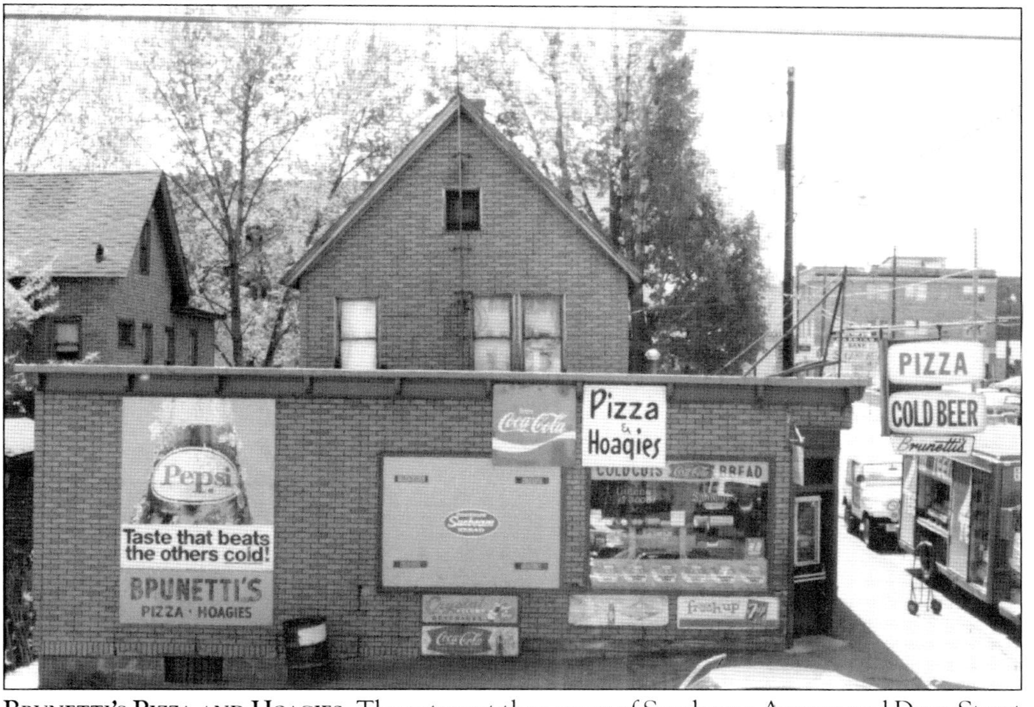

Brunetti's Pizza and Hoagies. The eatery at the corner of Sanderson Avenue and Dean Street opened in 1958 and is still going strong. The Brunetti family purchased the building in the 1980s. Michael Brunetti, proprietor, and his wonderful family make patrons feel right at home as soon as they walk through the door. They bring a little bit of Italy to Green Ridge. (Courtesy of the Brunetti family.)

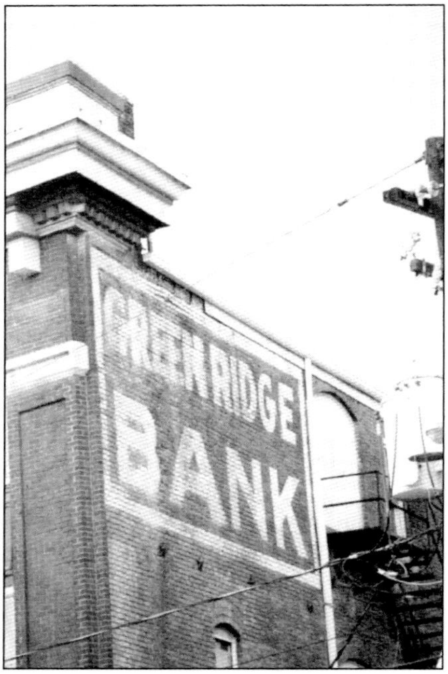

GREEN RIDGE BANK. Around the beginning of the 20th century, Green Ridge Corners began to flourish with businesses. The bank opened in 1910, the Howard M. Snowden Funeral Home in 1907, and the Roosevelt Theatre in 1925. (Courtesy of the author.)

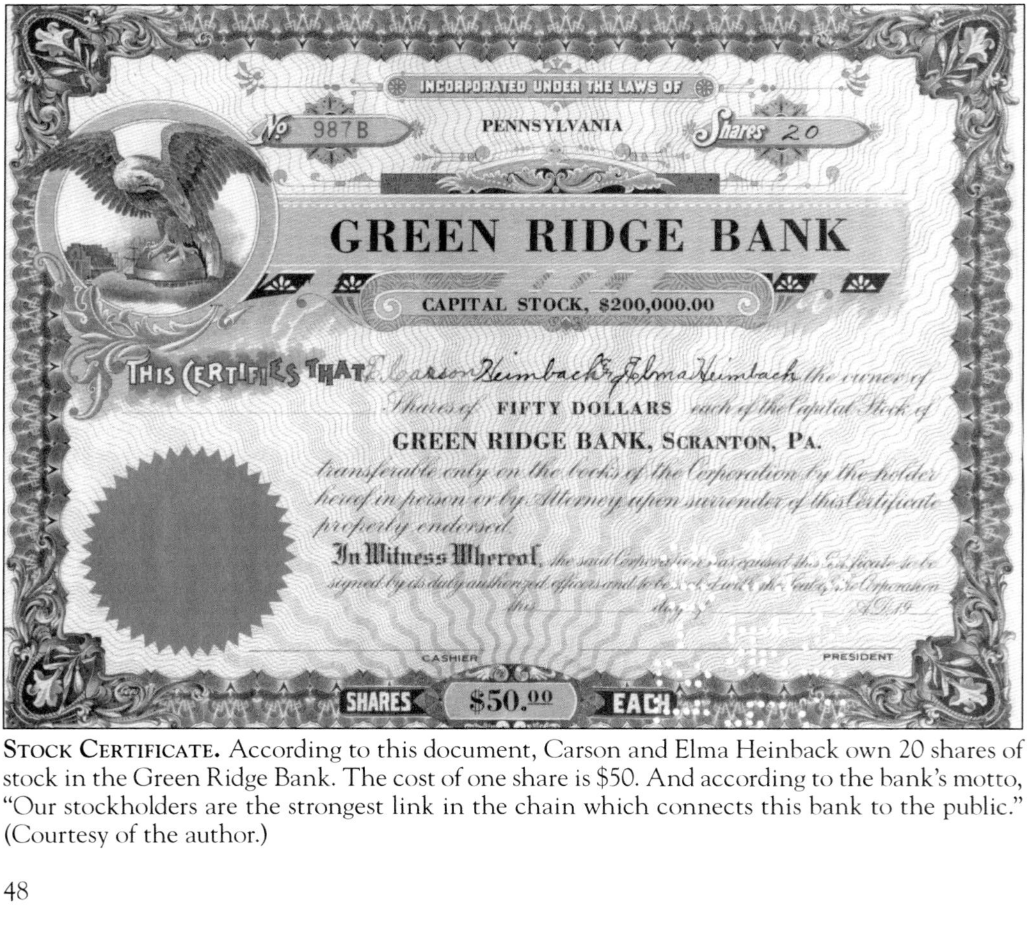

INCORPORATED UNDER THE LAWS OF

No 987B PENNSYLVANIA Shares 20

GREEN RIDGE BANK

CAPITAL STOCK, $200,000.00

THIS CERTIFIES THAT Carson Heimback & Elma Heimback the owner of Shares of FIFTY DOLLARS each of the Capital Stock of

GREEN RIDGE BANK, SCRANTON, PA.

transferable only on the books of the Corporation by the holder hereof in person or by Attorney upon surrender of this Certificate properly endorsed.

In Witness Whereof, the said Corporation has caused this Certificate to be signed by its duly authorized officers and to be sealed with the Seal of the Corporation this day of A.D. 19

CASHIER PRESIDENT

SHARES $50.00 EACH

STOCK CERTIFICATE. According to this document, Carson and Elma Heinback own 20 shares of stock in the Green Ridge Bank. The cost of one share is $50. And according to the bank's motto, "Our stockholders are the strongest link in the chain which connects this bank to the public." (Courtesy of the author.)

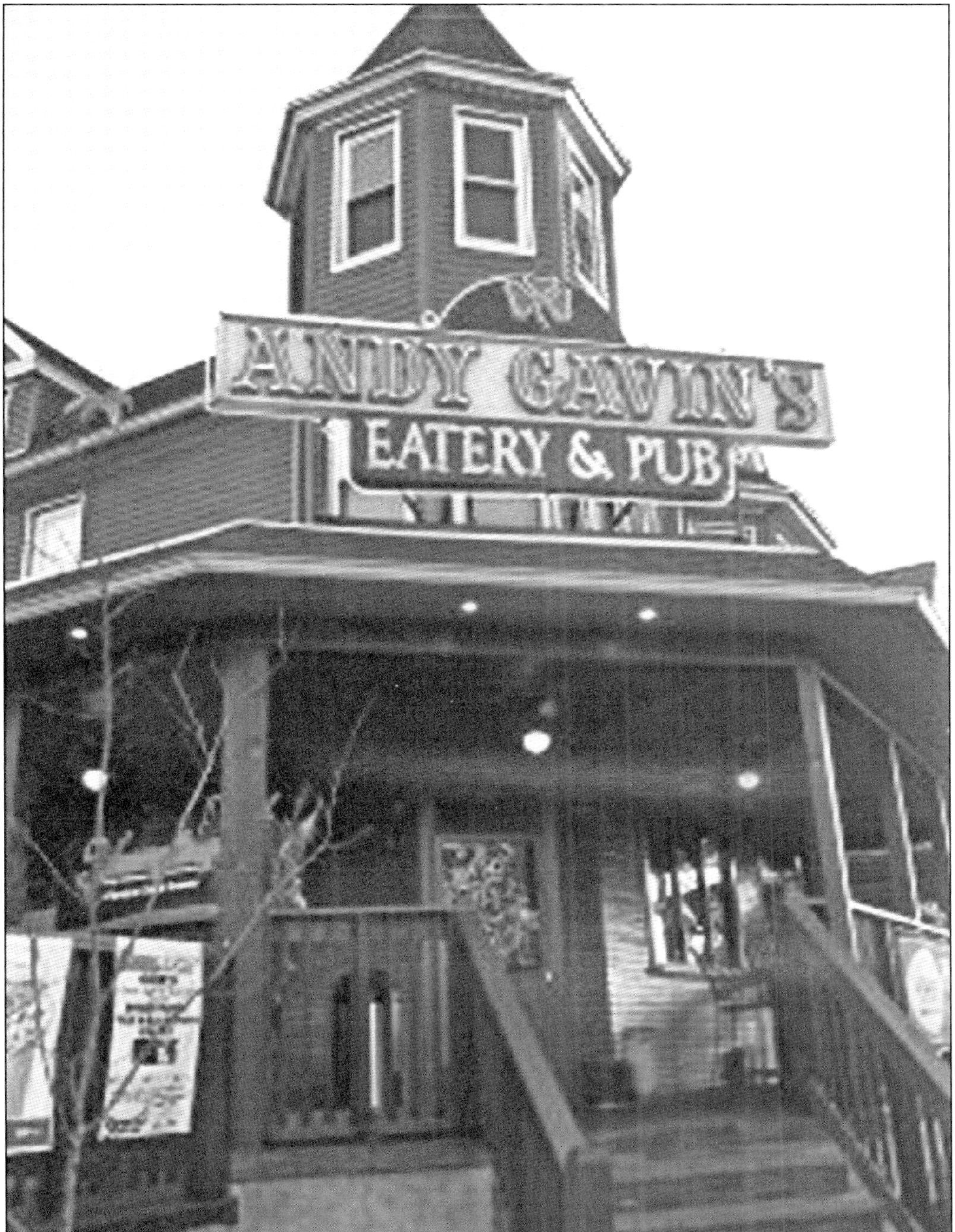

ANDY GAVIN'S. The iconic Green Ridge eatery and pub celebrated its 50th anniversary in 2010. Since 1988, Donnie Surace has run Andy Gavin's. The Victorian building dates back to 1903 and has seen its share of owners. But the one constant is George the miner, the ghost who is said to haunt the place. George likes to flick the lights on and off and pull customers' hair. (Courtesy of the author.)

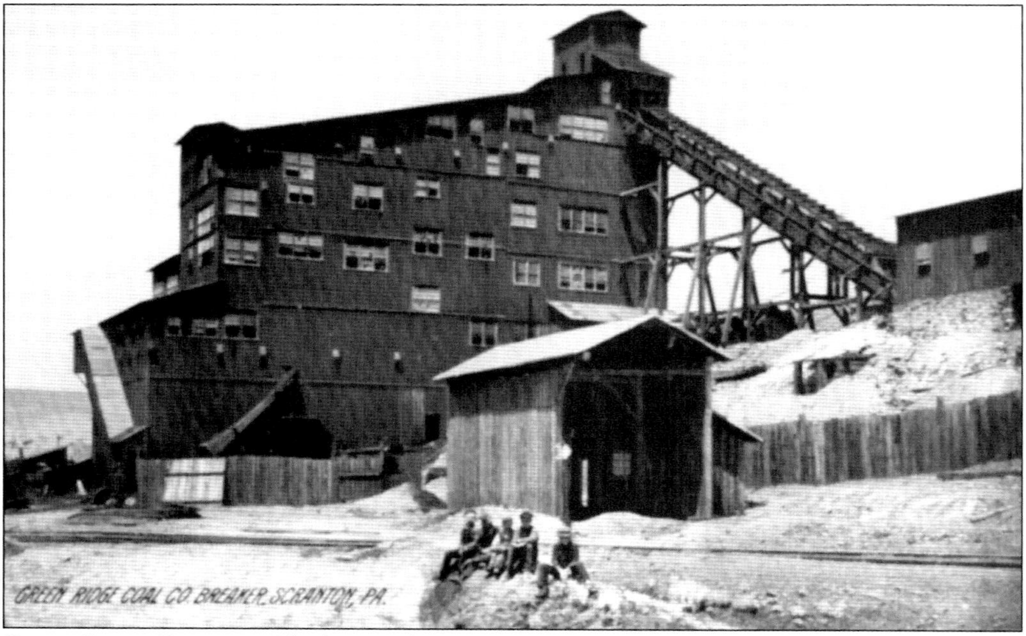

Green Ridge Breaker. The best anthracite coal was the bedrock of the Green Ridge section. The first to open mines was the Delaware & Hudson Railroad; the company built the Von Storch Breaker in 1859 on the Green Ridge Flats. The Green Ridge Breaker was opened in 1870 by George Filer, Frank Marsh, and James Riley. The shaft and breaker were located on North Washington Avenue at the intersection of Poplar Street. It was one of the oldest mine operations in the city. The Green Ridge Breaker closed in the early 1940s. (Courtesy of Mark Boock.)

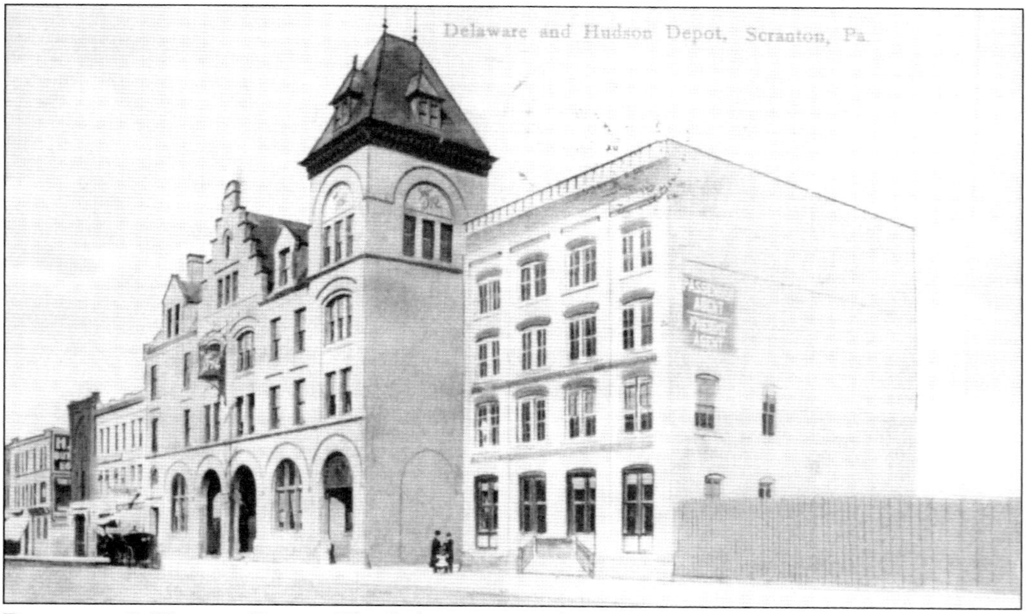

Delaware & Hudson Depot. The Delaware & Hudson Railroad line ran to East Market Street in 1860. The opening of the Von Storch Mine extended the line to central city in 1863. (Courtesy of Mark Boock.)

Five

Historical Mansions

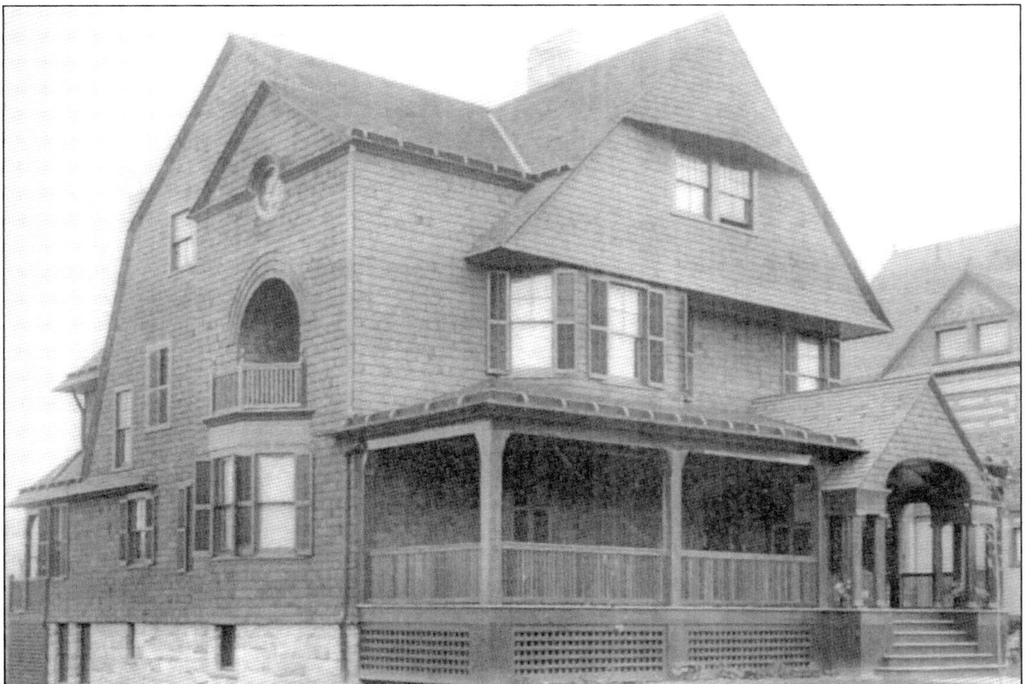

The Kennedy Mansion. This home, located at 1717 North Washington Avenue, was built in the late 1880s and belonged to Mr. and Mrs. William DeWitt Kennedy. On February 11, 1918, the couple celebrated their 50th wedding anniversary. The bride was the daughter of Mr. and Mrs. Pulaski Carter, a pioneer family in the valley with ancestors dating back to Colonial and Revolutionary times. The groom was a veteran of the Civil War and director of the Scranton Savings Bank. The couple resided in their Green Ridge home for 30 years until 1923, when Mrs. Kennedy passed away. (Courtesy of Susan White Pieroth.)

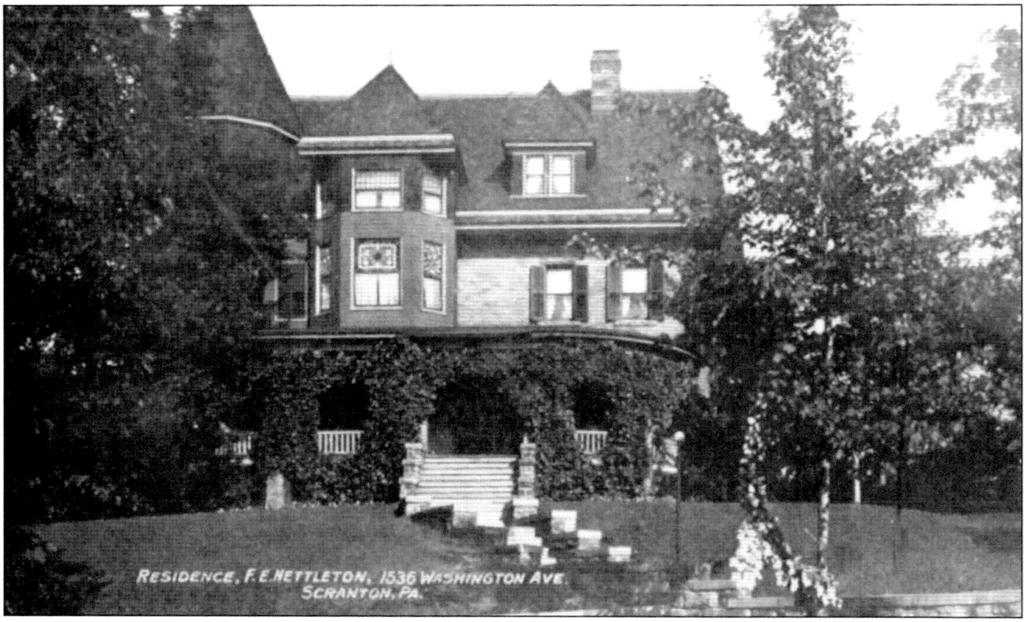

RESIDENCE OF F.E. NETTLETON. The mansion of Franklyn E. Nettleton was located at 1536 North Washington Avenue. Among his neighbors was Michael M. Bosak, a prominent banker in the city. Nettleton was engaged in the boot and shoe business before his retirement in 1886. He had the honor of calling the first meeting for the organization of the Young Men's Christian Association in Scranton. (Courtesy of Robert J. Walker.)

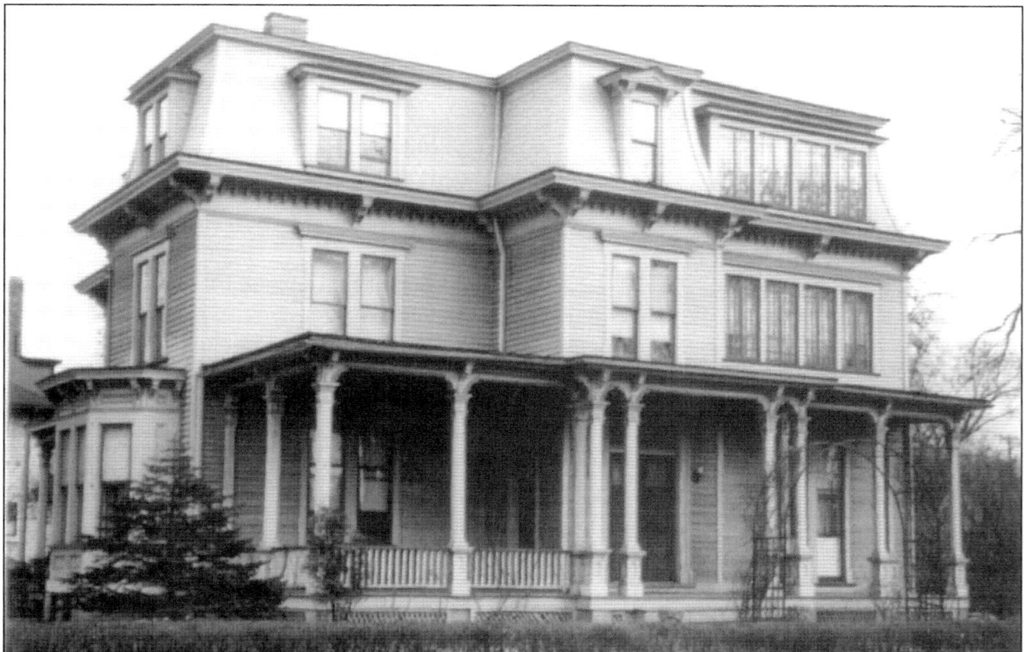

SANDERSON AVENUE RESIDENCE. The original owners of this beautiful home on the 1600 block of Sanderson Avenue are unknown. (Courtesy of Robert J. Walker.)

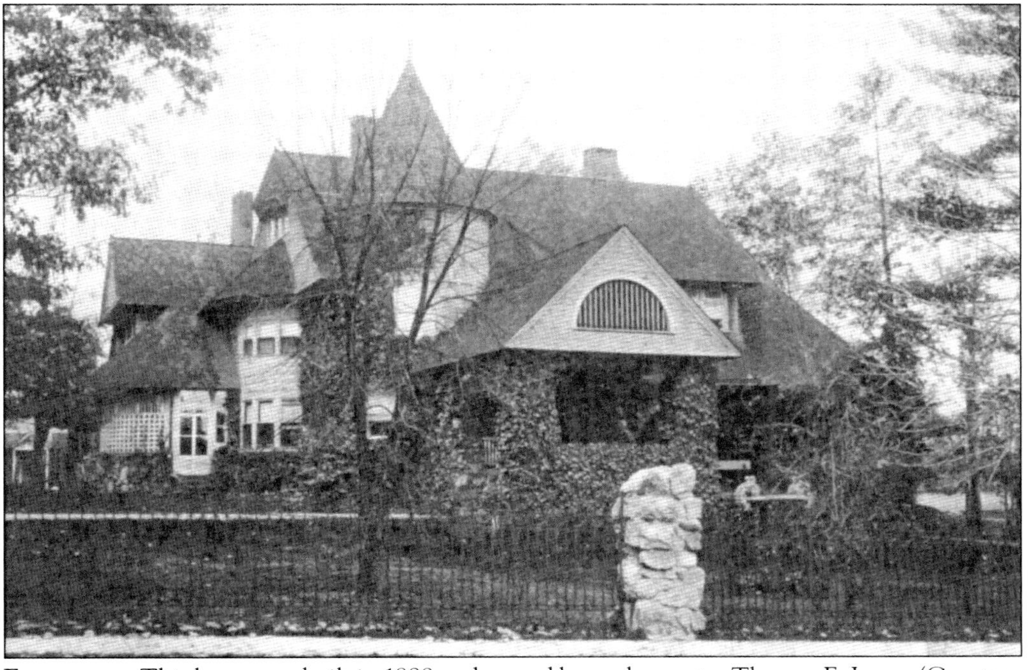

Fieldstone. This home was built in 1888 and owned by coal operator Thomas E. Jones. (Courtesy of Robert J. Walker.)

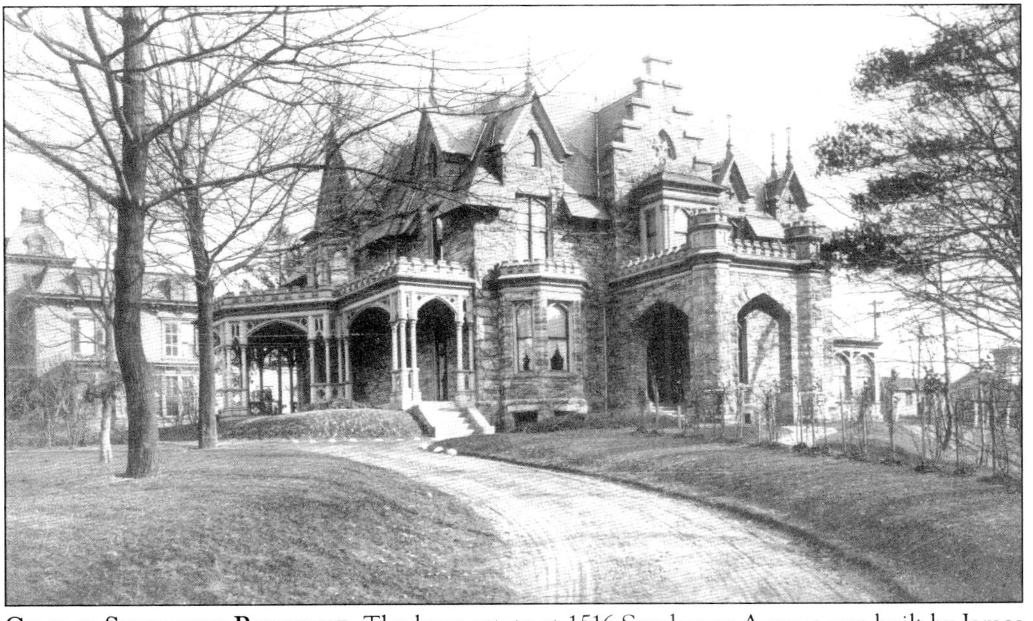

Conrad Schroeder Residence. The large estate at 1516 Sanderson Avenue was built by James G. Sanderson in the early 1870s. James lived in the "mansion house" until 1889. It was then sold to Conrad Schroeder, well-known contractor and president of the Carlucci Stone Company. He resided in the home until his death in 1903, and his widow remained until she passed away in 1941. The house was razed in 1947. (Courtesy of the Lackawanna Historical Society.)

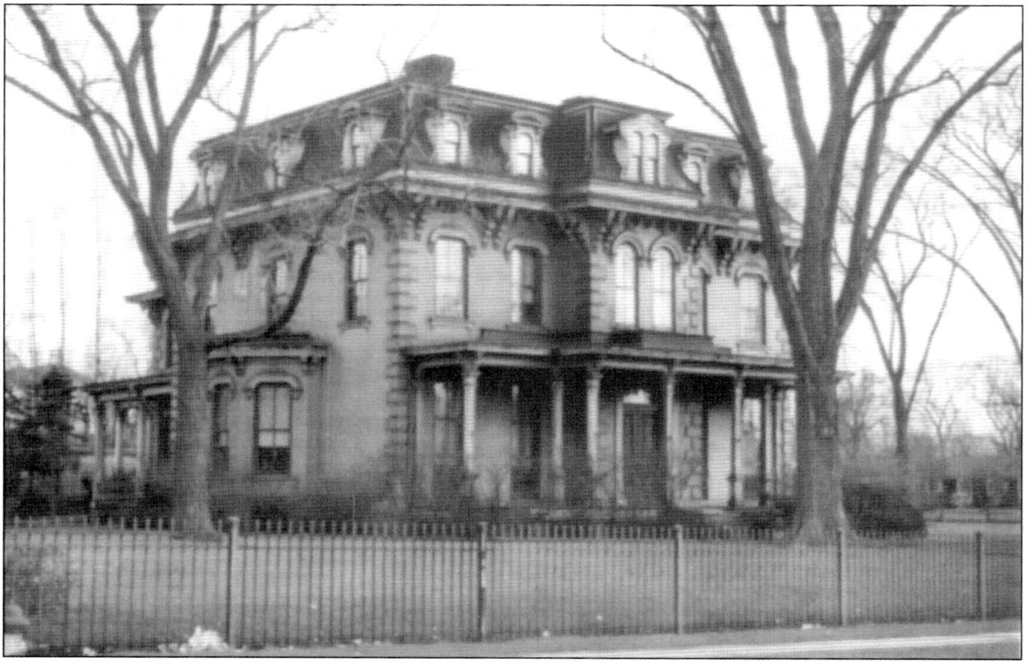

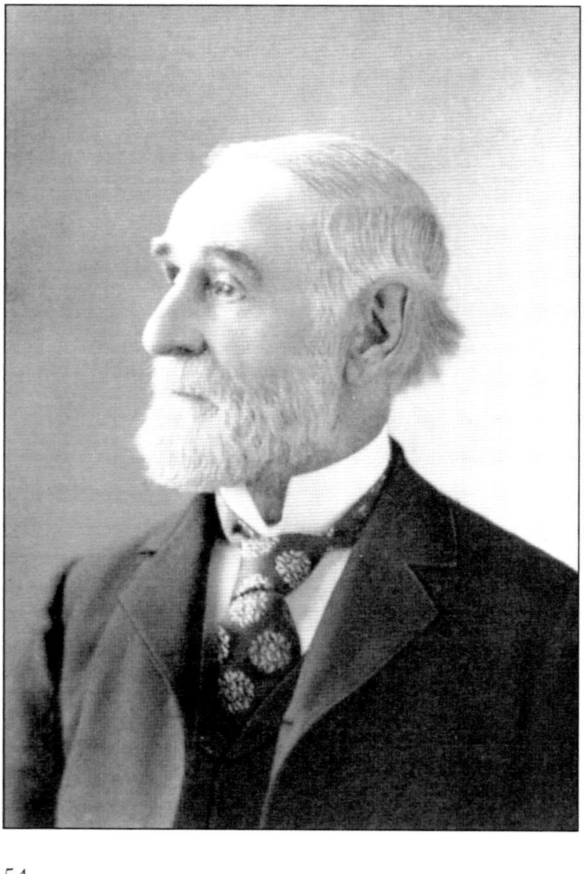

THE PAULI HOME. In 1897, Francis S. Pauli (pictured at left) was the oldest surviving resident in Green Ridge. He was born in 1823 and came to Scranton in 1857, where he opened a gentleman's hat and furnishing store on Lackawanna Avenue. He built the house at 1554 Sanderson Avenue, which was one of the first homes in Green Ridge. (Above, courtesy of Robert J. Walker; left, courtesy of the author.)

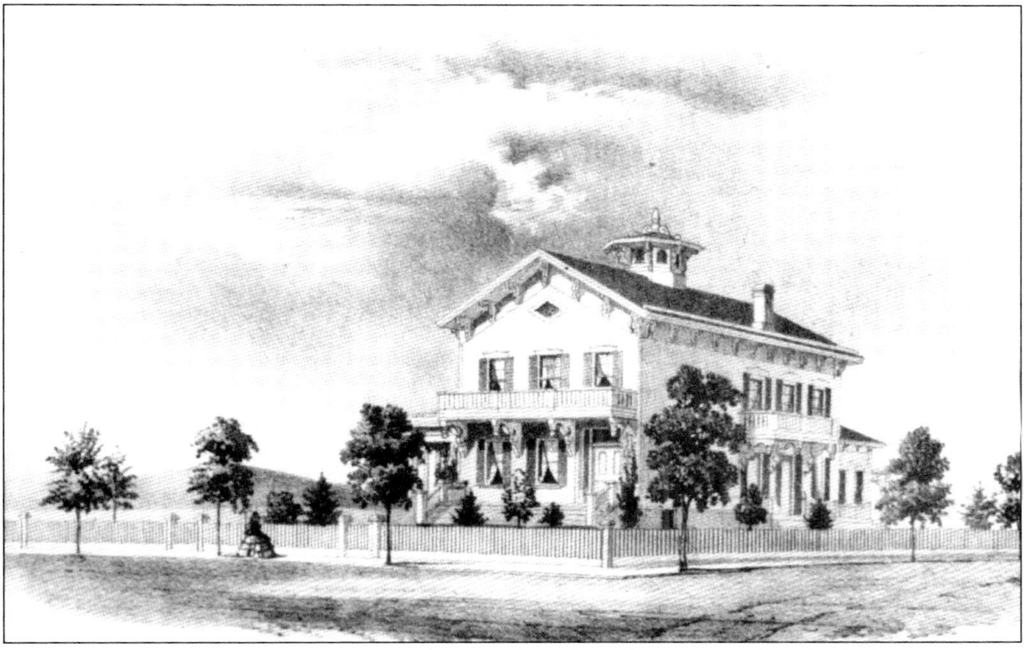

The Founder's Home. George Sanderson, founder of Green Ridge, built his Victorian home appropriately on Sanderson Avenue in 1865. He resided there until his death in 1886. Today, it is the current site of the Green Ridge Nursing Home. (Courtesy of the Lackawanna Historical Society.)

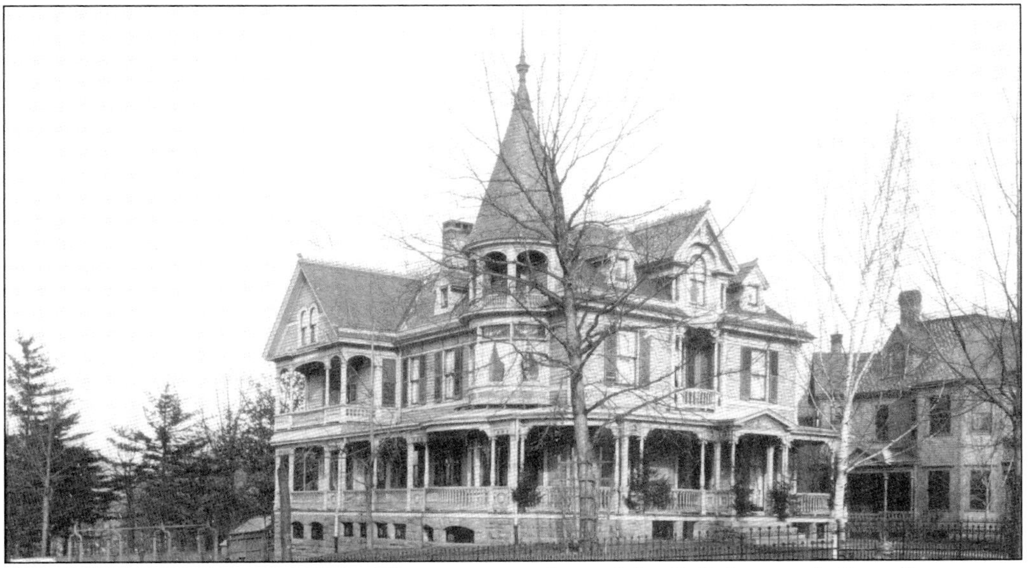

Charles Robinson's Residence. The superintendent of the E. Robinson & Sons Brewery on Seventh Street had his residence in Green Ridge on the 1500 block of North Washington Avenue. (Courtesy of the Lackawanna Historical Society.)

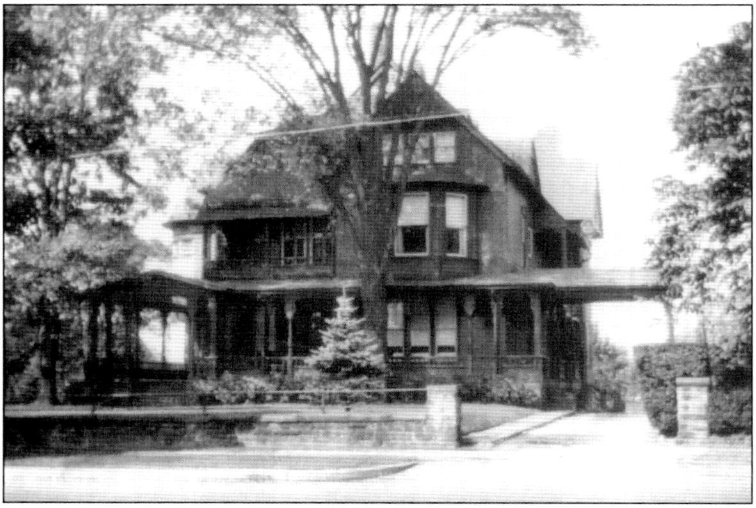

The Hemelright Home. The original owner of the 1545 Sanderson Avenue residence was Frank H. Hemelright. Members of the Winton family purchased the home in 1905. (Courtesy of Robert J. Walker.)

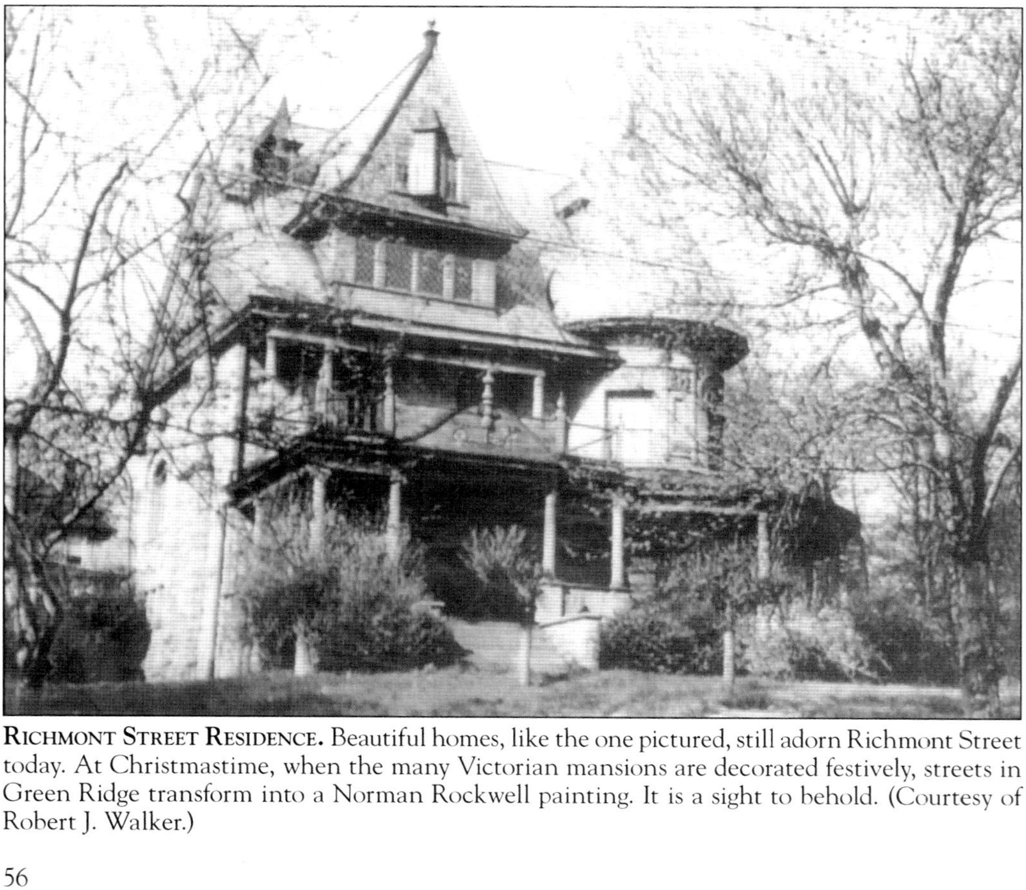

Richmont Street Residence. Beautiful homes, like the one pictured, still adorn Richmont Street today. At Christmastime, when the many Victorian mansions are decorated festively, streets in Green Ridge transform into a Norman Rockwell painting. It is a sight to behold. (Courtesy of Robert J. Walker.)

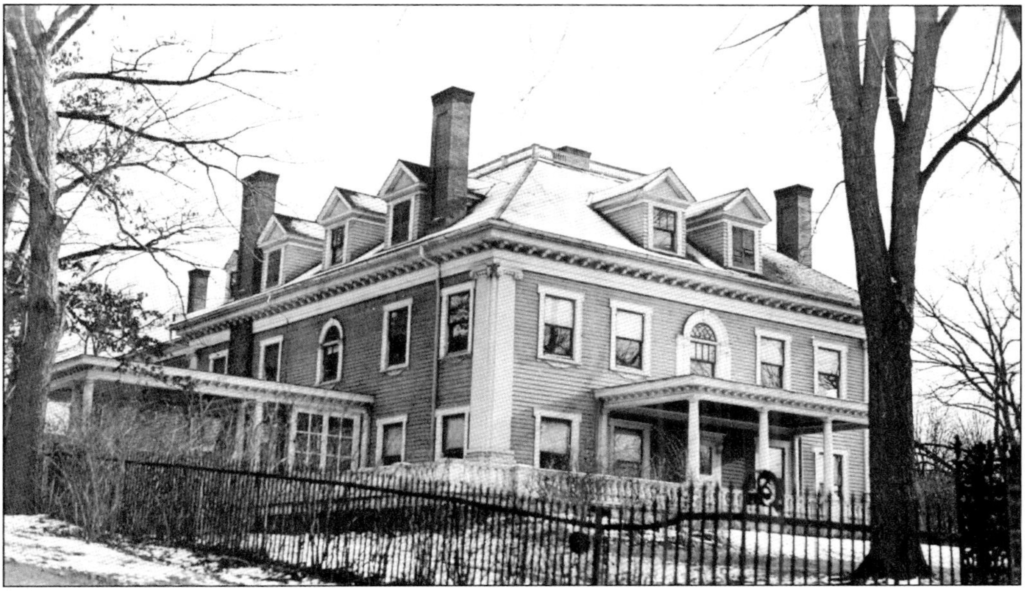

Residence of J. Benjamin Dimmick. The former mayor's home was located on the 1700 block of North Washington Avenue; J. Benjamin Dimmick and Scranton's mayor since 2002, Christopher Doherty, would have been neighbors 100 years ago. Pictured below is the extraordinary rear view of the residence around 1897. (Both, courtesy of the Lackawanna Historical Society.)

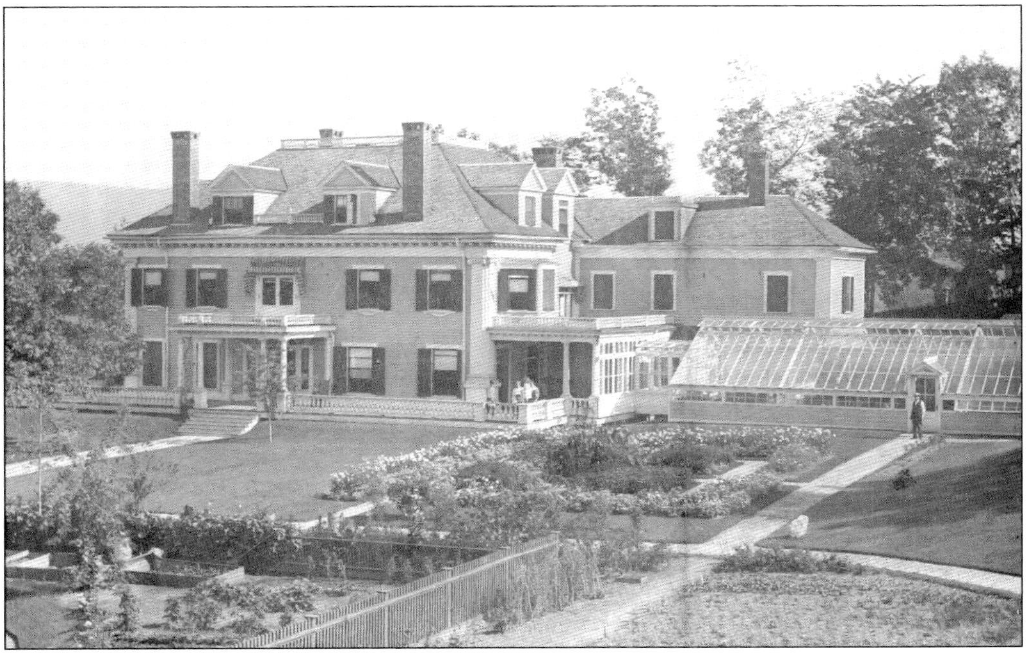

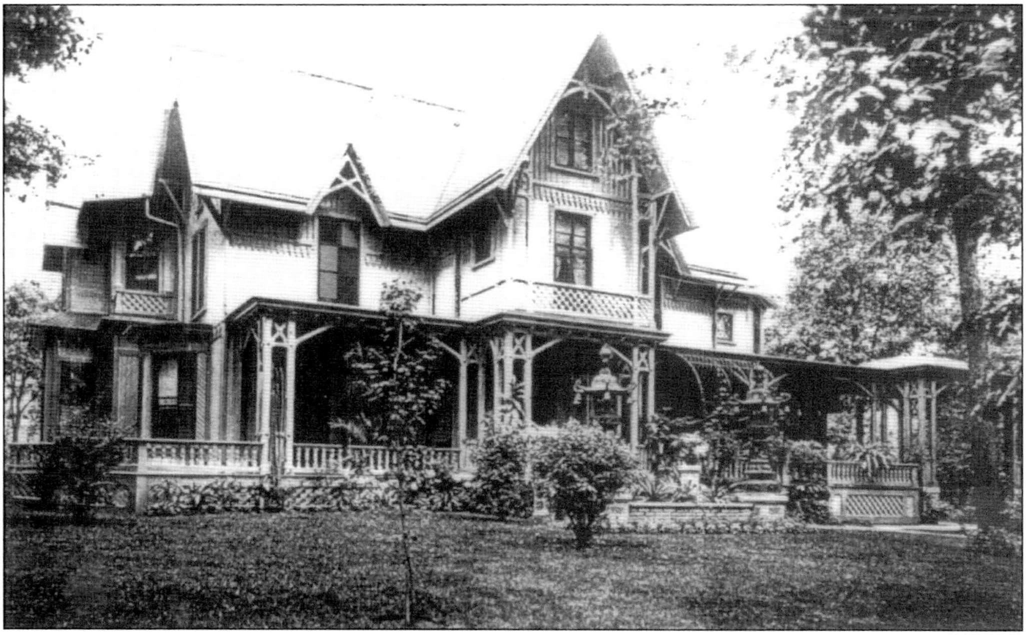

Sturges and Walker Mansion. E.B. Sturges had the magnificent mansion shown above built on the 1600 block of North Washington Avenue in 1875. It was the first and only home on the block at the time. He and his wife, Marion, and their children resided there until 1924. Flash forward 83 years and four owners later, local businessman and Green Ridge historian R.J. Walker purchased the property shown below and had the home restored to its original beauty. (Both, courtesy of Robert J. Walker.)

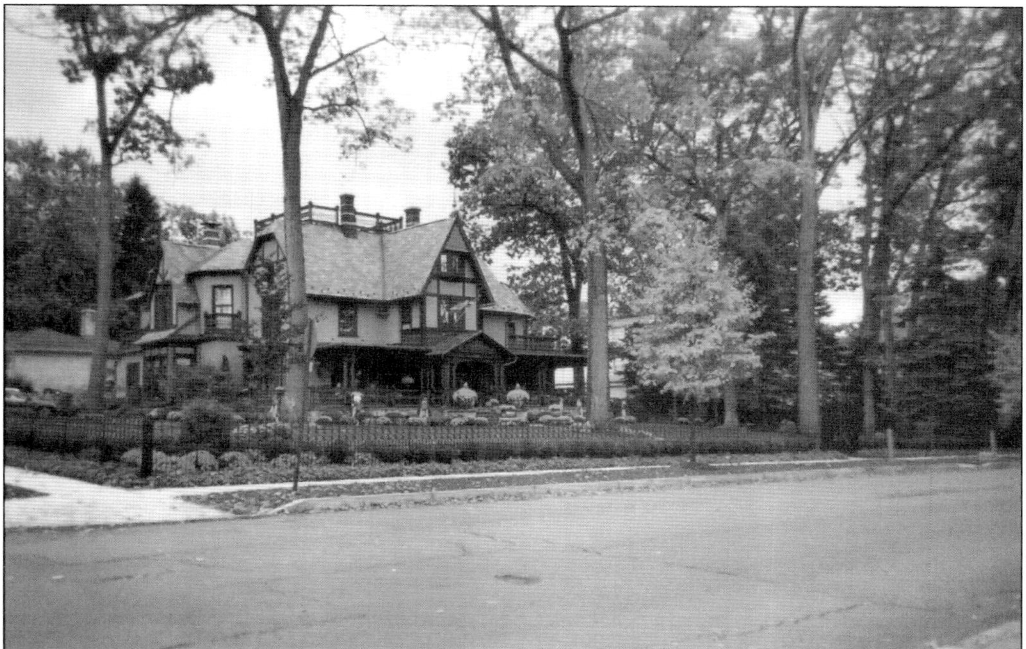

Six

Learning My ABCs

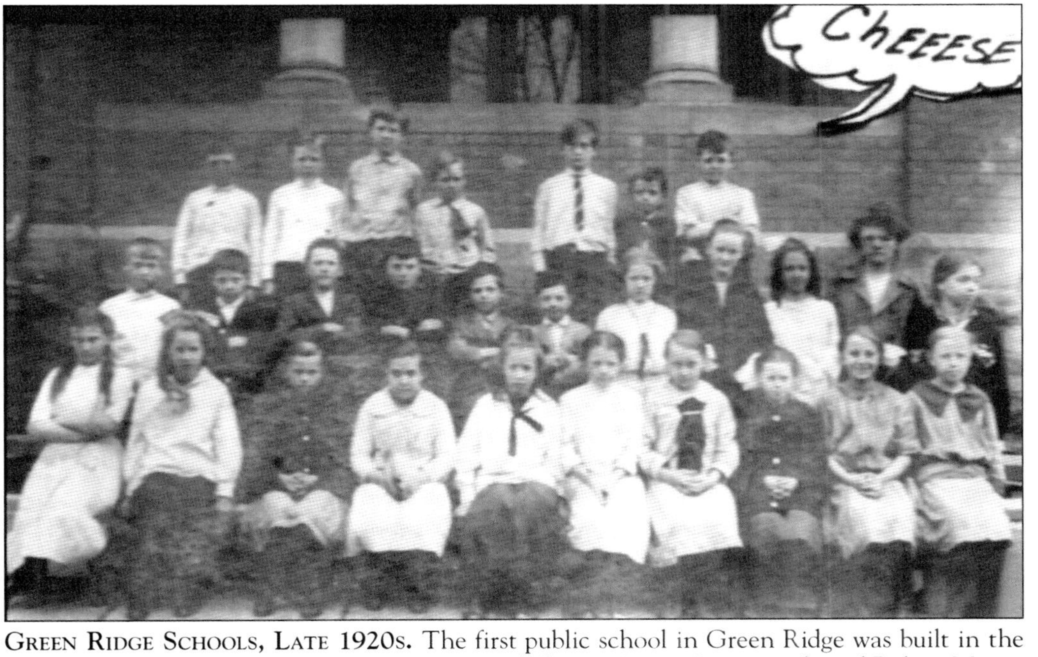

Green Ridge Schools, Late 1920s. The first public school in Green Ridge was built in the early 1870s on the corner of Dickson Avenue and Electric Street. It was used until Robert Morris No. 27 School was built in 1897. This class picture is of students who attended the Robert Morris School. (Courtesy of the Brunetti family.)

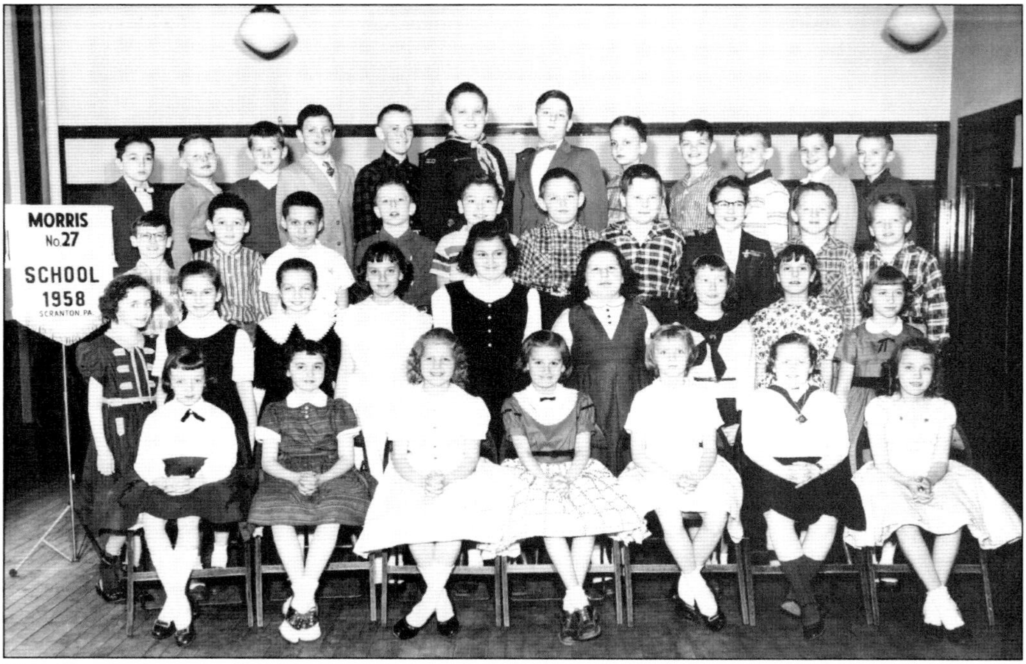

THE CLASSES OF 1958 AND 1960. Here is picture day at Robert Morris School on two different occasions. Many children who lived in the Green Ridge area attended the elementary school. Robert Morris was built in 1897. Eventually, all Green Ridge schools were consolidated into No. 27 at Green Ridge Corners. (Both, courtesy of the Brunetti family.)

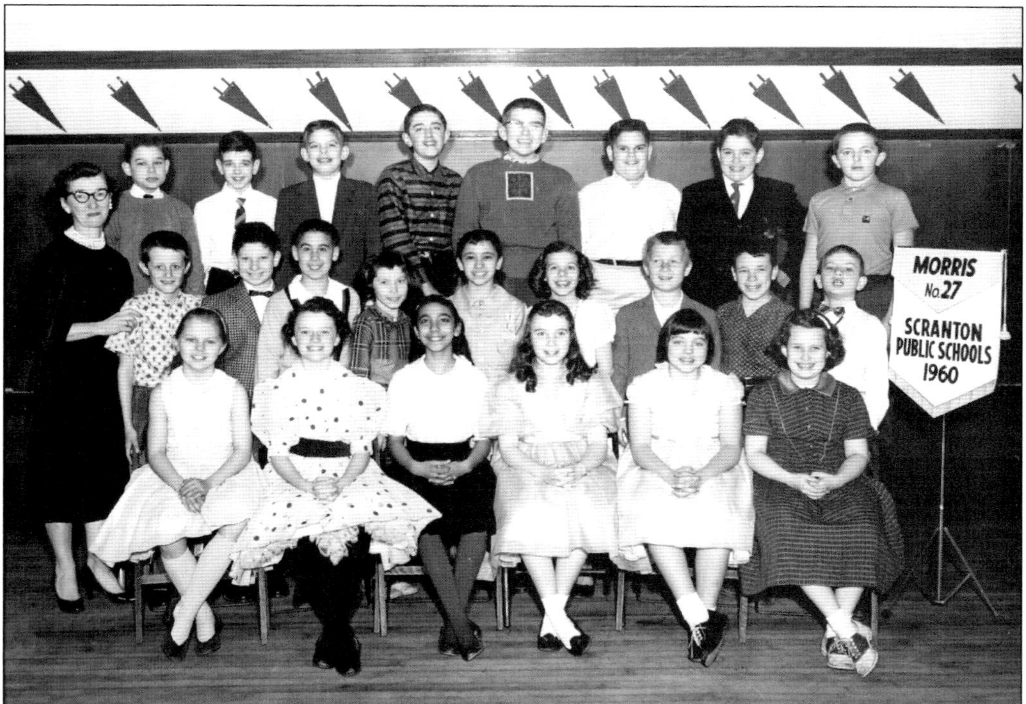

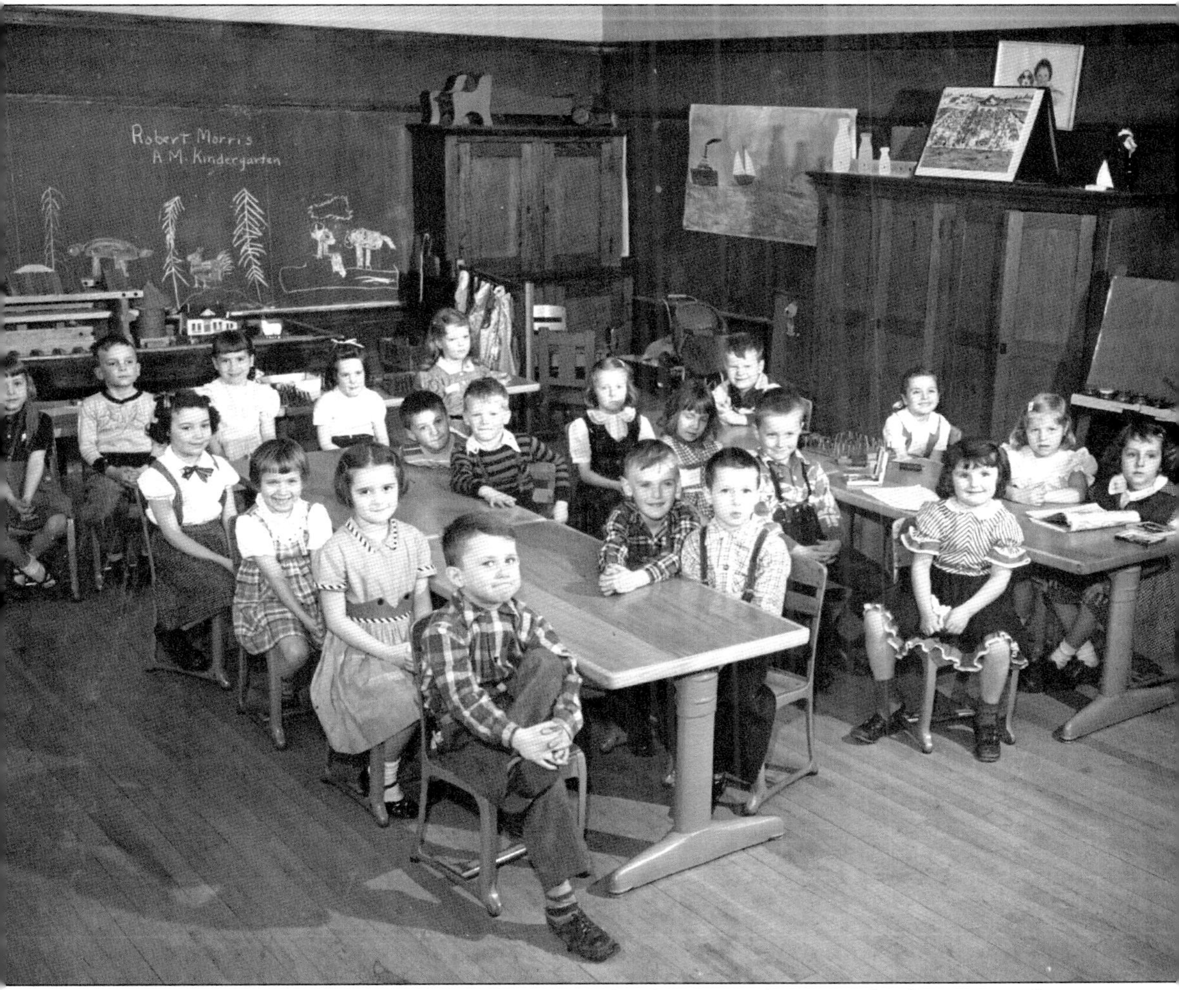

A Well-Behaved Class. Robert Morris's morning kindergarten class poses for the camera. Some of the children's artwork is shown in the background on the blackboard. Judging by their angelic smiles, they were a very well-behaved class. (Courtesy of the Brunetti family.)

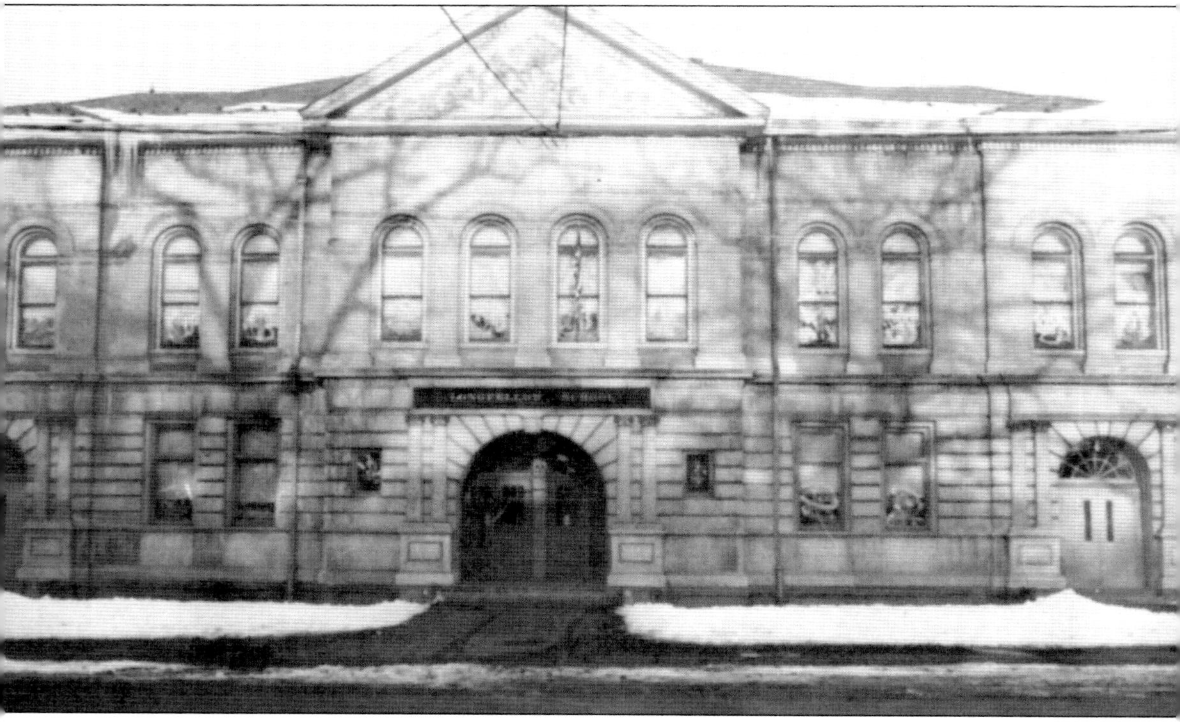

HENRY LONGFELLOW SCHOOL. Another school in Green Ridge was Henry Longfellow No. 28 on Wyoming Avenue. The school opened in 1891 along with Emerson School No. 34 on Albright Avenue. Today, both schools are closed. (Courtesy of Joanne Hector.)

Seven

SERVANTS OF THE IMMACULATE HEART OF MARY

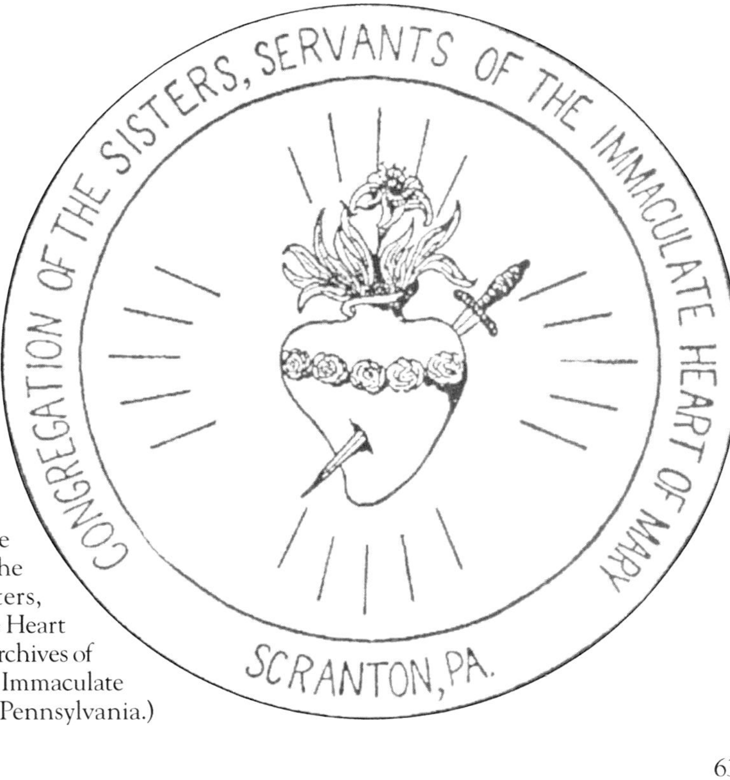

THE CONGREGATION'S SEAL. The artist is unknown, but the design intends to capture in an image with words the meaning of the title of the congregation of the Sisters, Servants of the Immaculate Heart of Mary. (Courtesy of the Archives of the Sisters, Servants of the Immaculate Heart of Mary, Scranton, Pennsylvania.)

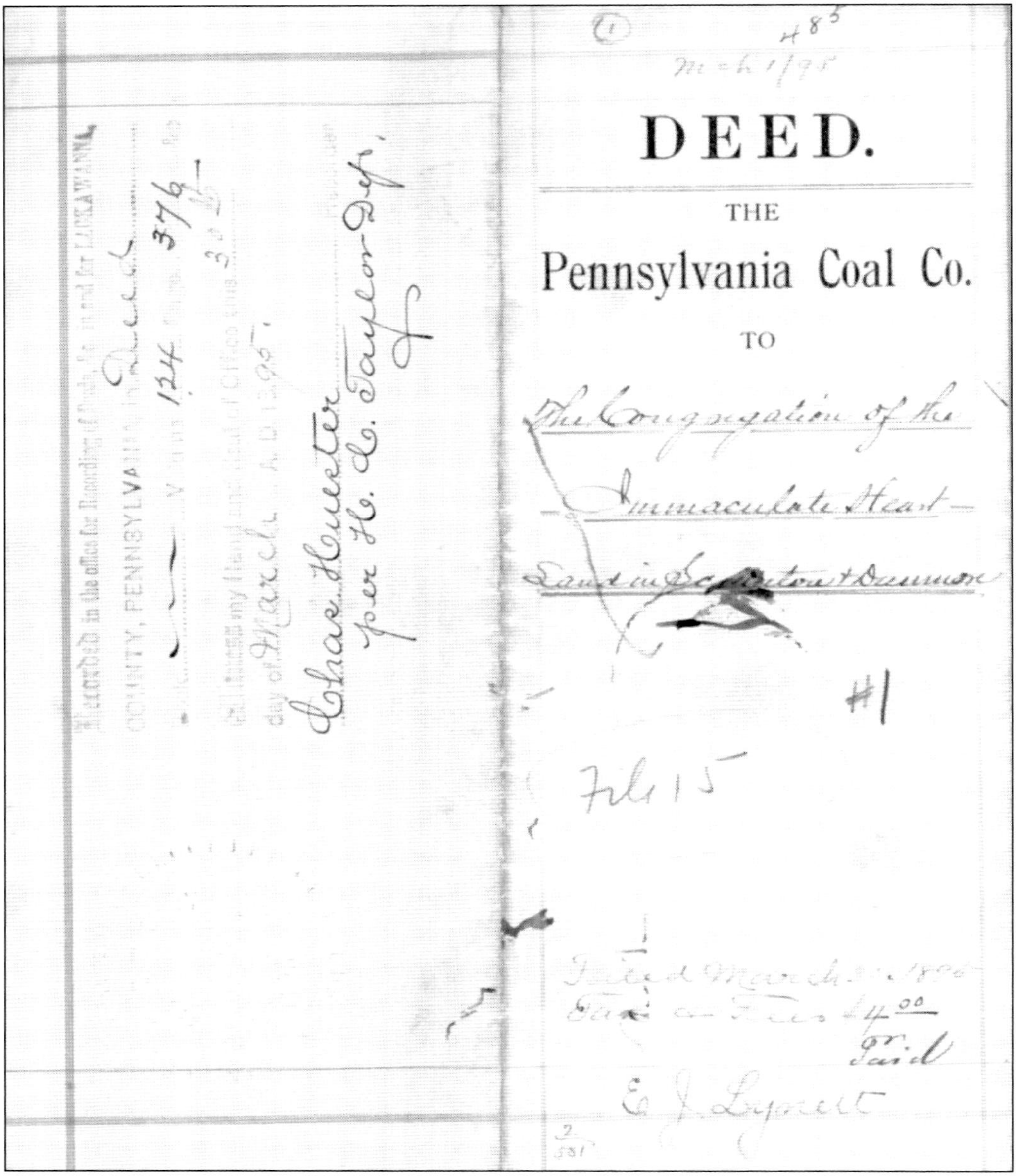

DEED.

THE

Pennsylvania Coal Co.

TO

The Congregation of the Immaculate Heart

Land in Scranton & Dunmore

#1

DEED FOR 30 ACRES. Here is a copy of the deed from the Pennsylvania Coal Company to the IHM congregation, dated March 30, 1895, and signed by Mother Mary Jackson, IHM, and by Samuel Thorne, president of the coal company. The purchase price was $24,000. (Courtesy of the Archives of the Sisters, Servants of the Immaculate Heart of Mary, Scranton, Pennsylvania.)

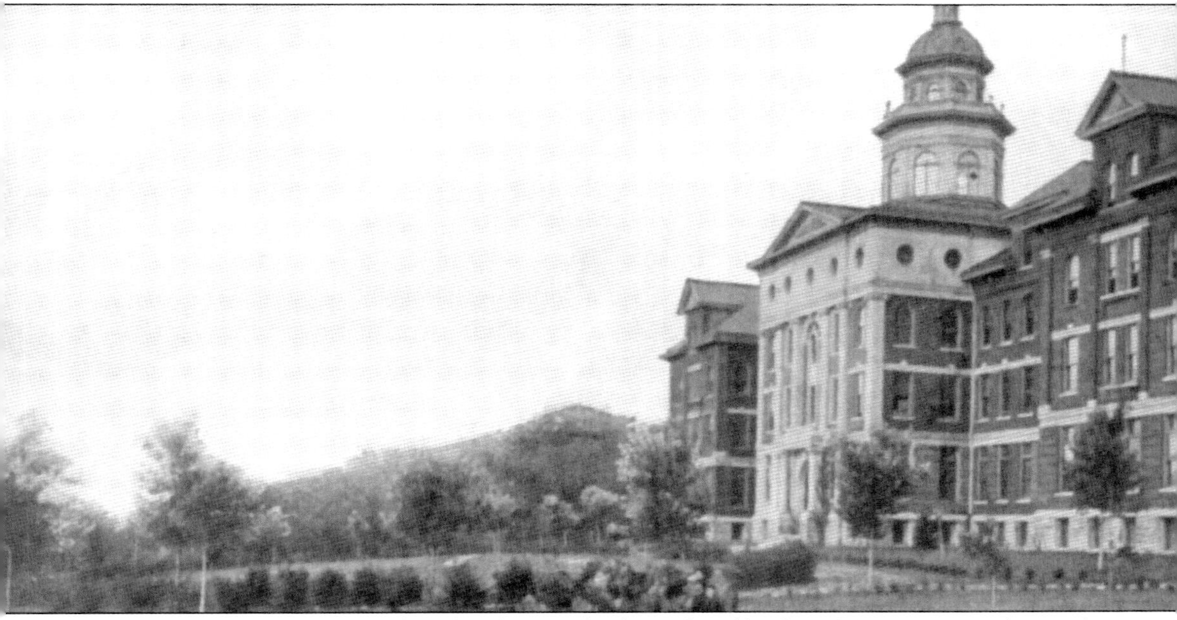

Mount St. Mary's. Victor Koch and Bishop Michael J. Hoban (for the IHM congregation) signed the deed for Mount St. Mary's on September 21, 1903. The purchase price for 54,908.7 square feet of land at the intersection of Adams Avenue and Seminary Street was $6,500. (Courtesy of the Archives of the Sisters, Servants of the Immaculate Heart of Mary, Scranton, Pennsylvania.)

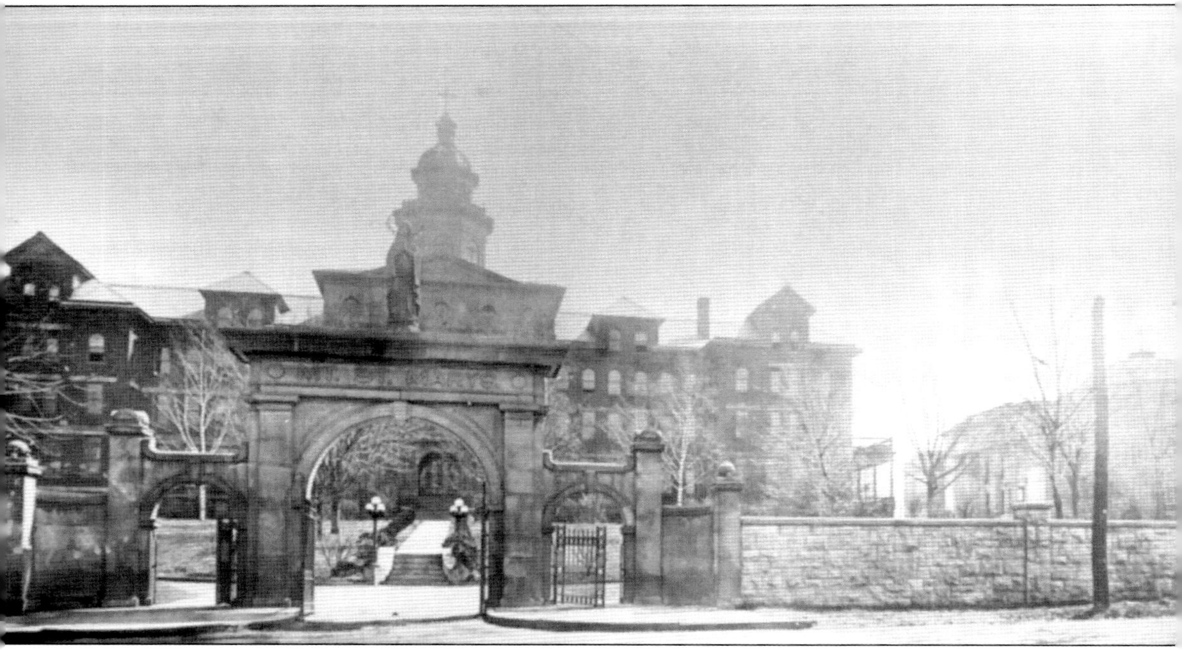

Original Motherhouse. The cornerstone for Mount St. Mary's, the original motherhouse of the sisters of IHM, was laid on November 3, 1900. The four-story structure included a wing for Marywood Seminary, a beautiful chapel, space for the novitiate classrooms, dining rooms, dormitories, and housing for the faculty of both Marywood Seminary and College. The building was destroyed by fire in 1971. (Courtesy of the Archives of the Sisters, Servants of the Immaculate Heart of Mary, Scranton, Pennsylvania.)

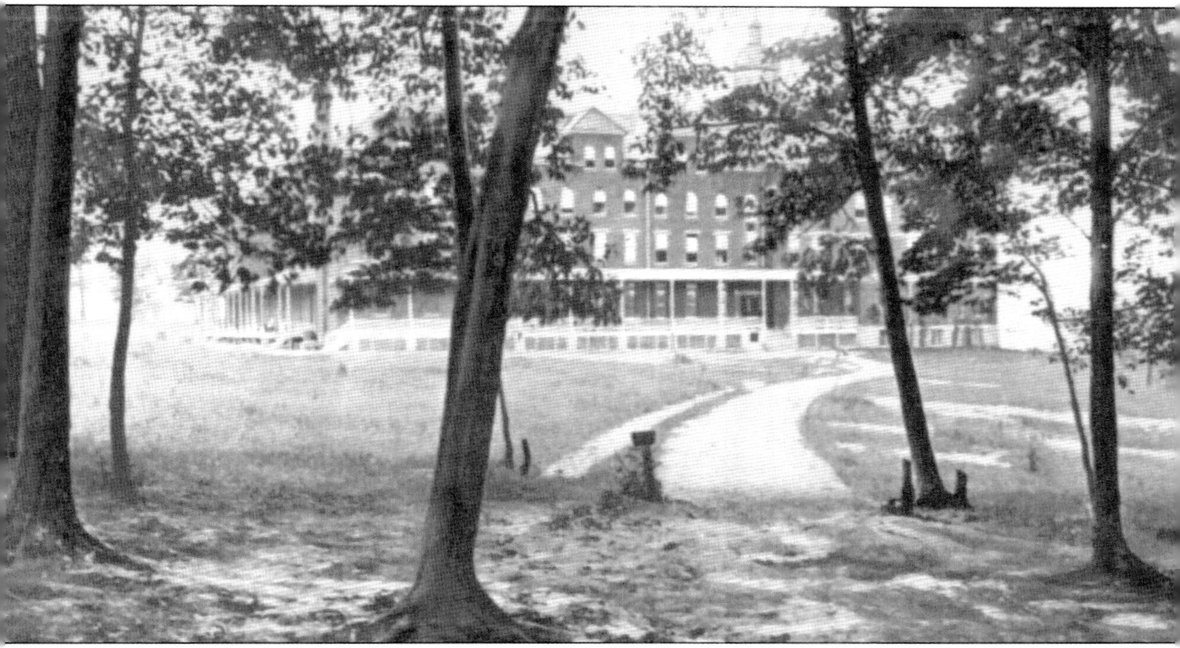

MARYWOOD SEMINARY. Marywood Seminary opened as a wing of the new motherhouse of the Sisters, Servants of the Immaculate Heart of Mary, in September 1902. It was an all-girl elementary and high school facility that was open to both day and boarding students. Its high school curriculum was classical, preparing young women for entrance into college. By 1914, it was fully accredited by the Pennsylvania School Board of Education. Its motto, *Orare et Laborare* (to pray and to work), was introduced by Bishop Michael J. Hoban. The elementary school was closed in 1965, and the seminary high school was closed in 1971 due to the fire that destroyed the entire motherhouse building. (Courtesy of the Archives of the Sisters, Servants of the Immaculate Heart of Mary, Scranton, Pennsylvania.)

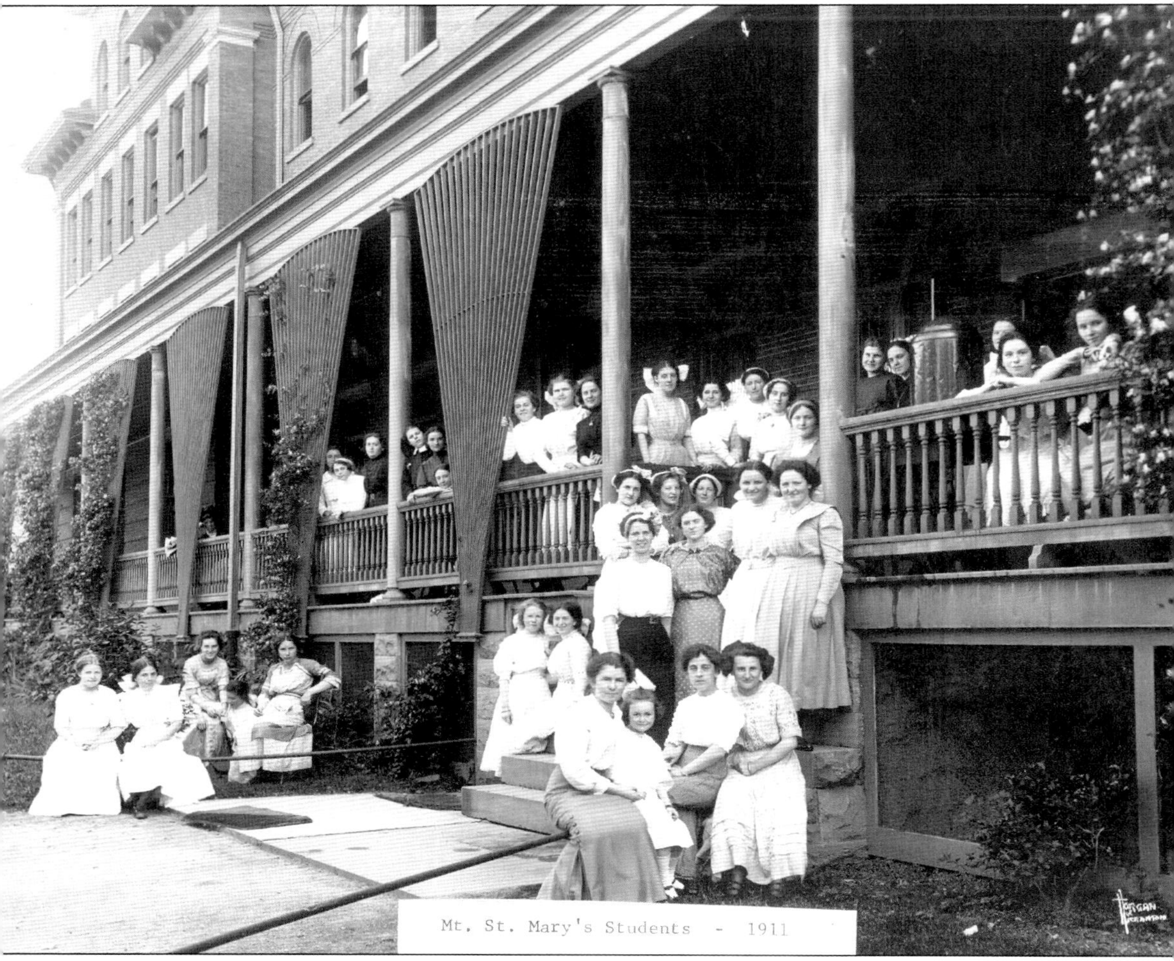

MARYWOOD SEMINARY VERANDA. Marywood students are shown being photographed on the east veranda of Mount St. Mary's motherhouse. The verandas were added in 1904 due to a generous gift from the priests of the Scranton Diocese after their first retreat held in the new motherhouse building. (Courtesy of the Archives of the Sisters, Servants of the Immaculate Heart of Mary, Scranton, Pennsylvania.)

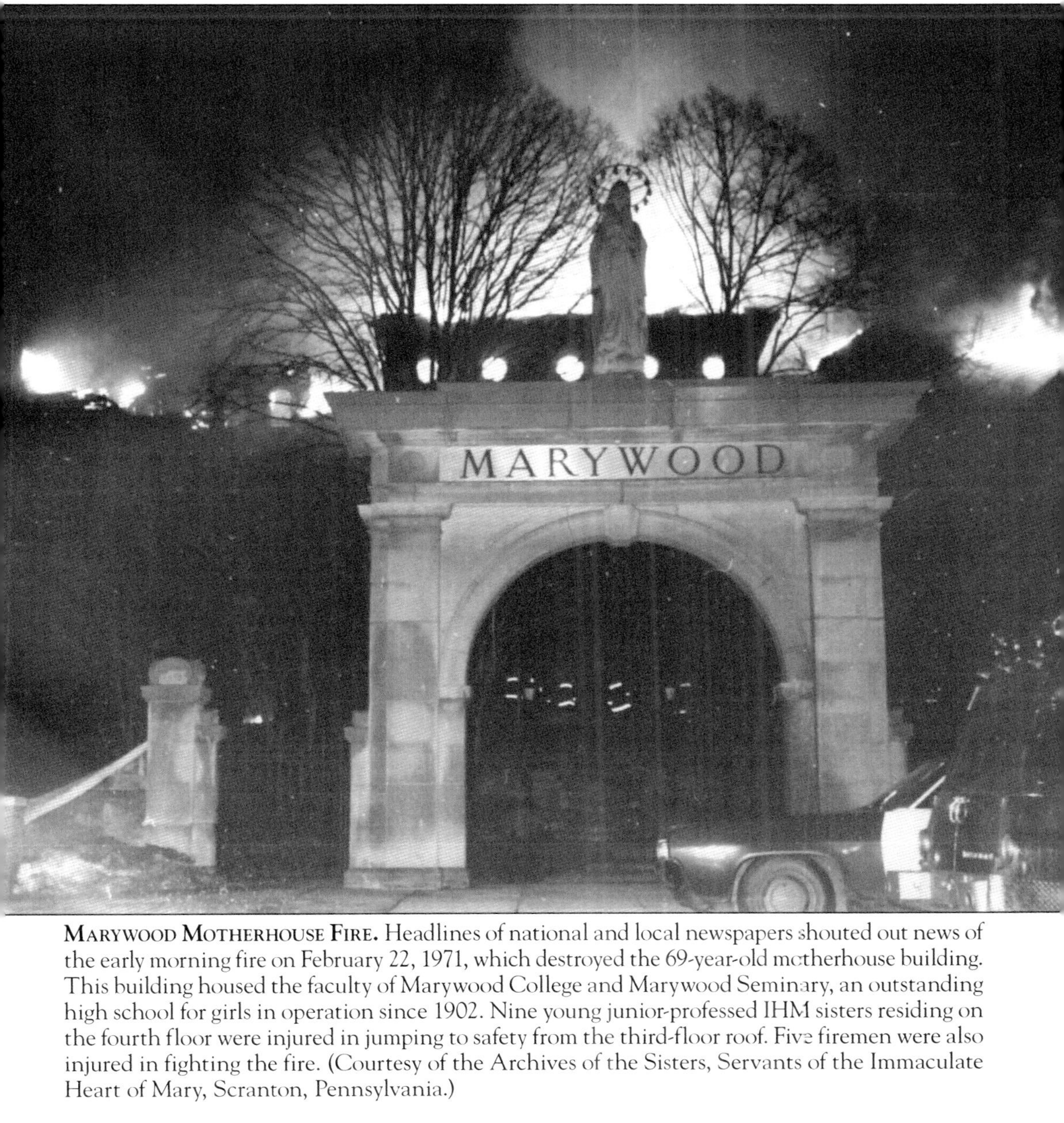

MARYWOOD MOTHERHOUSE FIRE. Headlines of national and local newspapers shouted out news of the early morning fire on February 22, 1971, which destroyed the 69-year-old motherhouse building. This building housed the faculty of Marywood College and Marywood Seminary, an outstanding high school for girls in operation since 1902. Nine young junior-professed IHM sisters residing on the fourth floor were injured in jumping to safety from the third-floor roof. Five firemen were also injured in fighting the fire. (Courtesy of the Archives of the Sisters, Servants of the Immaculate Heart of Mary, Scranton, Pennsylvania.)

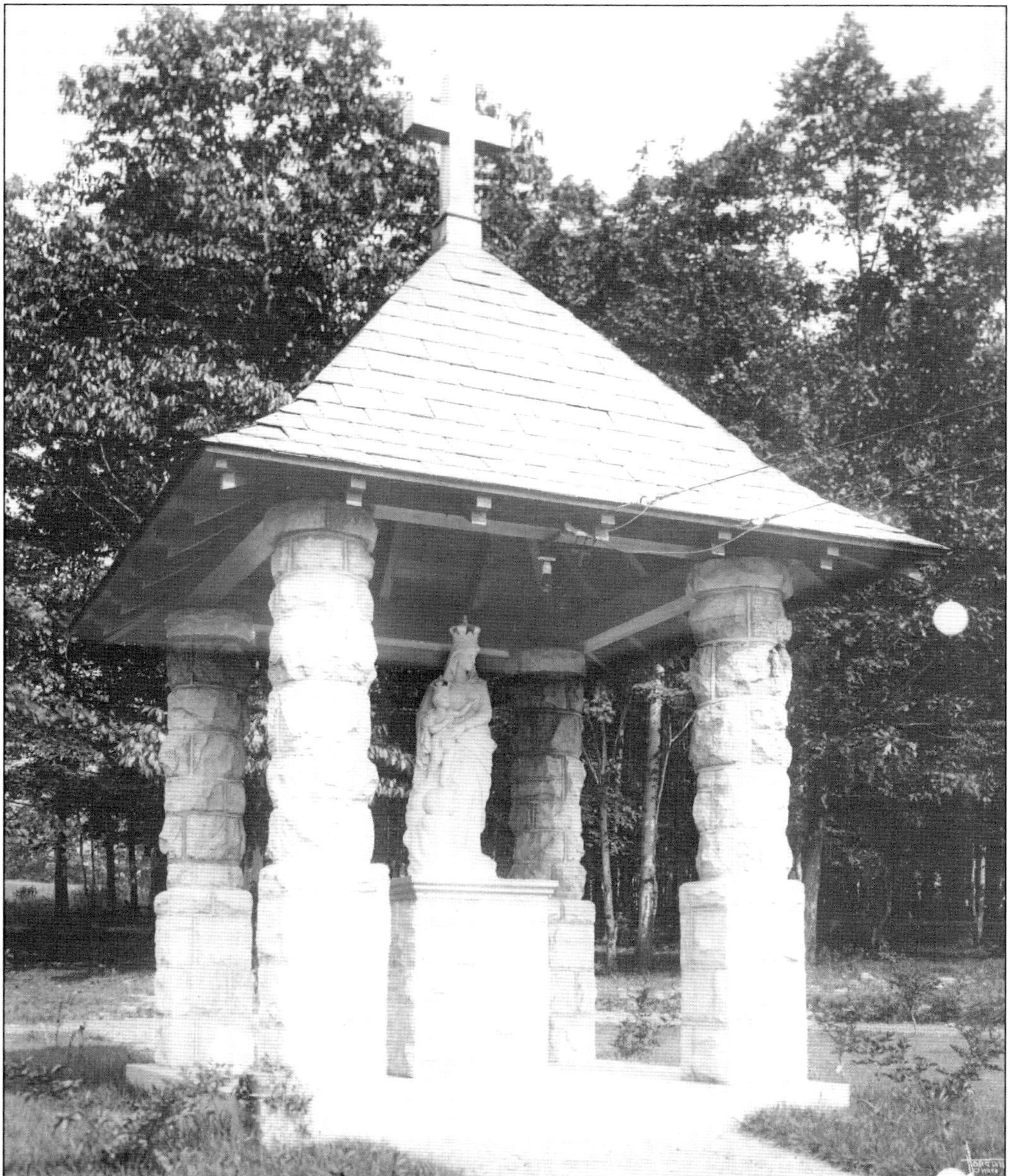

OUR LADY OF VICTORY SHRINE STORY, C. 1901. The Lackawanna & Wyoming Railroad Company was planning an extension between Scranton and Carbondale. It had surveyed the land and acquired the right of eminent domain to run the railroad through the motherhouse grounds. Mother Cyril met with the railroad officials to voice objections to their invasion of Mount St. Mary's property. Her pleadings were heard. This rather miraculous result was attributed to the prayers of the sisters and the promise made to build a shrine to Our Lady of Victory if the proposed railroad did not go through. Three years later, about 1904, Bishop Hoban dedicated the shrine. The shrine was the gift of two priests of the Scranton Diocese, Revs. John and Daniel Dunn. (Courtesy of the Archives of the Sisters, Servants of the Immaculate Heart of Mary, Scranton, Pennsylvania.)

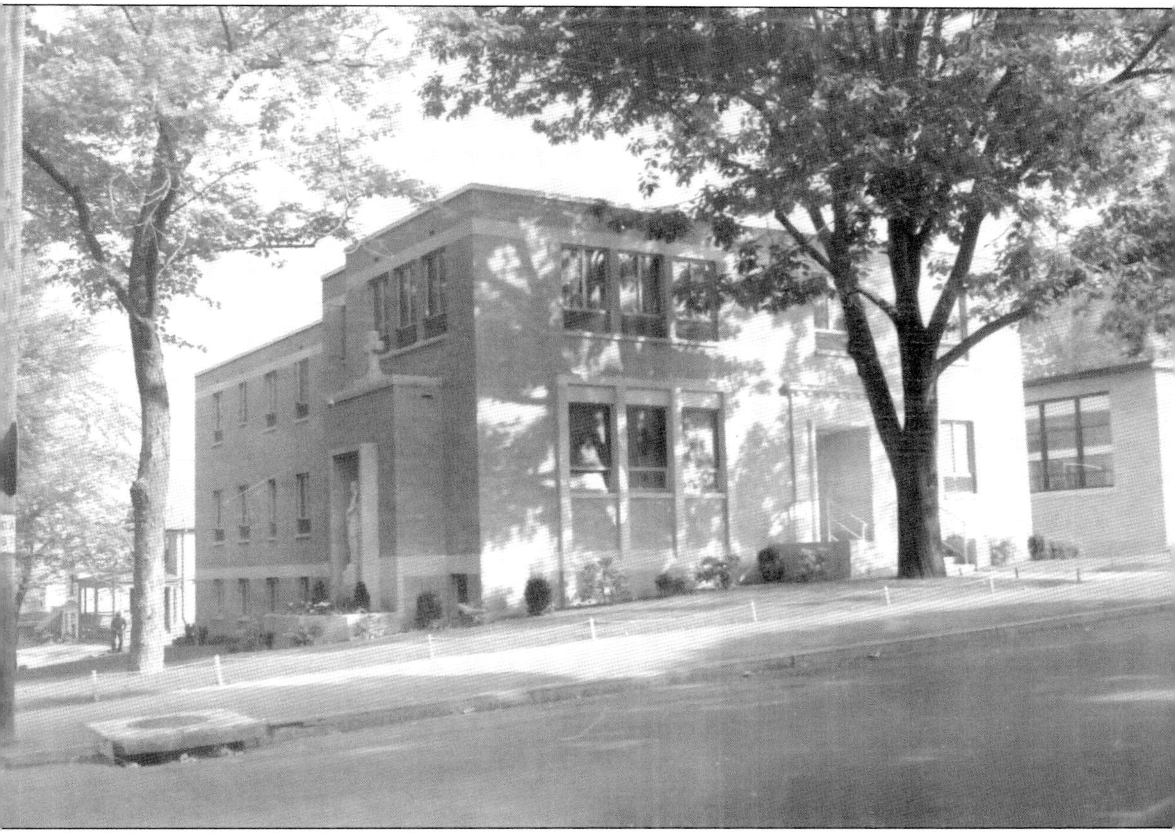

St. Clare Convent. When St. Clare School opened in 1954, there was no convent. The sisters teaching there were housed at St. Paul's Convent or at the motherhouse. The convent was opened on February 10, 1959. (Courtesy of the Archives of the Sisters, Servants of the Immaculate Heart of Mary, Scranton, Pennsylvania.)

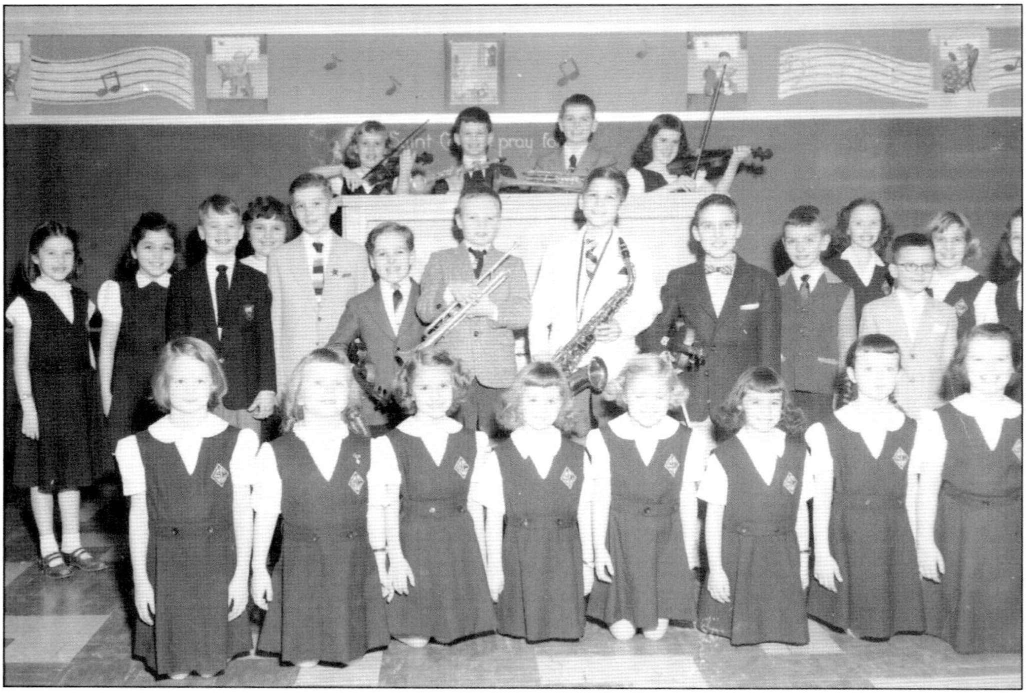

Music and Orchestra at St. Clare. Students at St. Clare School involved in both private music lessons and group activities, such as glee club and orchestra, were under the direction of Sr. Maryla Farfour, who also served as music instructor at nearby Marywood Seminary. (Both, courtesy of the Archives of the Sisters, Servants of the Immaculate Heart of Mary, Scranton, Pennsylvania.)

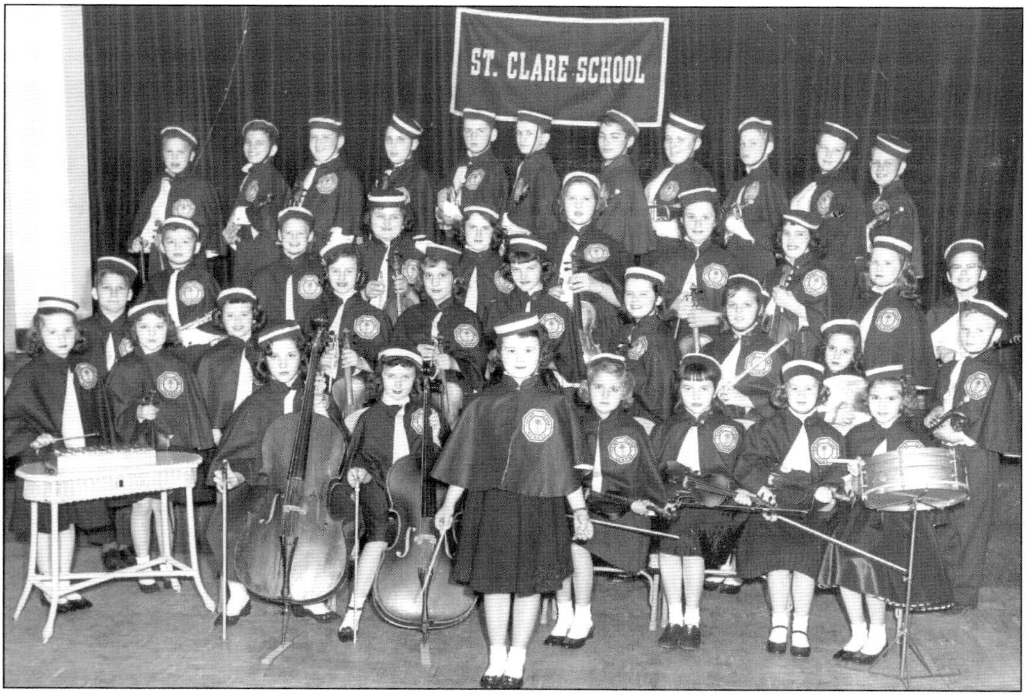

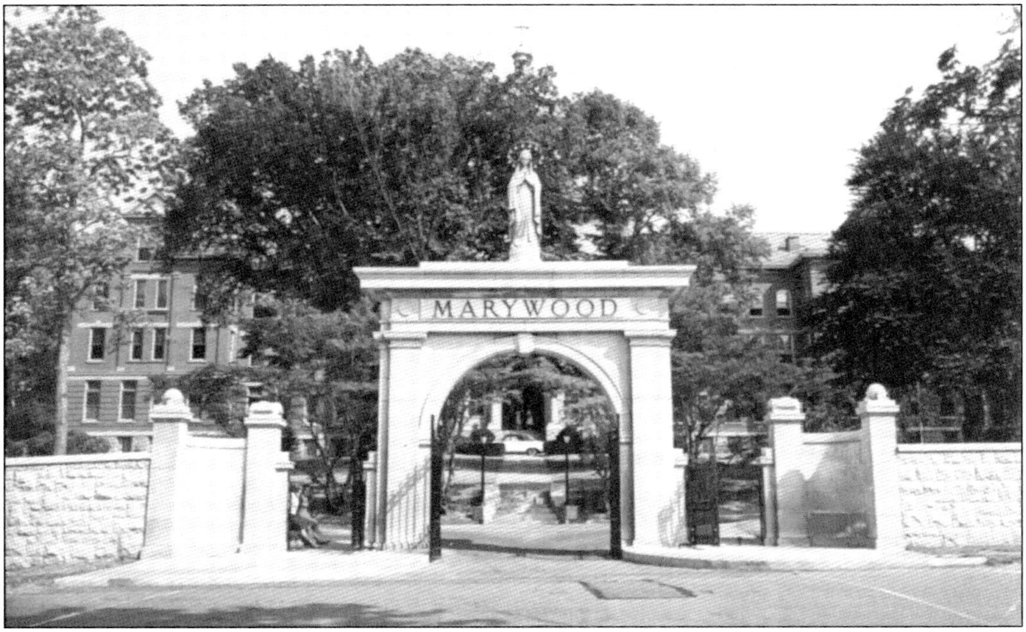

MARYWOOD COLLEGE/UNIVERSITY. Marywood College opened in 1915 in the motherhouse building, admitting 34 women students. Marywood was the first Catholic college for women in the state of Pennsylvania. Mother M. Germaine O'Neil, MA, as superior general of the IHM congregation, was also the first president of the college. Sr. Immaculata Gillespie, MA, was its first dean. There were 10 full-time faculty members, including two priests, one laywoman, and seven IHM sisters. The motto chosen was *Sanctitas, Scientia, Sanitas*, which translates to "Holiness, Knowledge, Health." (Courtesy of Mark Boock.)

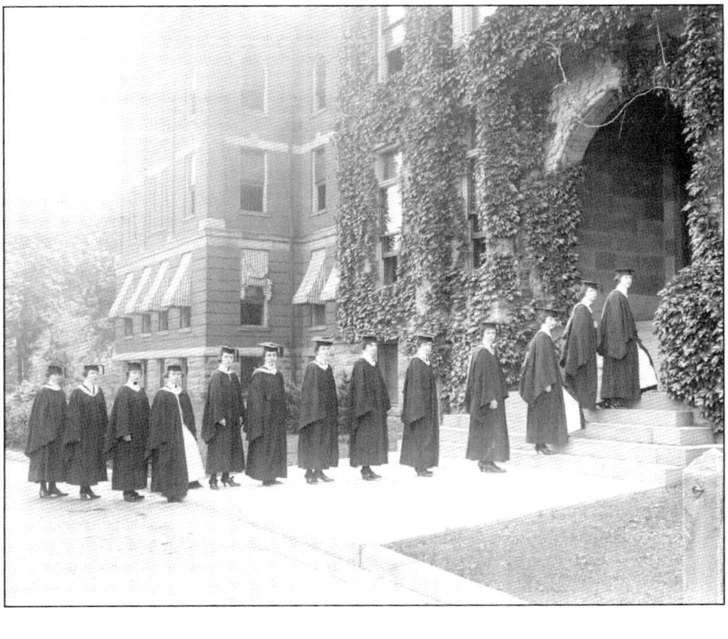

FIRST COMMENCEMENT. Seventeen of the original 34 students, including four IHM sisters, completed the four-year curriculum, which led to a degree in the bachelor of arts, music, or science. The first commencement was held in June 1919. (Courtesy of the Archives of the Sisters, Servants of the Immaculate Heart of Mary, Scranton, Pennsylvania.)

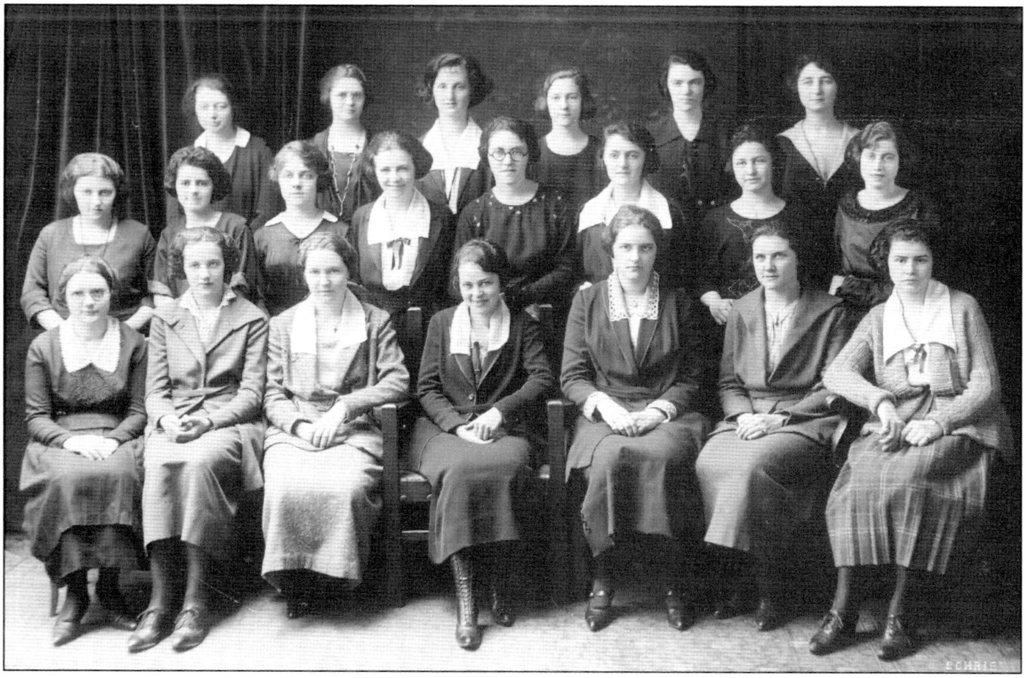

Bay Leaf Staff, 1921. The *Bay Leaf*, a quarterly literary magazine, had its start in 1919. It derived its name from the ancient Greek and Roman custom of crowning heroes and poets with wreaths of bay leaves. Moderators, such as Sister Charitas and Dr. Philip Tama, guided talented student writers, earning the first-place award in the Columbia University, New York, collegiate competition in 1969. (Courtesy of the Archives of the Sisters, Servants of the Immaculate Heart of Mary, Scranton, Pennsylvania.)

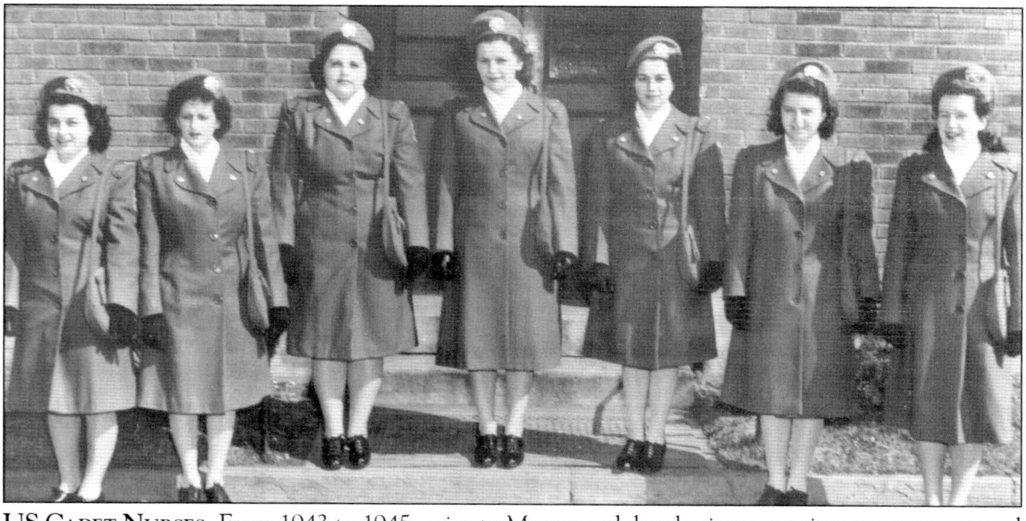

US Cadet Nurses. From 1943 to 1945, prior to Marywood developing a nursing program, several groups of US Cadet Nurses attended the college for a semester of accelerated liberal arts courses. At the conclusion of these intensive courses, they returned to their home schools of nursing at Pittston City Hospital and St. Joseph's Hospital in Carbondale, Pennsylvania. (Courtesy of the Archives of the Sisters, Servants of the Immaculate Heart of Mary, Scranton, Pennsylvania.)

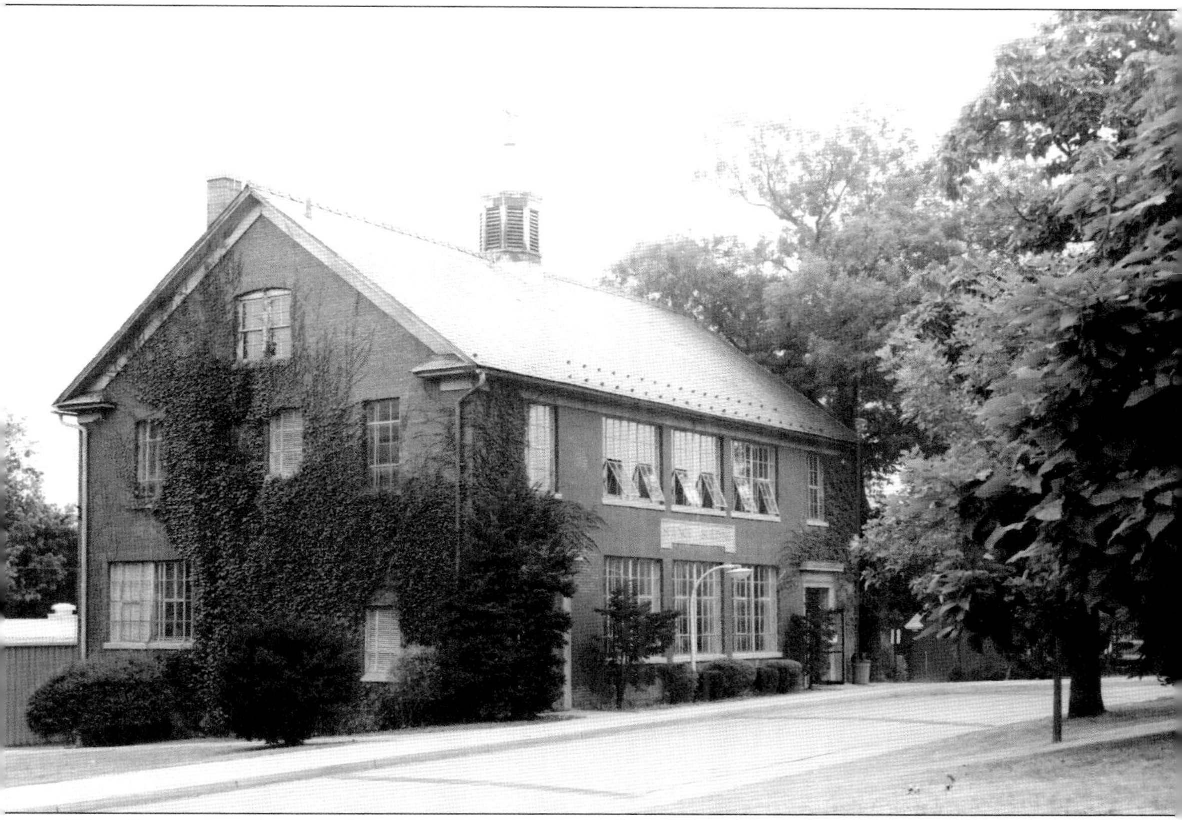

The Carriage House. Three structures were on the land purchased in 1895 as the future site of the motherhouse of the sisters of the IHM and Marywood College and Seminary. These included the carriage house, a small cottage, and a greenhouse. In 1926, the carriage house was converted into the two-story Science Building, and it served in that capacity until after World War II. (Courtesy of the Archives of the Sisters, Servants of the Immaculate Heart of Mary, Scranton, Pennsylvania.)

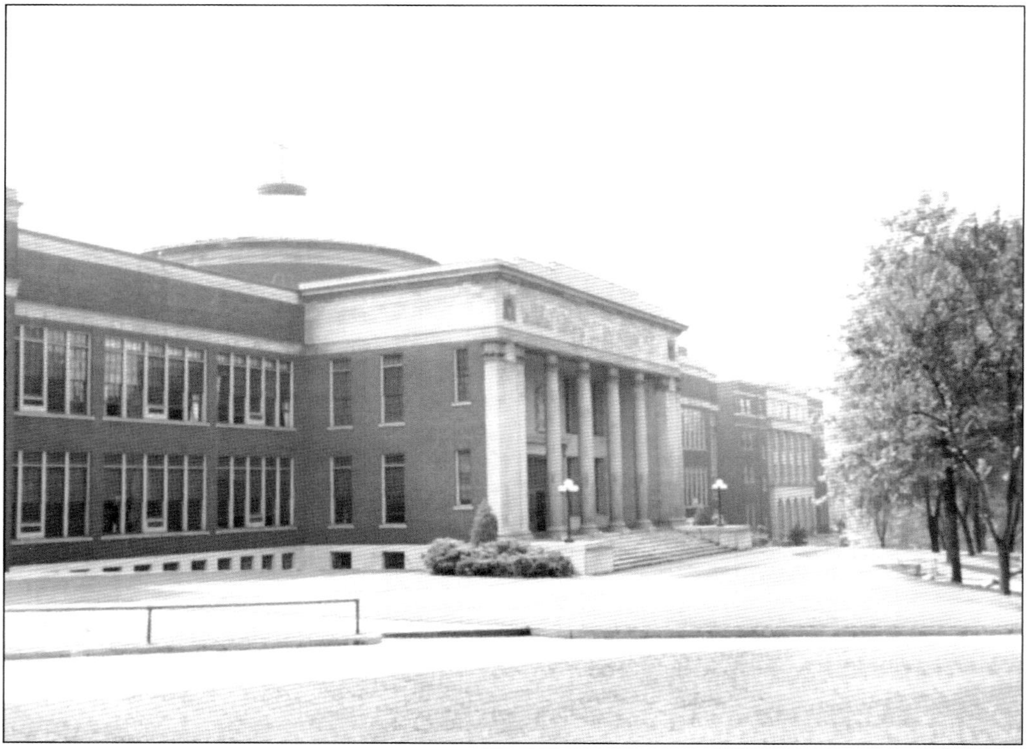

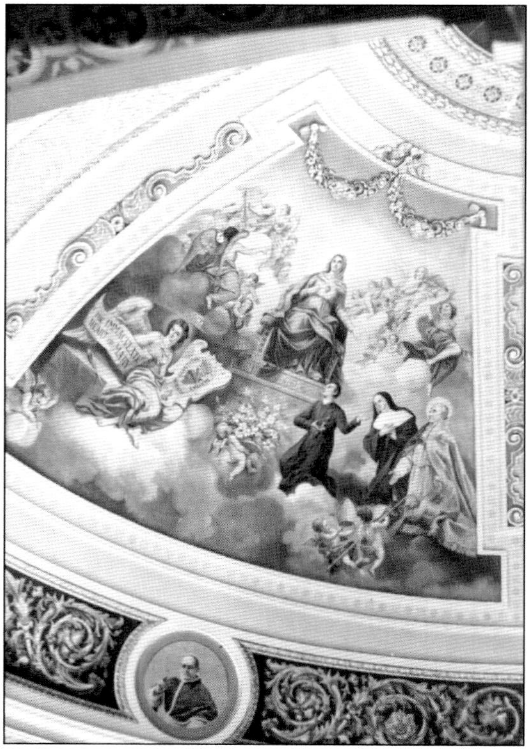

Liberal Arts Building and Rotunda. The Liberal Arts Building, the first of the Marywood College buildings, was dedicated on March 25, 1924. A focal point of the campus, the two-story Liberal Arts Building, with its enormous gold-leafed dome and striking marble and terrazzo floors, originally contained administrative and faculty offices, the library, and the cafeteria. The rotunda remained unfinished until 1937. Mother Josepha Hurley conducted work on this imposing space from 1935 through 1937, when it reached completion. Architect Anthony dePace was the designer. The beautiful Italian marble columns, Tennessee pink marble floor, and 16 paintings referencing the arts and sciences and Biblical themes astound visitors to this day. (Both, courtesy of the Archives of the Sisters, Servants of the Immaculate Heart of Mary, Scranton, Pennsylvania.)

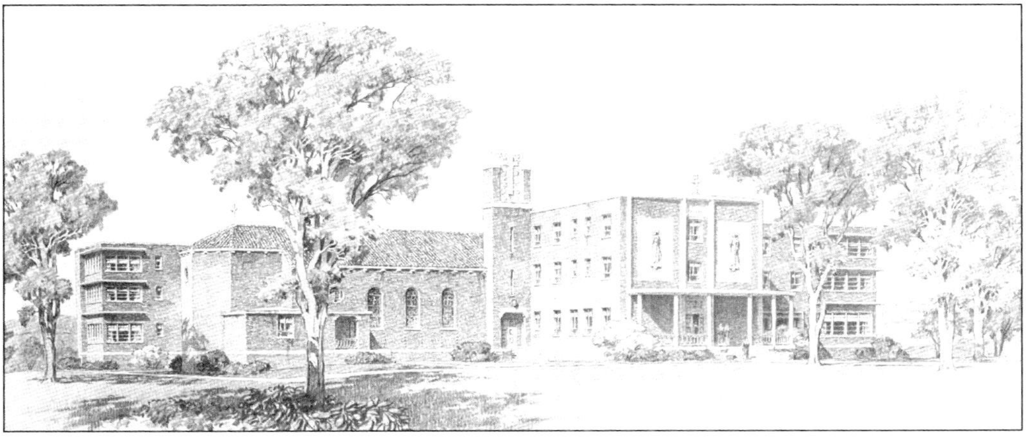

MARIAN CONVENT. Built on the Marywood campus as a facility for the care of the aged and ill members of the sisters of the IHM, the Marian Convent was planned by Mother Marcella Gill, who died on September 14, 1955. Her successor, Mother Kathleen Hart, saw the Marian Convent to completion, opening on April 9, 1956. With 40 IHM sisters entering this facility, it had reached 50-percent capacity within its opening two weeks. The first administrator and superior was Sr. Alphonsus McGoldrick, who served until her death in 1961. (Both, courtesy of the Archives of the Sisters, Servants of the Immaculate Heart of Mary, Scranton, Pennsylvania.)

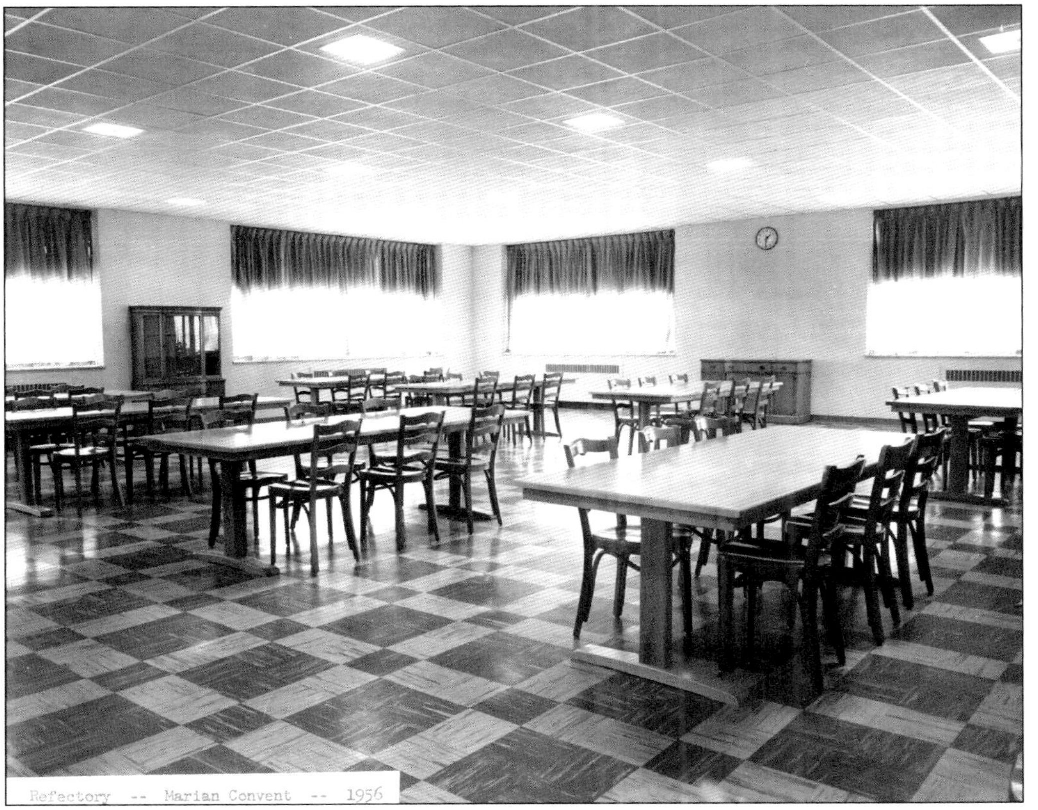

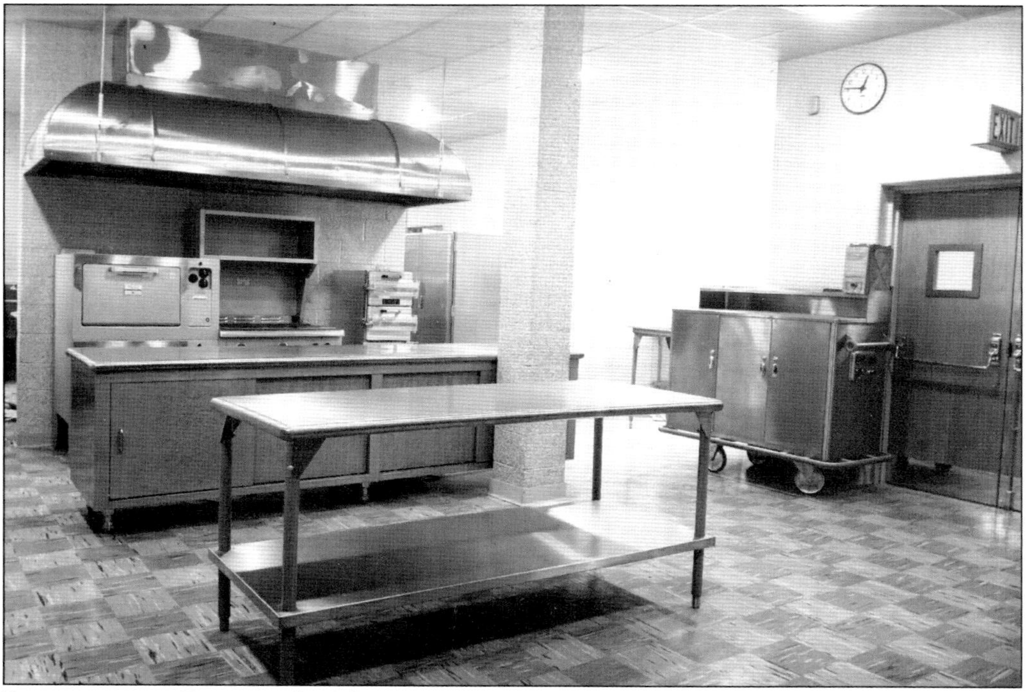

POWERHOUSE OF PRAYER. The following words of Mother Kathleen in 1961 are often repeated in reference to the Marian Convent: "The Marian Convent is a powerhouse of prayer, a source of grace and blessings for the entire Congregation." A 50-bed wing, pharmacy, and other improvements were added in 1971. When the congregation built its new retirement facility, Our Lady of Peace, in 2006, Marywood University purchased the Marian Convent for use as a residence hall. (Both, courtesy of the Archives of the Sisters, Servants of the Immaculate Heart of Mary, Scranton, Pennsylvania.)

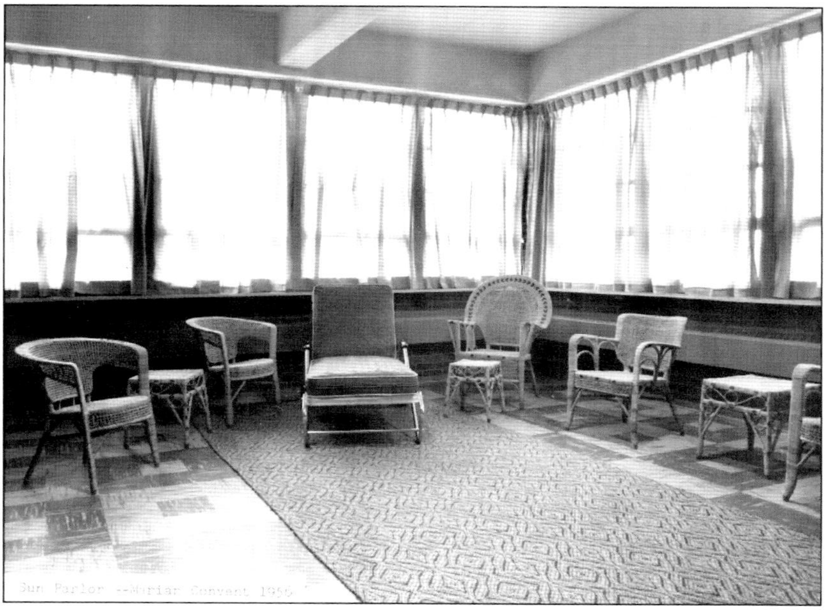

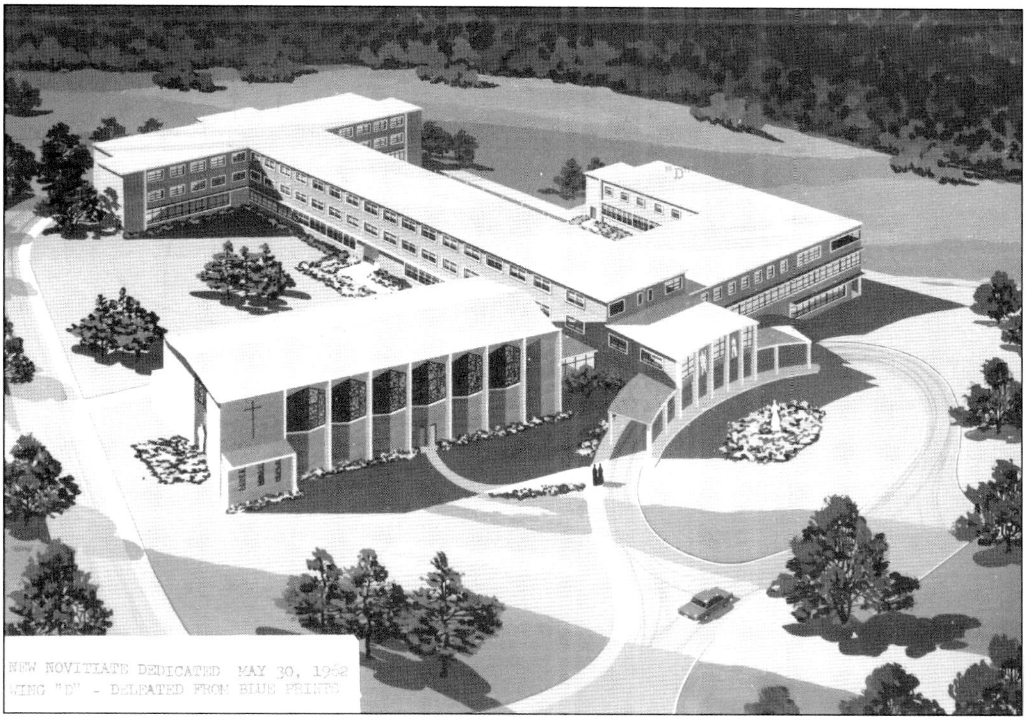

Ground-Breaking of Novitiate Building. The IHM Novitiate Building, designed by Valverde and Franco, architects from Scranton, Pennsylvania, was built to house approximately 168 novices and 10 professed sisters of the IHM congregation. The imposing 103,000-square-foot building of redbrick and cast-stone trim included within its space a beautiful chapel with a magnificent pipe organ, stained-glass windows depicting biblical scenes of the life of the Blessed Virgin Mary, and warm wood-paneled walls; classrooms; a library; recreation, dining, laundry, and music practice rooms; and administrative offices. Ground-breaking was held on May 30, 1960, with Mother Kathleen, who had planned the facility. The dedication on May 30, 1962, was presided over by Mother Beata Wertz, just four months after Mother Kathleen's death. The Fathers and Friends of the Marywood Novitiate, founded in 1958, raised nearly $1 million over a 10-year period for the building. (Both, courtesy of the Archives of the Sisters, Servants of the Immaculate Heart of Mary, Scranton, Pennsylvania.)

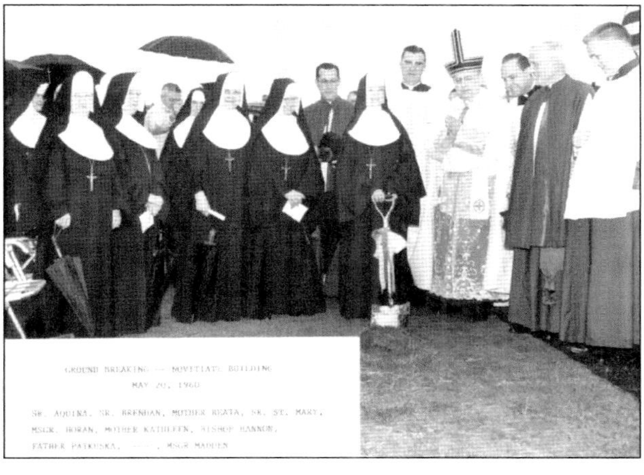

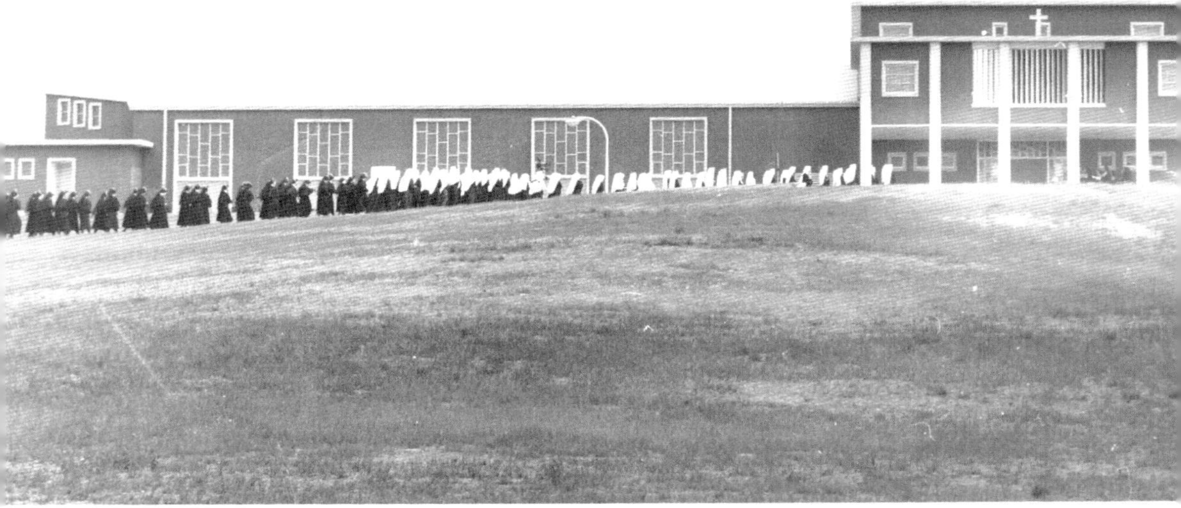

On arrival at Novitiate, the Postulants and Novices
are greeted by Mother M. Beata and the Council members.

PROCESSION FROM THE MOTHERHOUSE TO THE NOVITIATE. On June 4, 1962, at 2:00 p.m., 71 novices and 30 postulants, together with seven professed sisters, moved from the motherhouse to the new Novitiate Building. This building was to be the congregation's novitiate for 28 years, until July 27, 1990, when the novices moved to the IHM Convent on River Street, Scranton, and the candidates to St. Rose Convent, Carbondale. At that time, the name of the building was changed to the IHM Center. (Courtesy of the Archives of the Sisters, Servants of the Immaculate Heart of Mary, Scranton, Pennsylvania.)

Eight

Welcome to the Neighborhood

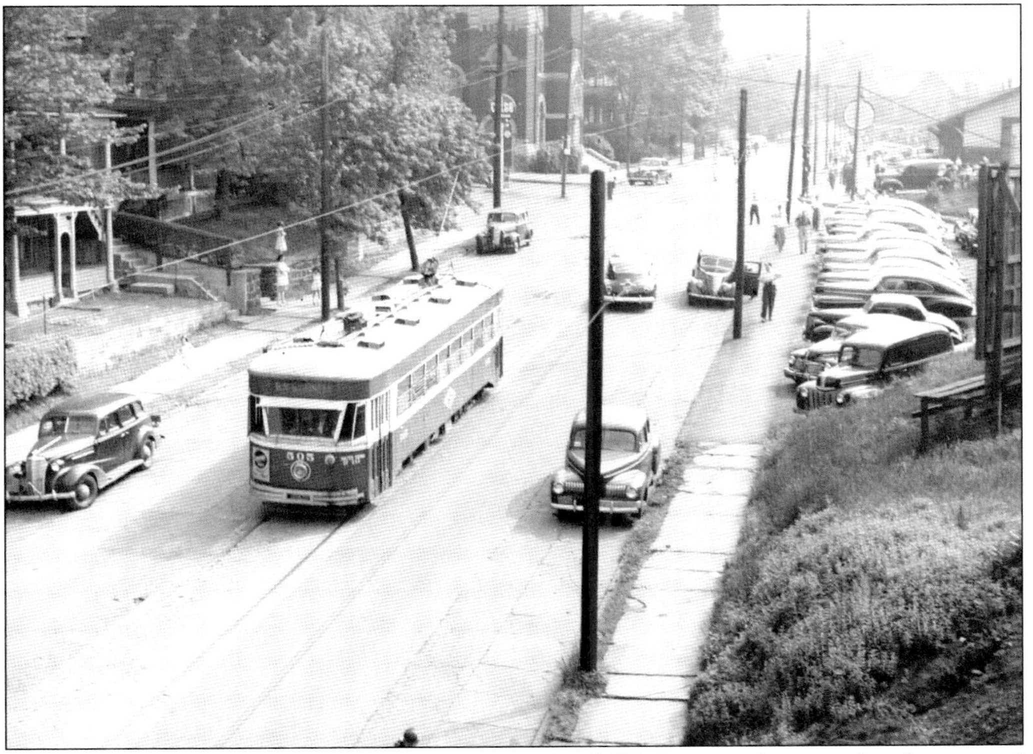

Green Ridge Suburban, c. 1951. Car No. 505 on North Washington Avenue is heading toward its destination of Green Ridge. In the days of horse-drawn cars, the trip from downtown Scranton to Green Ridge took between 90 minutes and two hours. (Courtesy of Mark Boock.)

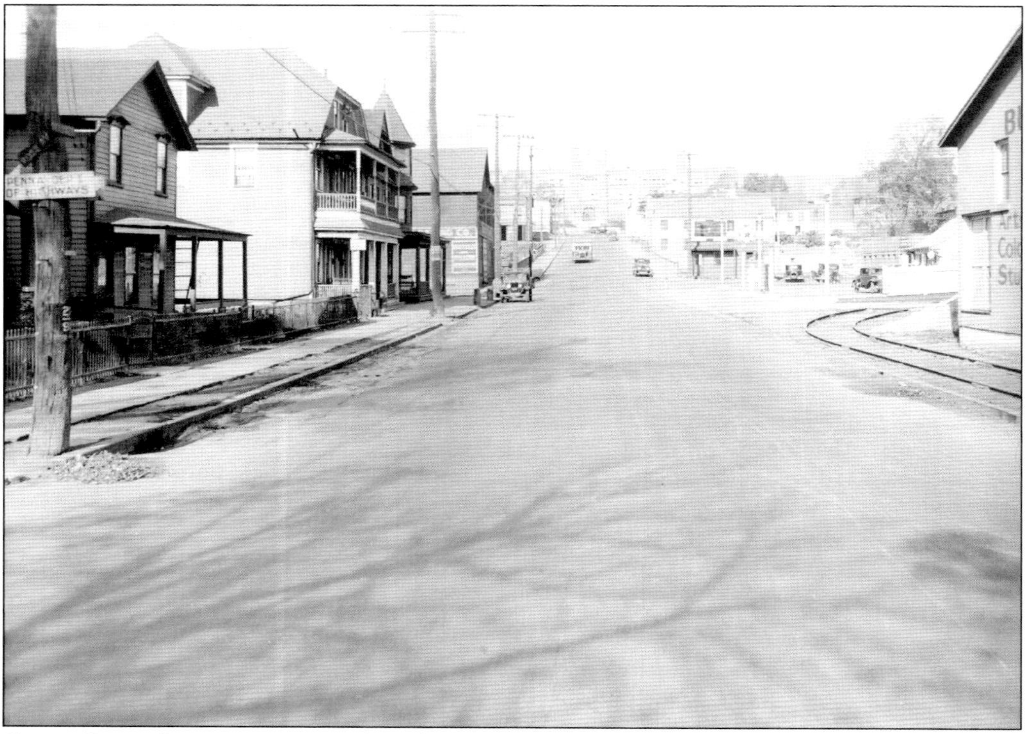

Green Ridge Street, c. 1930. Though the buildings have changed, this is still a familiar sight to anyone who lives in and around the historic neighborhood. Green Ridge Street was and still is a busy thoroughfare. Many of the businesses have come and gone, like the Paragon Plaster and Supply Company or more recently the Green Ridge Lanes. Today, a CVS is on one corner and a Walgreens on the other, not to mention the slew of stores in the Green Ridge Shopping Center. Shown above and below at the very end of the block is the grand sight of the North Scranton Junior High School, one of the only buildings that still remains, reminding people that no matter how much things change, they still stay the same. (Both, courtesy of Mark Boock.)

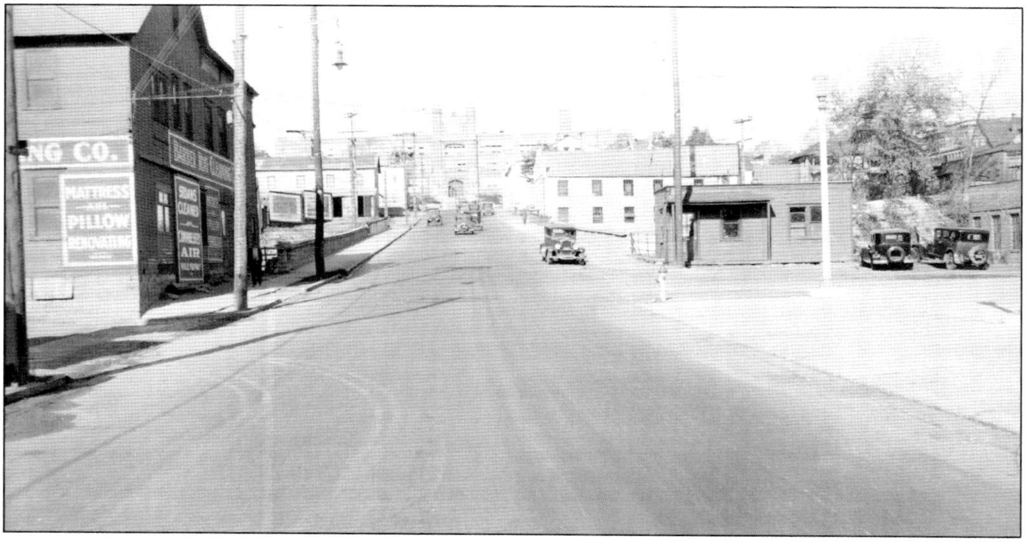

Green Ridge Hotel. The Green Ridge Hotel was located at the corner of Green Ridge Street and Dickson Avenue, near the Delaware & Hudson roundhouse and station. It was a favorite social spot for people in the neighborhood. (Courtesy of Mark Boock.)

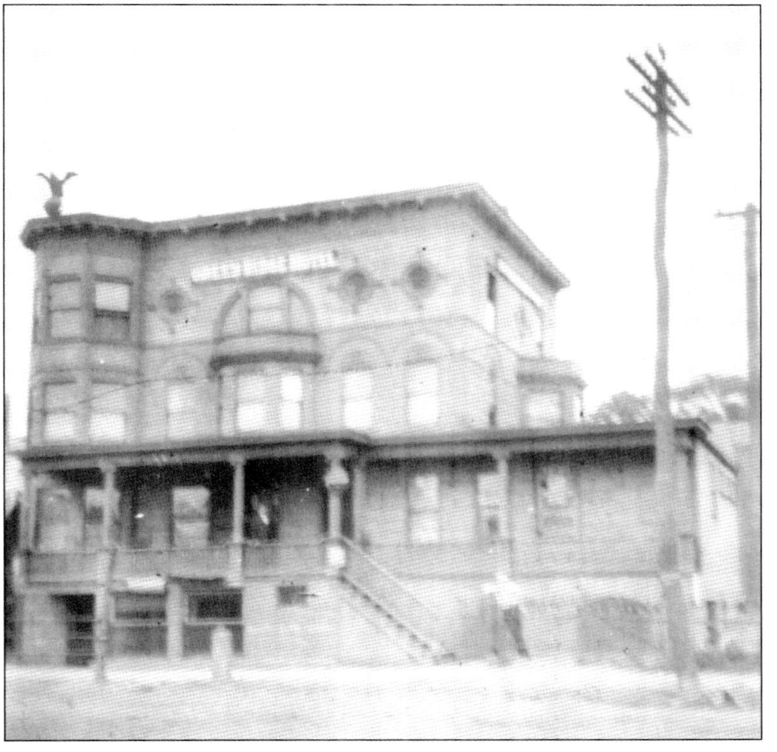

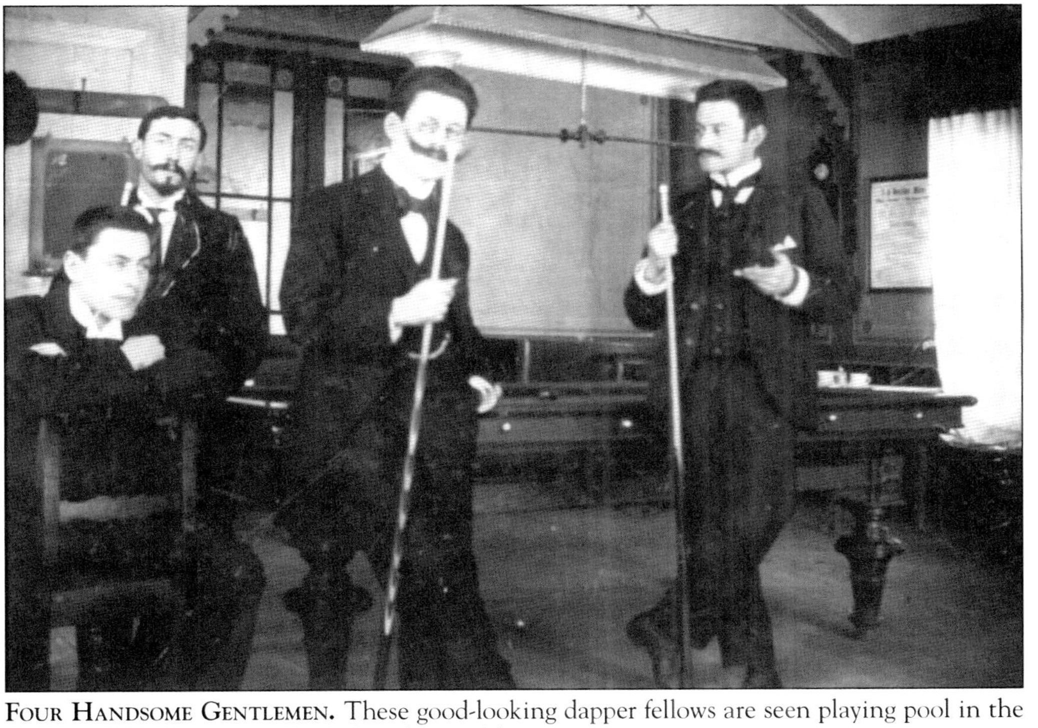

Four Handsome Gentlemen. These good-looking dapper fellows are seen playing pool in the Green Ridge Hotel. (Courtesy of Mark Boock.)

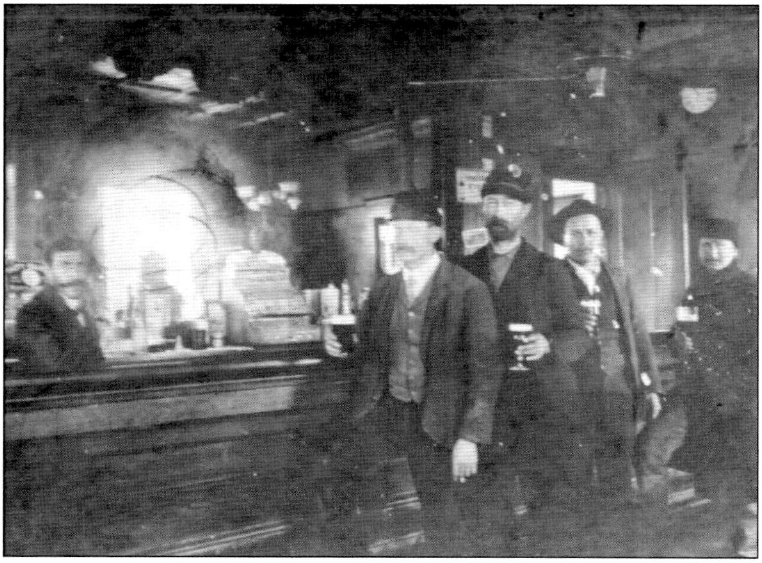

"It's 5 O'clock Somewhere." These men are enjoying a drink in the Green Ridge Hotel after a long day of work in the mines or perhaps the lace works. In 1893, the proprietor was John Horn. The hotel changed owners quite frequently. (Courtesy of Mark Boock.)

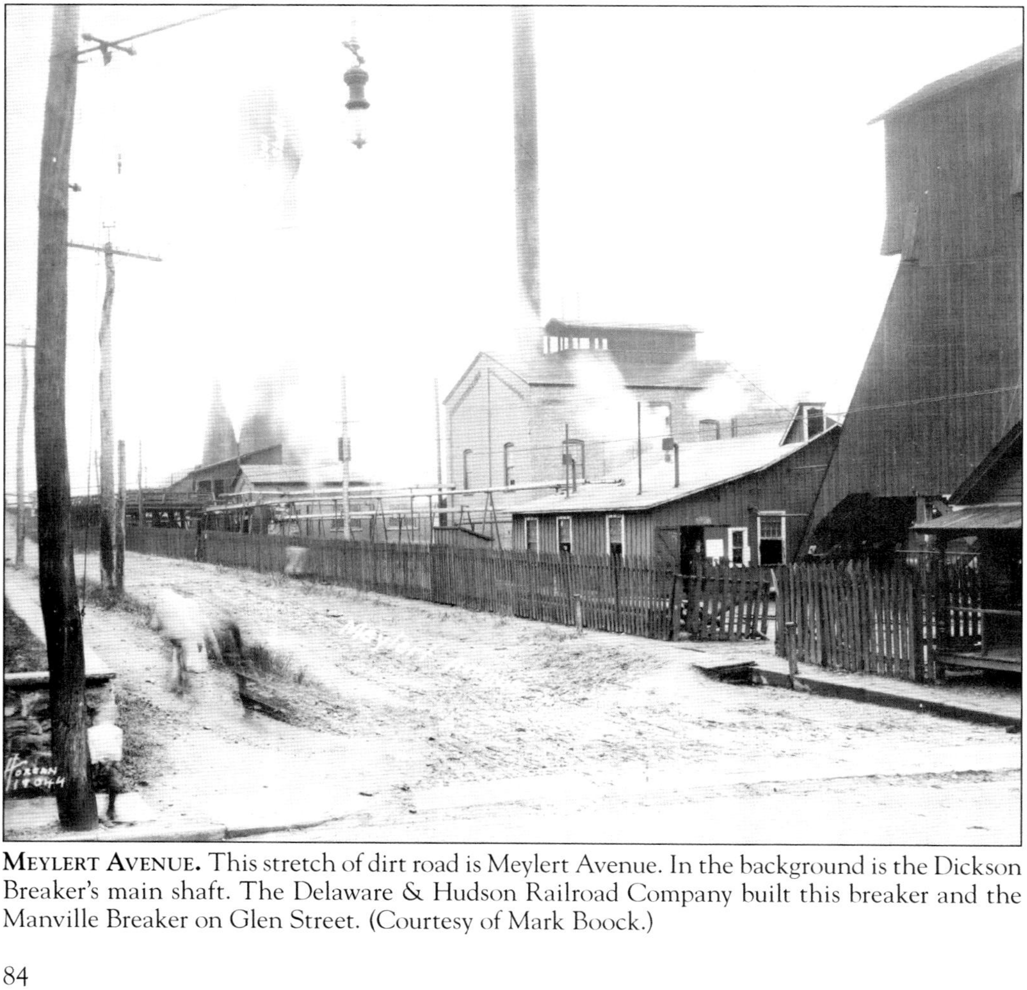

Meylert Avenue. This stretch of dirt road is Meylert Avenue. In the background is the Dickson Breaker's main shaft. The Delaware & Hudson Railroad Company built this breaker and the Manville Breaker on Glen Street. (Courtesy of Mark Boock.)

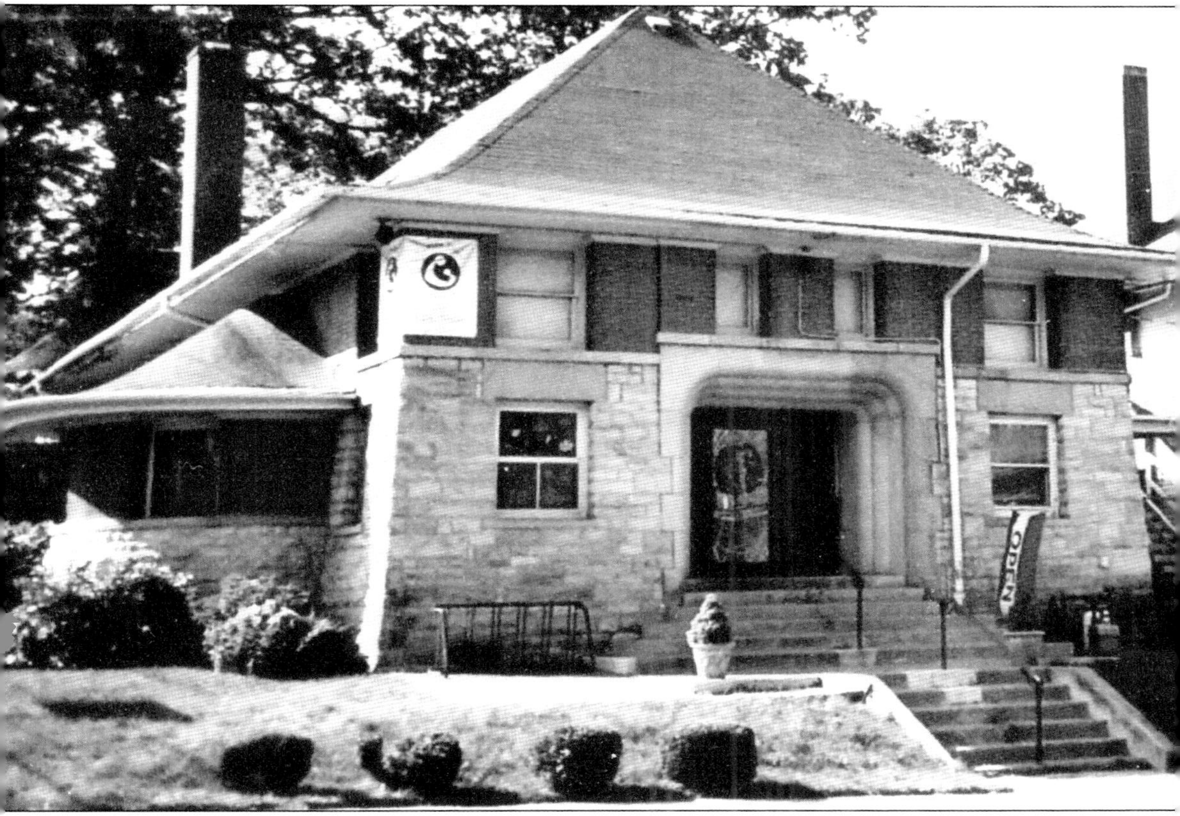

The Green Ridge Library. Around 1881, Green Ridge residents organized a book club, which consisted of 50 members. The hall of E.C. Dimmick's home was used as a library. As the number of members grew, so did the need for more space. A public library was suggested and met with much approval. The result of this suggestion is the beautiful stone-and-brick building on the corner of Wyoming Avenue and Green Ridge Street. The Sanderson estate donated the lot. The charter was granted on June 27, 1881, and it holds the distinction of being the first public library in the city of Scranton and the last neighborhood library to remain open. Today, it is known as the Nancy K. Holmes Library, Green Ridge Branch of the Scranton Public Library. (Courtesy of the author.)

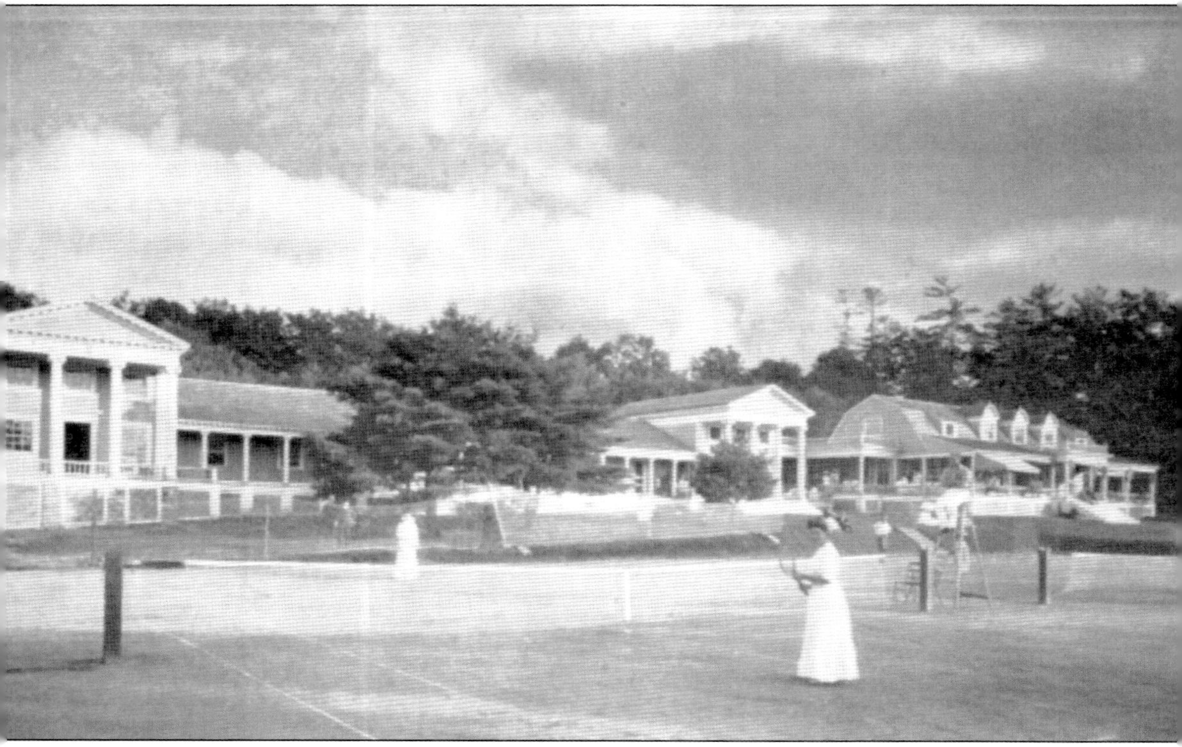

SCRANTON COUNTRY CLUB. The luxurious country club was originally established at the end of North Washington Avenue. Its founding members, J. Benjamin Dimmick, W.W. Scranton, C.S. Weston, and E.B. Sturges, organized it on October 5, 1896. The club introduced golf to Lackawanna County on its 18-hole course, which measured 4,273 yards. Due to mine cave-ins threatening various parts of Green Ridge in 1925, a committee was appointed the job of looking for a new, safer location. Land in South Abington and Newton was chosen as the Scranton Country Club's new location. (Courtesy of the author.)

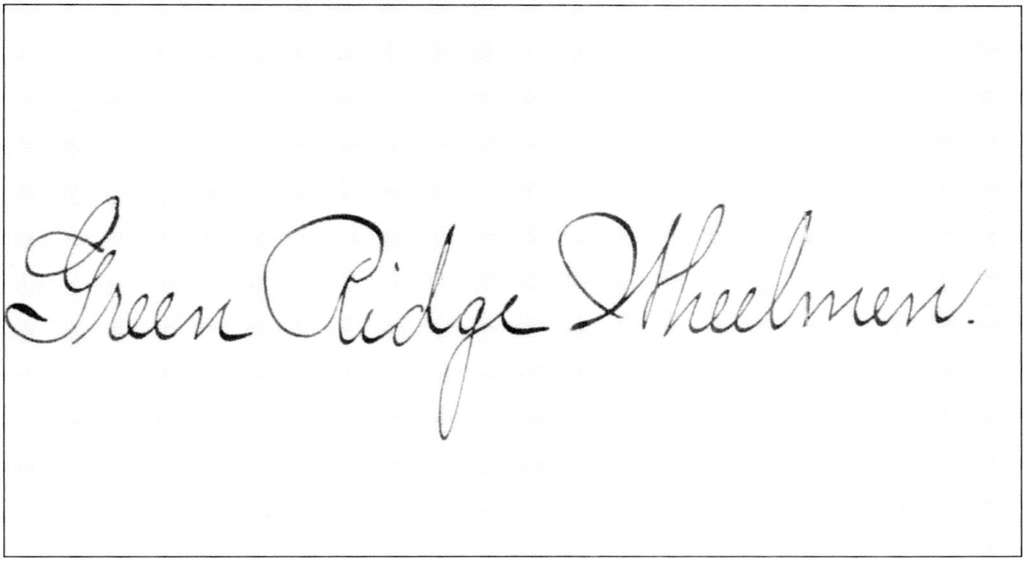

Green Ridge Club. The club was organized on June 28, 1892, under the name of the Green Ridge Wheelmen; its calling card is pictured above. Only cyclists were admitted. Its mission was to "advocate the principles of good roads and labor for the pleasure and welfare of its members." There were 14 original members, all bicycle owners. In January 1894, the club's rules changed to include non-cyclists, and membership increased. At the beginning of the 20th century, they built their clubhouse at 1645 Wyoming Avenue. E.B. Sturges donated $1,000 toward the purchase price with the conditions that no gambling and no liquor were allowed on the premises. Membership climbed to 200, and the name was changed to the Green Ridge Club, pictured below, in 1906. Today, the full-service banquet facility is run by the Sinkaus family and is known for its delectable cuisine. (Both, courtesy of the Sinkaus family.)

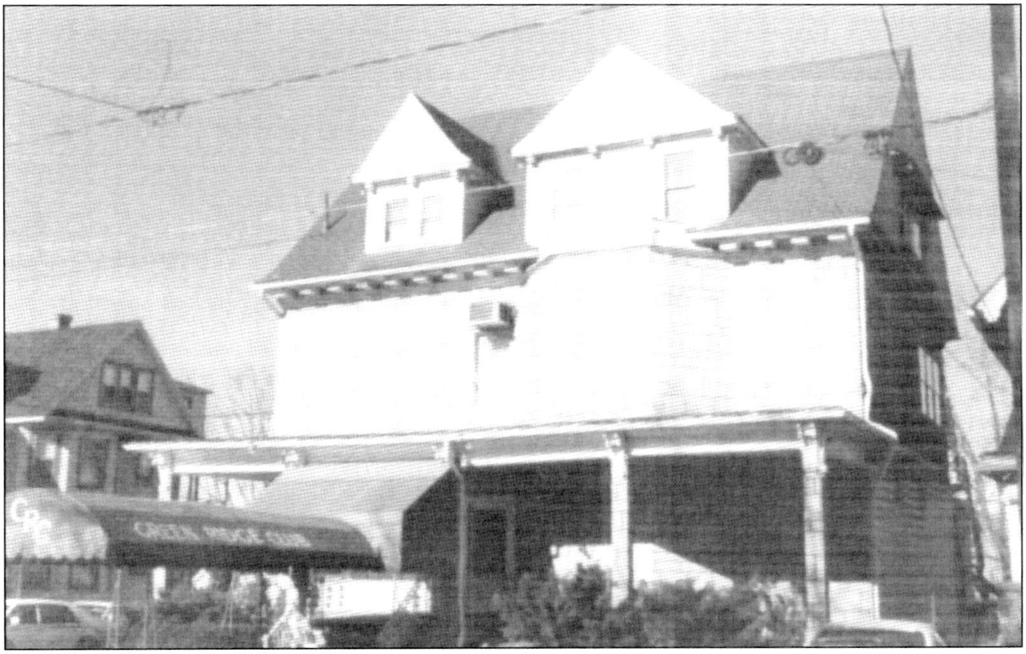

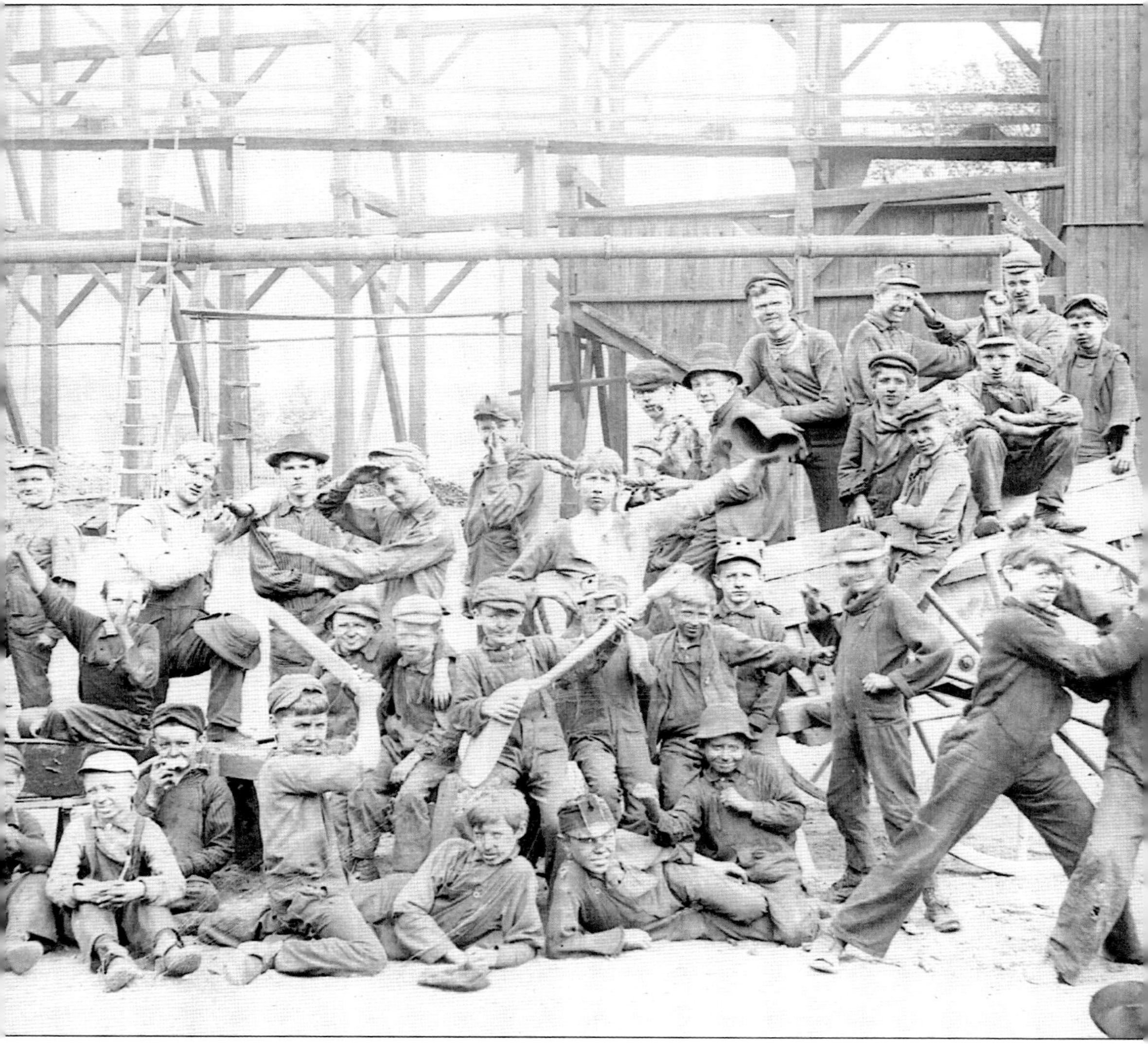

Breaker Boy . . . Breaker Boy. Young men and boys pose outside the Green Ridge Breaker. Some as young as nine years old worked in the coal mines in order to support their families in the anthracite region. (Courtesy of Mark Broock.)

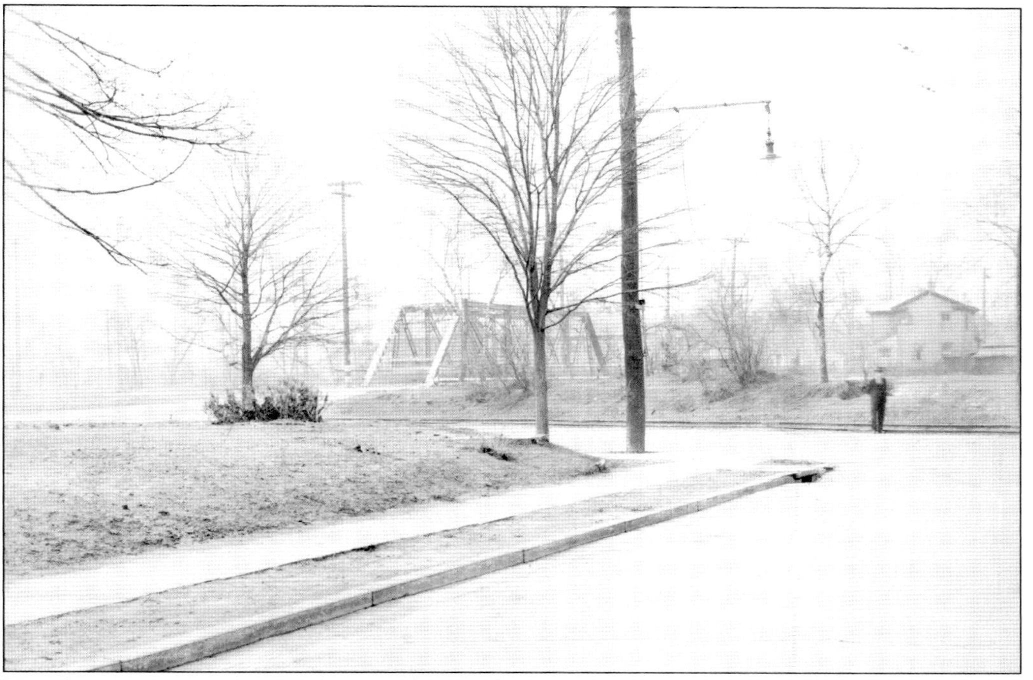

Nay Aug and Albright Avenues. This gentleman is enjoying a walk on a sunny spring day in April 1936. Floods have plagued this section of lower Green Ridge for many years. Pictured below, the Scranton Lace Company has also fallen victim to the Lackawanna River's rising waters. A levee system constructed by the US Army Corps of Engineers now protects the area from such destruction. (Both, courtesy of Mark Boock.)

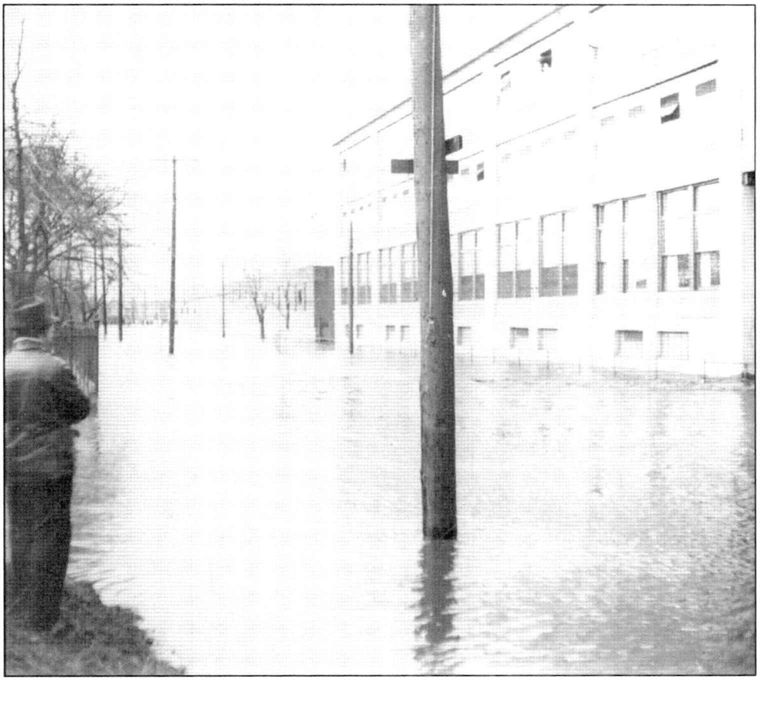

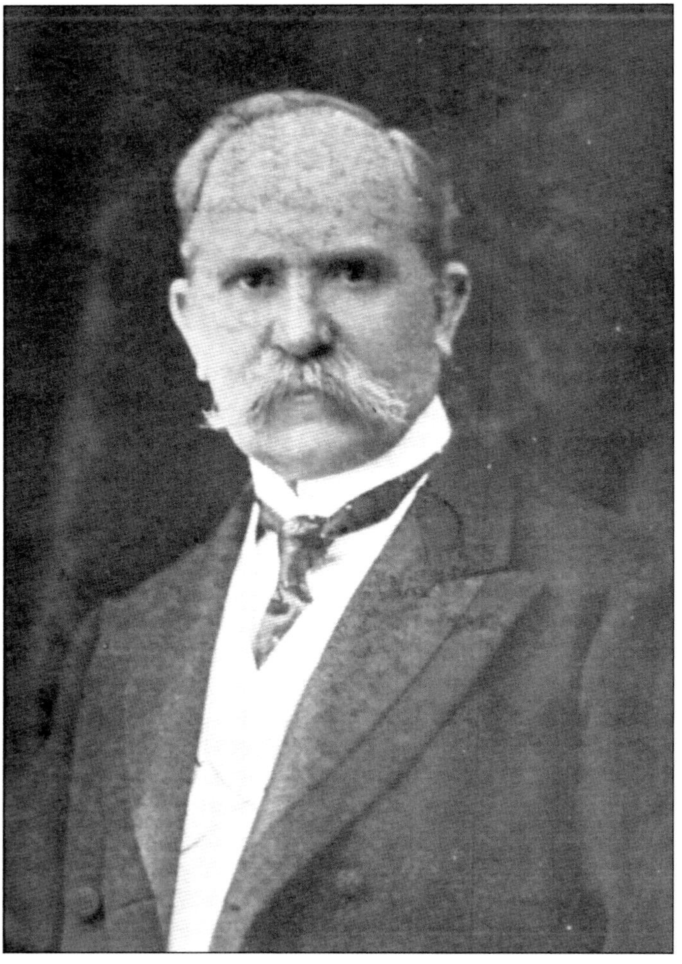

Martin J. Maloney. Maloney was an entrepreneur who invented the gas streetlights used in Scranton. These lights eventually were replaced with electric lamp stands. Maloney was prominently connected to many corporations. He lived in Scranton for a time before relocating to Philadelphia. (Courtesy of the author.)

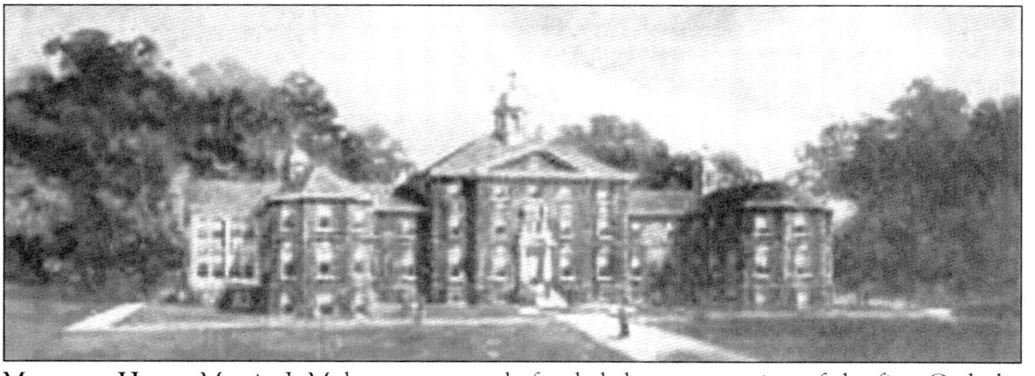

Maloney Home. Martin J. Maloney generously funded the construction of the first Catholic home dedicated to caring for the elderly poor in Scranton. In June 1908, Mother Provincial and six Little Sisters arrived at the Maloney Home with an offer to care for the home's elderly residents. Their offer was accepted immediately. The Maloney Home was blessed and the altar consecrated on June 24, 1908. In 1976, the Holy Family Residence was built on the same property where the Little Sisters of the Poor continue the work of the Maloney Home. (Courtesy of the author.)

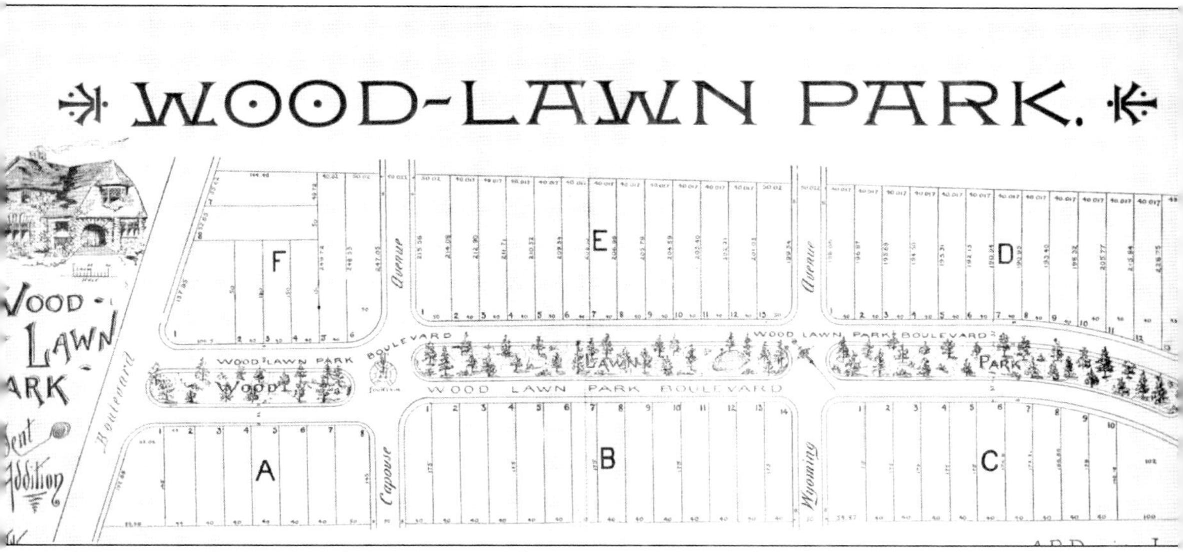

WOODLAWN PARK. The advertisement reads, "A New Departure for Attractive Homes." The tract of land was situated in Green Ridge, ranging four blocks along Washington Avenue to North Park Street and extending west to old Boulevard Avenue. It was precisely 900 feet from the corner of East Market Street and Sanderson Avenue. The plot, containing 17 acres is laid out as per cut. It represents a large public park and 67 of the finest lots in the Green Ridge area. The owners include G.R. Clark, Hanson Carpenter, G.W. Finn, S.H. Finn, and M.W. Finn. (Courtesy of Mark Boock.)

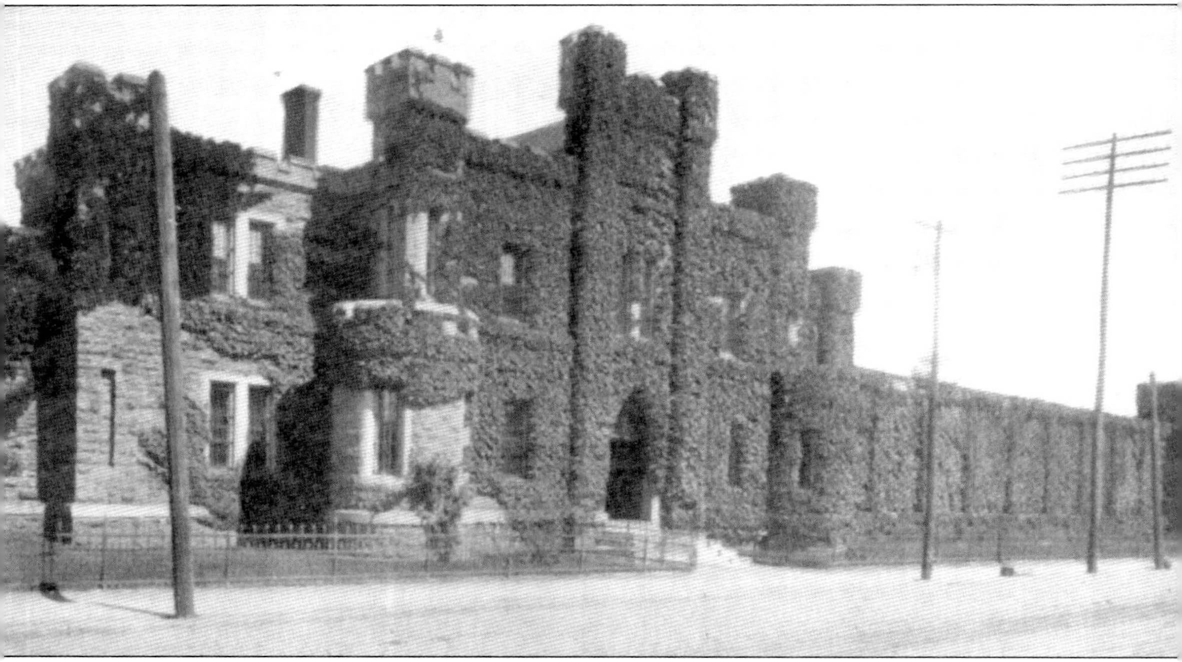

Lackawanna County Prison. The prison was originally built in the mid-1880s to hold a population of 110 prisoners. A major expansion and renovations took place in 1999, and today, the prison can have up to 1,200 prisoners at a time. Beyond the prison's walls, there is a laundry, canteen, medical services, chapel, gymnasium, food service, and housing units. The prison houses both male and female pretrial detainees and sentenced inmates up to one day less than five years. (Courtesy of the author.)

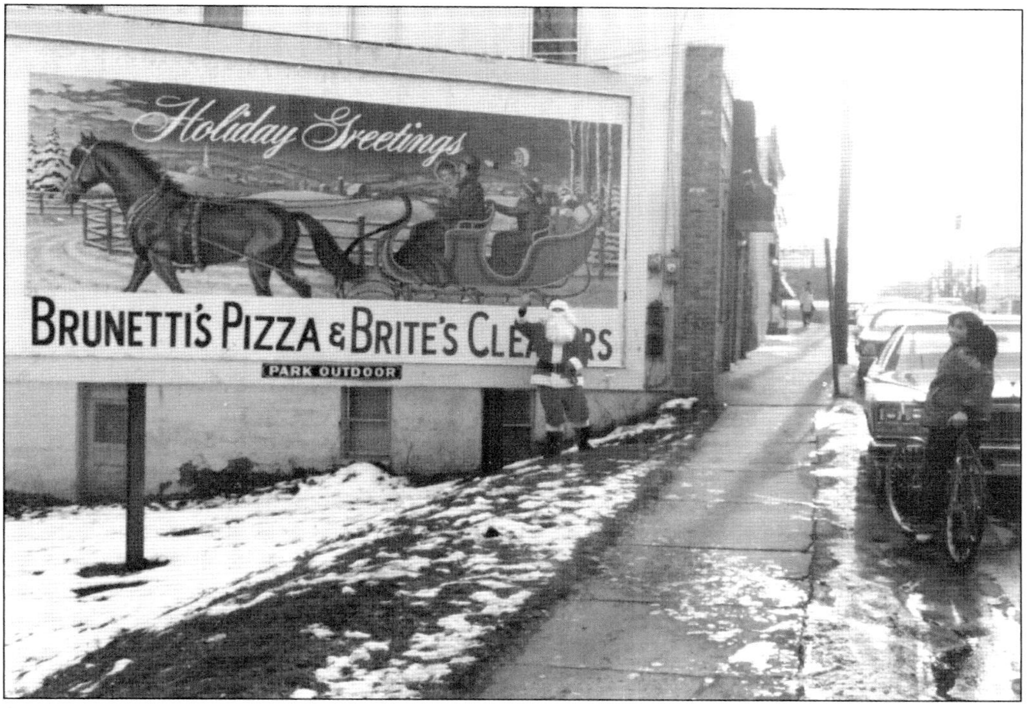

SANTA COMES TO GREEN RIDGE. Santa (Michael Brunetti) poses in front of a billboard advertisement for Brunetti's Pizza. Brites Cleaners (background) is another business establishment on Green Ridge Corners. (Courtesy of the Brunetti family.)

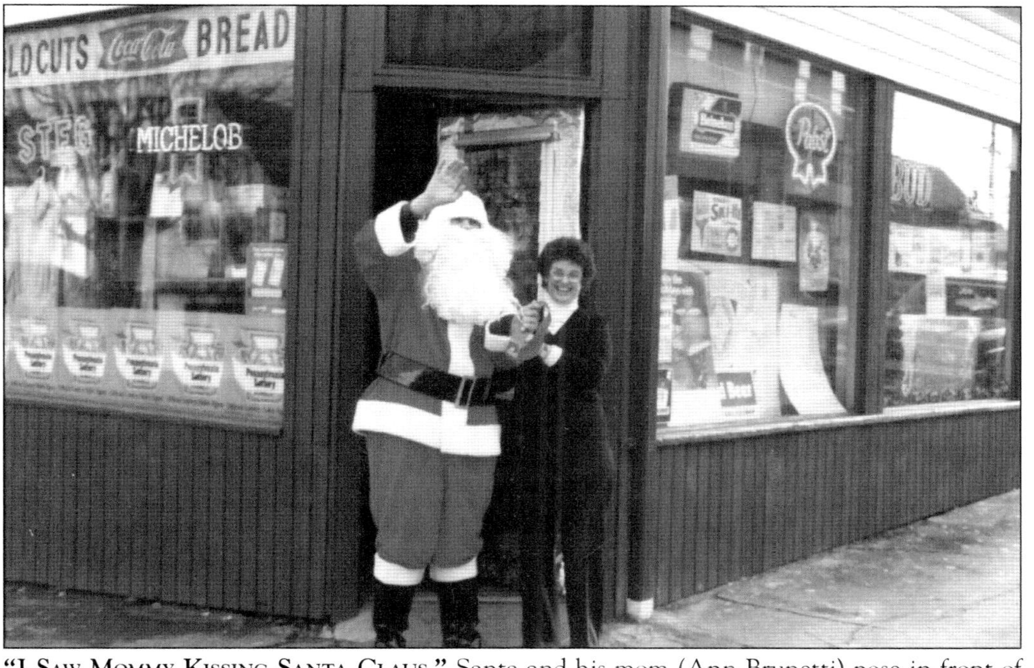

"I SAW MOMMY KISSING SANTA CLAUS." Santa and his mom (Ann Brunetti) pose in front of their place of business while greeting the customers. (Courtesy of the Brunetti family.)

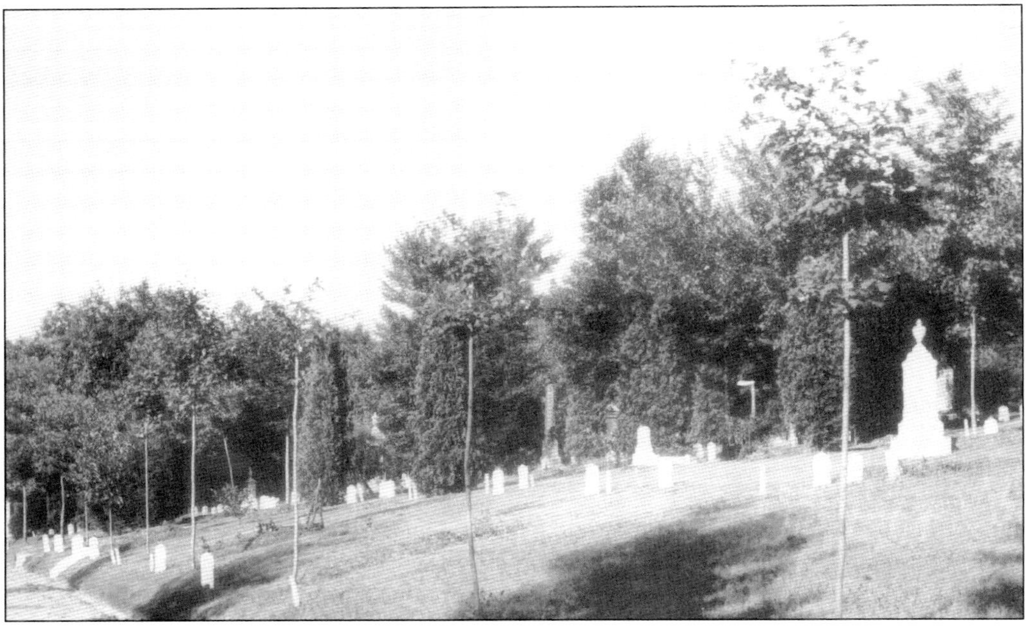

Forest Hill Cemetery. The development of the cemetery began in 1868. The first burial took place in May 1870. Forest Hill founders are as follows: Hon. George Sanderson, James G. Sanderson, George Scott Kingsbury, Elisha Phinney, J. Atticus Robertson, and William DuPont Breck. All were residents of Green Ridge with the exception of Breck. Today, Forest Hills is a part of the borough of Dunmore, but at the time of its charter, the area was still considered Green Ridge. (Both, courtesy of the author.)

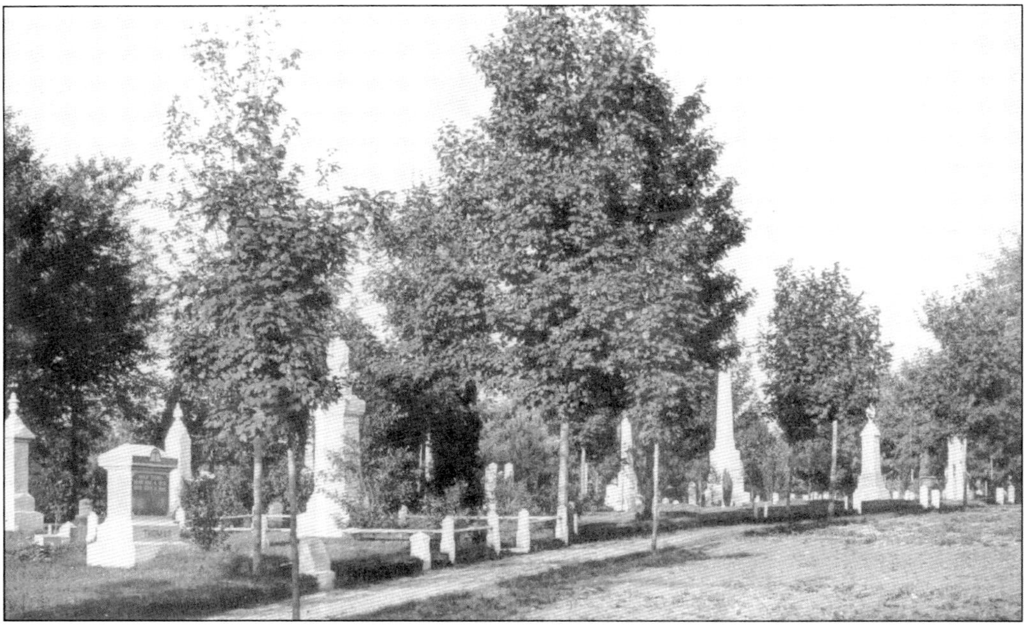

NOVEMBER 30, 1886. The first trolley system to run completely on electricity was invented by Green Ridge resident E.B. Sturges. The Suburban Passenger Railway Electric Trolley's first run was on November 30, 1886. A trial run occurred the day before. It traveled from the corner of Franklin Avenue to Lackawanna Avenue. It then returned up Franklin Avenue to Spruce Street, across Penn and Wyoming Avenues, and up to Adams Avenue, where it turned the corner and traveled the rest of the way to Green Ridge Street. At times, the trolley could hit a speed of 12 miles per hour. The cost to travel by streetcar was 5¢. (Courtesy of the author.)

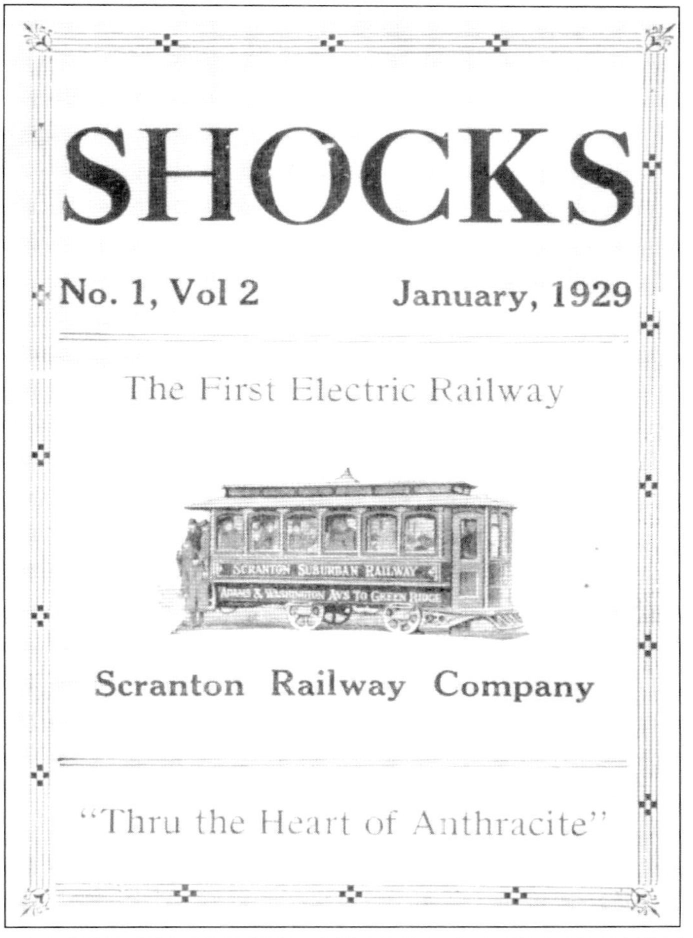

SHOCKS

No. 1, Vol 2 January, 1929

The First Electric Railway

Scranton Railway Company

"Thru the Heart of Anthracite"

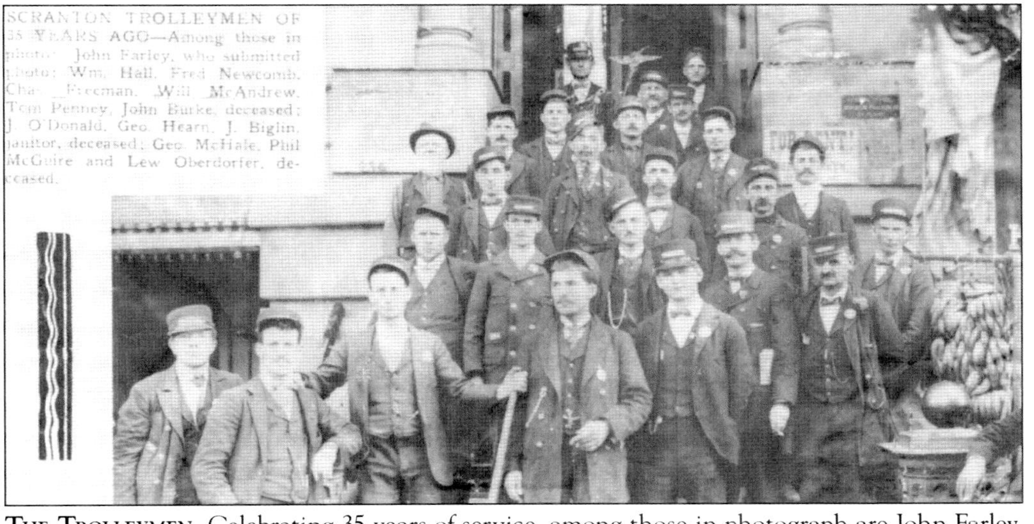

SCRANTON TROLLEYMEN OF 35 YEARS AGO—Among those in photo: John Farley, who submitted photo; Wm. Hall, Fred Newcomb, Chas. Freeman, Will McAndrew, Tom Penney, John Burke, deceased; J. O'Donald, Geo. Hearn, J. Biglin, janitor, deceased; Geo. McHale, Phil McGuire and Lew Oberdorfer, deceased.

THE TROLLEYMEN. Celebrating 35 years of service, among those in photograph are John Farley, William Hall, Fred Newcomb, Tom Penney, and Lew Oberdofer. (Courtesy of Mark Boock.)

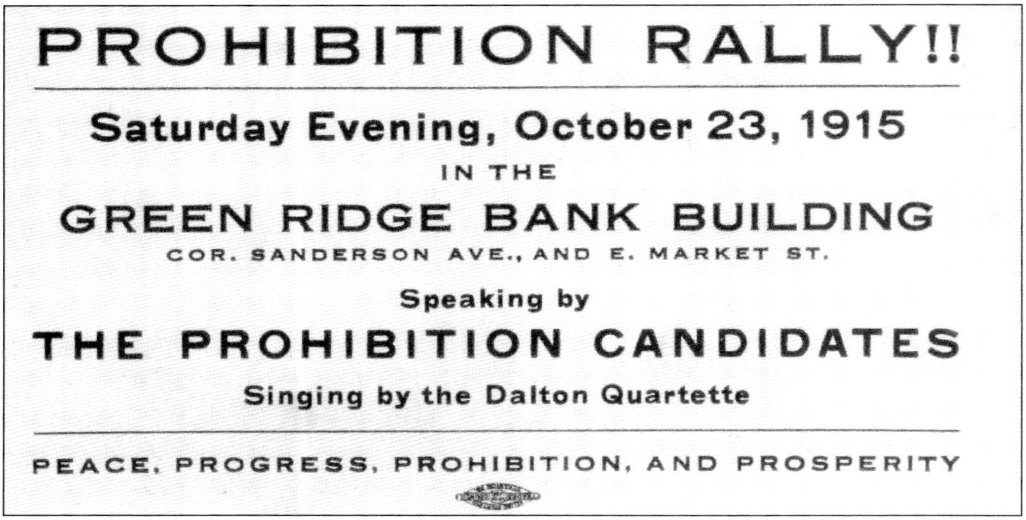

PROHIBITION RALLY!!

Saturday Evening, October 23, 1915

IN THE

GREEN RIDGE BANK BUILDING

COR. SANDERSON AVE., AND E. MARKET ST.

Speaking by

THE PROHIBITION CANDIDATES

Singing by the Dalton Quartette

PEACE, PROGRESS, PROHIBITION, AND PROSPERITY

PROHIBITION RALLY. While the 18th Amendment took away the right of individuals to drink alcohol in 1919, the 21st Amendment repealed the 18th Amendment and ended Prohibition in 1933. This rally was held at the Green Ridge Bank Building. (Courtesy of Mark Boock.)

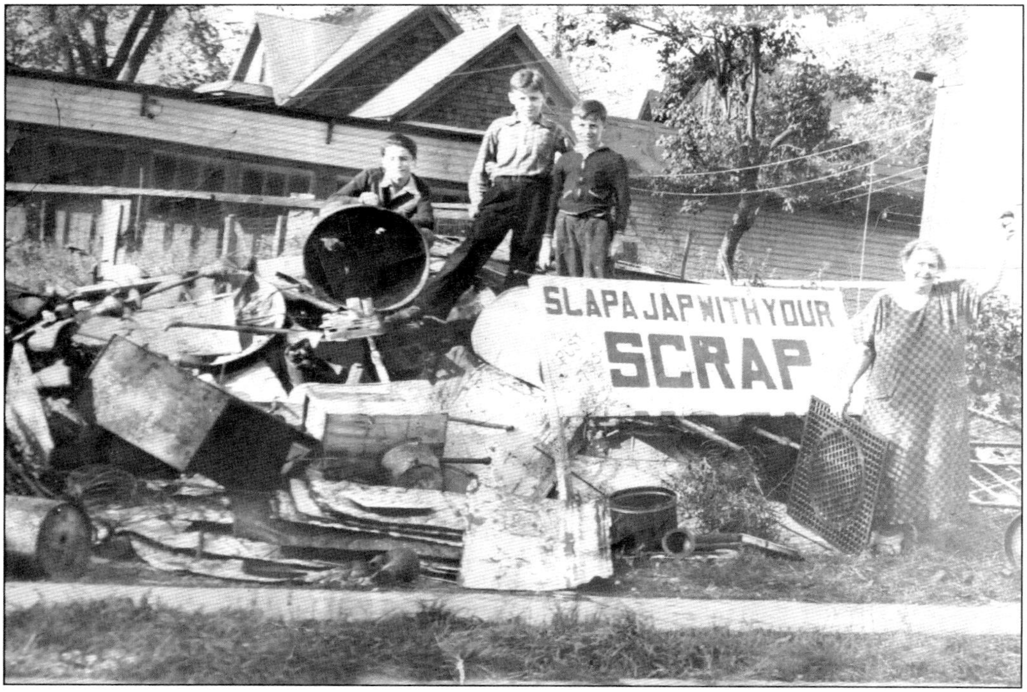

WORLD WAR II. In an effort to raise money for the war, the Green Ridge VFW collected scrap metal, as did other VFWs. The slogan "Slapa Jap with Your Scrap," though politically incorrect today, was known nationally at the time. Pictured is Mary Ricardo (right) with unidentified children. (Courtesy of the Brunetti family.)

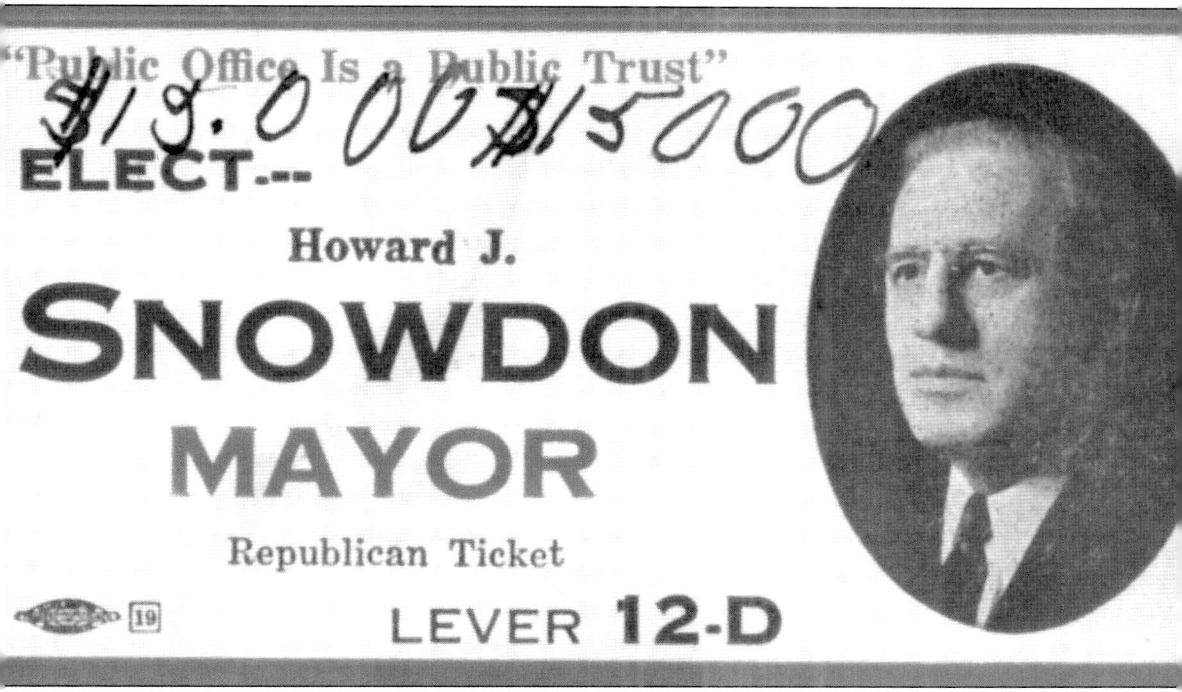

HOWARD J. SNOWDON. Howard J. Snowdon was the 20th mayor of Scranton. He was in office from 1942 to 1946. After graduating from Embalming College in Philadelphia, Snowdon opened the funeral home on Sanderson Avenue in 1907. (Courtesy of Mark Boock.)

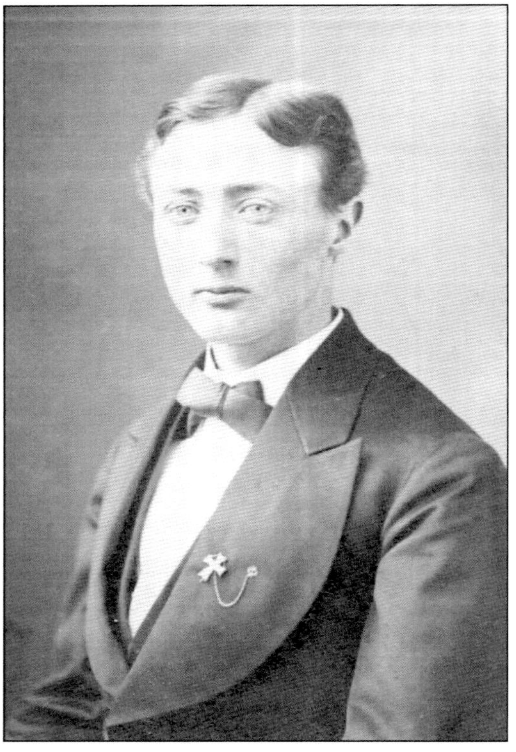

The Rittenhouse Family. These photographs are of a young James H. Rittenhouse (left) and Ida Cole (below) of Montrose, Pennsylvania. The pair met after James graduated from Lafayette College and were married on April 10, 1878. They made their home on the 1600 block on North Washington Avenue in the early 1880s. (Both, courtesy of the Lackawanna Historical Society.)

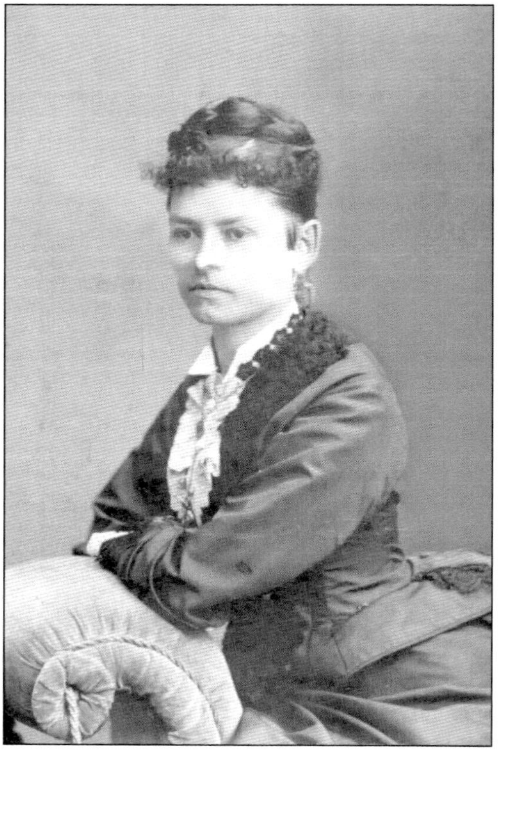

MOTHER AND DAUGHTER. Ida Rittenhouse (right) and her oldest child, Lucia, pose for a family portrait. Ida bore James four children, Lucia, Ralph, Karl, and Leonard. Sadly, Ida passed away on April 20, 1893, after a long illness and never saw her children grow up. (Courtesy of the Lackawanna Historical Society.)

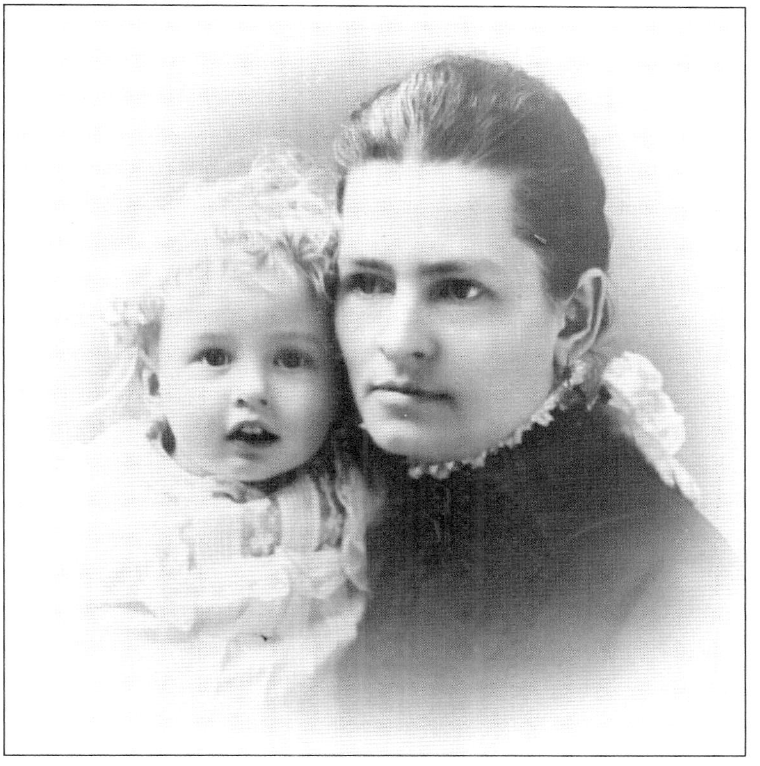

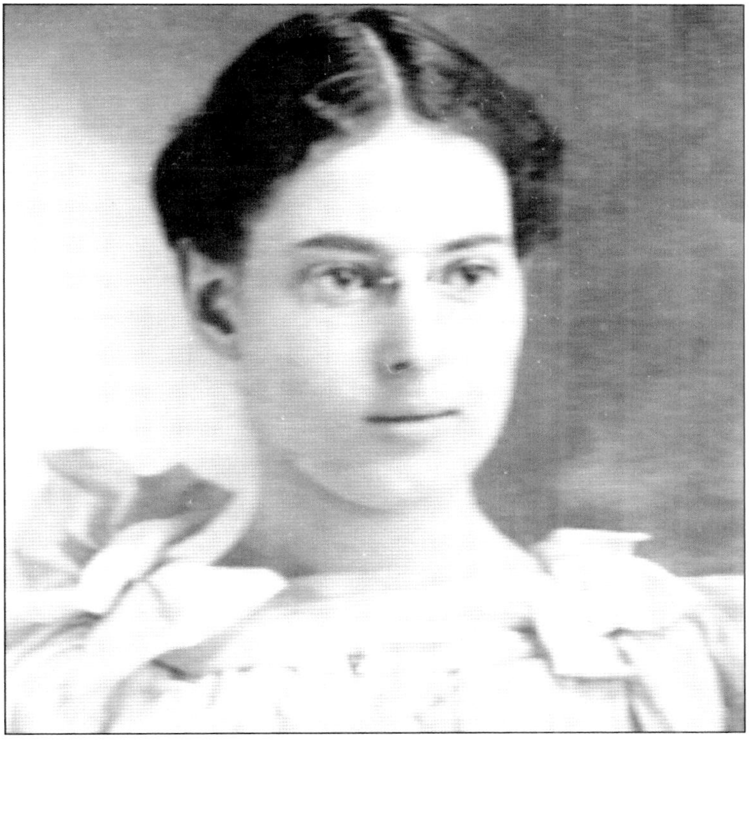

LUCIA RITTENHOUSE. James and Ida's oldest child attended the Academy of Music and was gifted with an artist's soul. In the early 1900s, she moved out of her Green Ridge childhood home to Washington, DC, where she married George Shoemaker. (Courtesy of the Lackawanna Historical Society.)

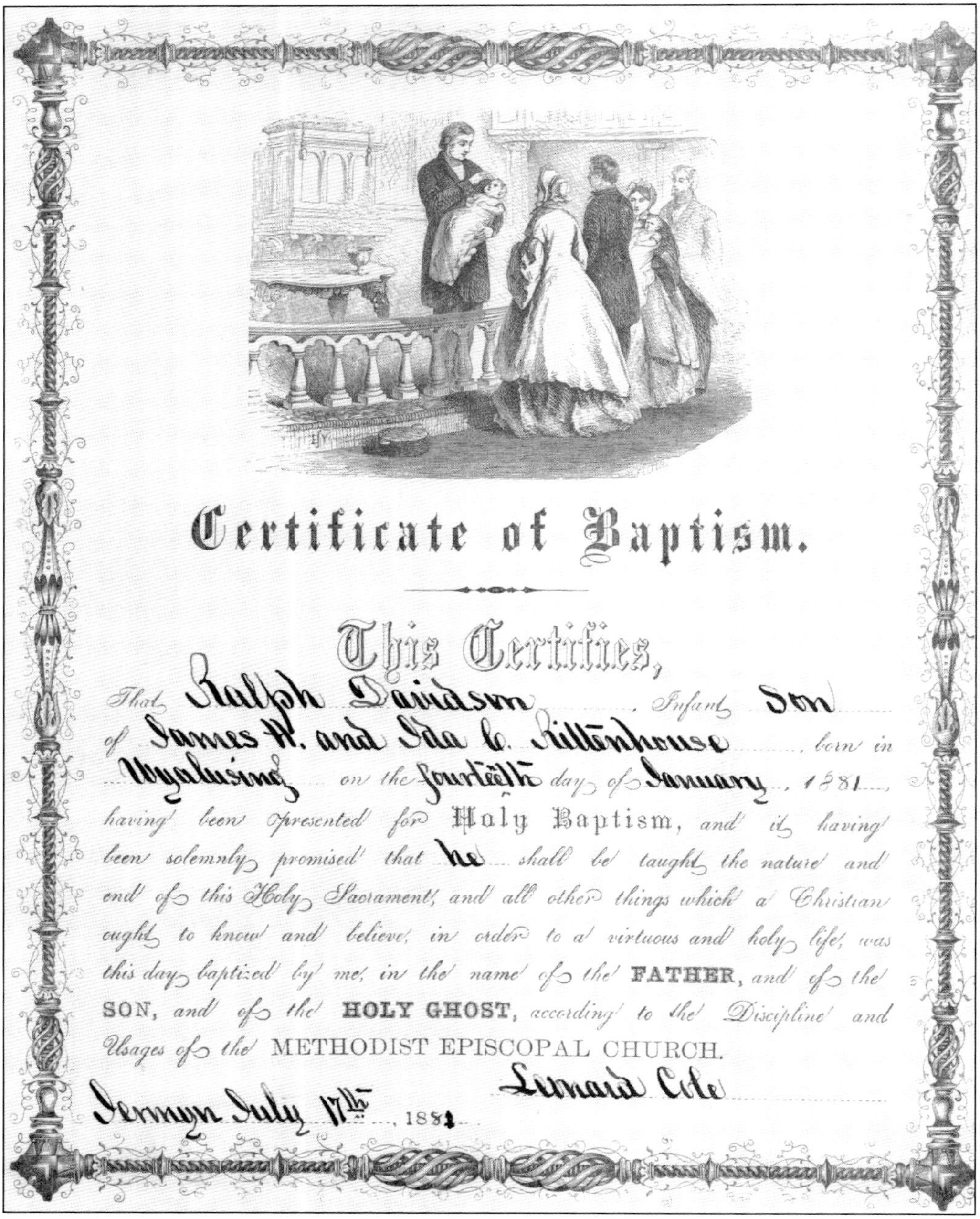

Certificate of Baptism.

This Certifies,

That Ralph Davidson, Infant Son of James H. and Ida C. Rittenhouse, born in Wyalusing on the fourteenth day of January, 1881, having been presented for Holy Baptism, and it having been solemnly promised that he shall be taught the nature and end of this Holy Sacrament, and all other things which a Christian ought to know and believe, in order to a virtuous and holy life, was this day baptized by me, in the name of the FATHER, and of the SON, and of the HOLY GHOST, according to the Discipline and Usages of the METHODIST EPISCOPAL CHURCH.

Leonard Cole

Jermyn July 17th, 1881

19TH-CENTURY BIRTH CERTIFICATE. The birth certificate of Ralph Rittenhouse, the oldest son of James and Ida, is dated July 17, 1881. Ralph was following in his father's footsteps when his dreams of becoming a civil engineer were shattered suddenly. He retired one evening in 1903 not feeling well and woke up the next morning paralyzed. At first, it was suspected the young man of only 22 years of age suffered a stroke, but it was meningitis. He died after only a week. (Courtesy of the Lackawanna Historical Society.)

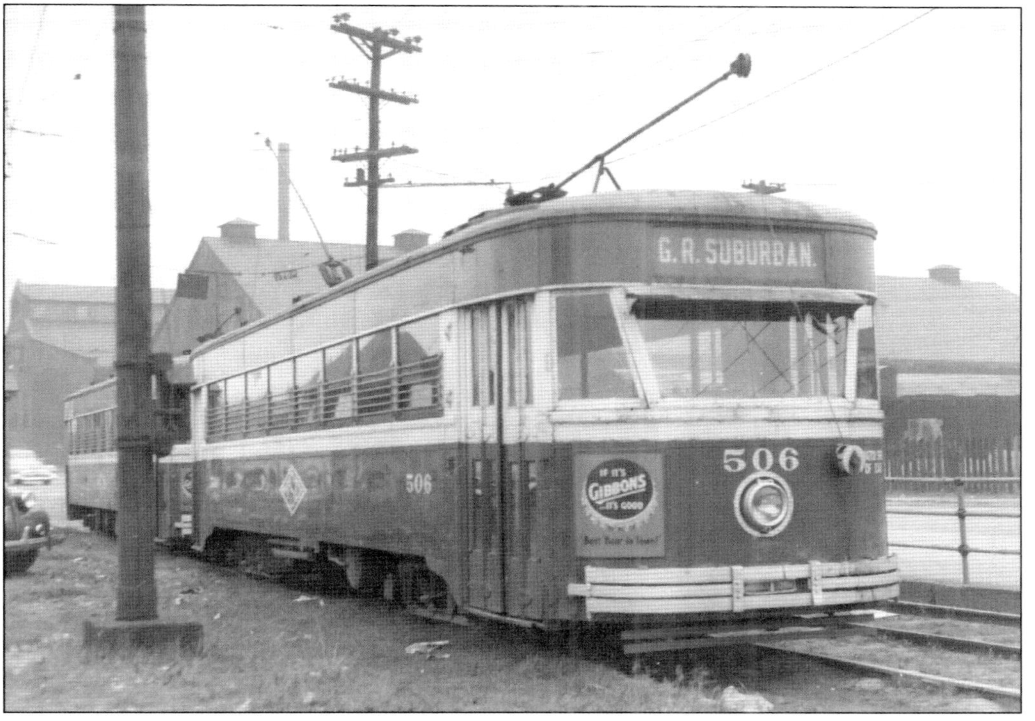

Car No. 506. Car No. 506 was used for the Green Ridge Suburban run. It was owned by the Scranton Transit Company. (Courtesy of Mark Boock.)

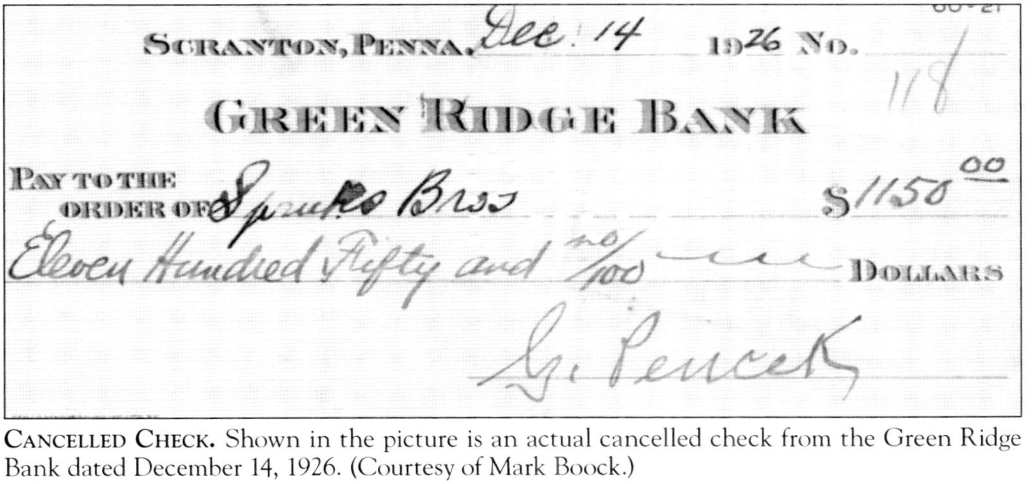

Scranton, Penna, Dec. 14 1926 No. 118

Green Ridge Bank

Pay to the order of Spruks Bros $1150 00

Eleven Hundred Fifty and no/100 Dollars

Cancelled Check. Shown in the picture is an actual cancelled check from the Green Ridge Bank dated December 14, 1926. (Courtesy of Mark Boock.)

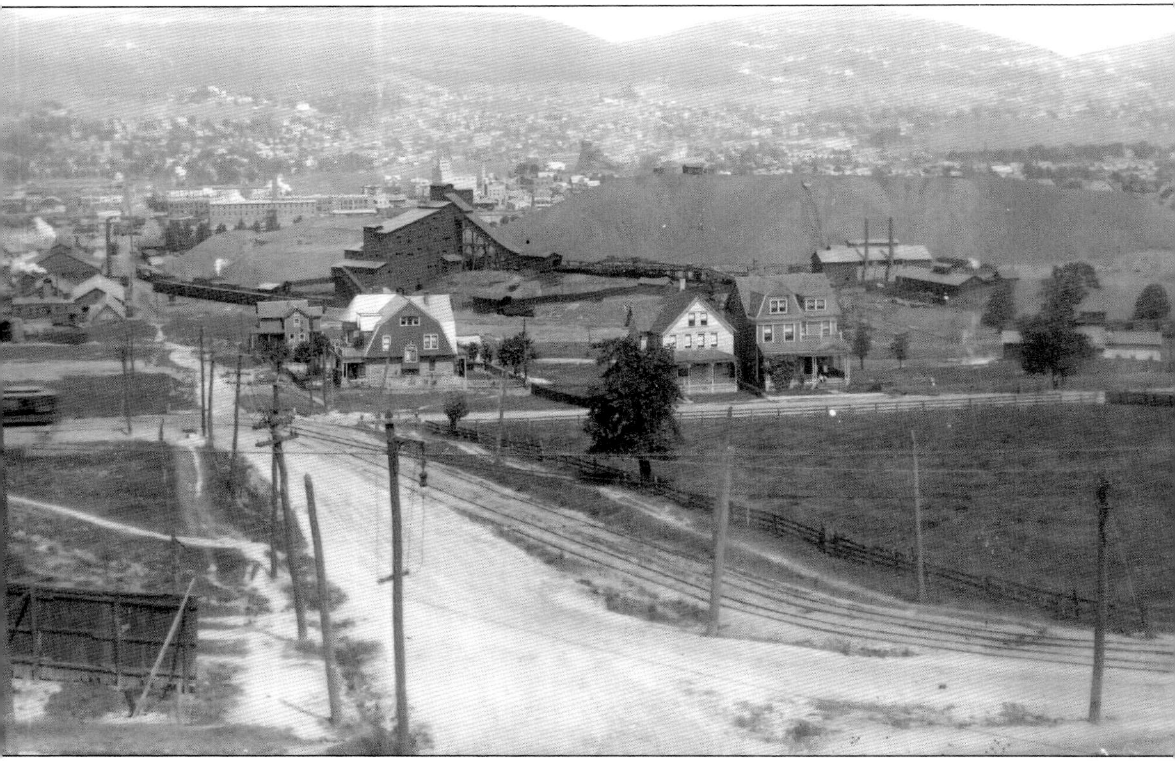

VIEW FROM CLAY AVENUE. In this panoramic view is the trolley traveling over Quincy Avenue in order to turn up Poplar Street. In the background is the Green Ridge Breaker. (Courtesy of the Lackawanna Historical Society.)

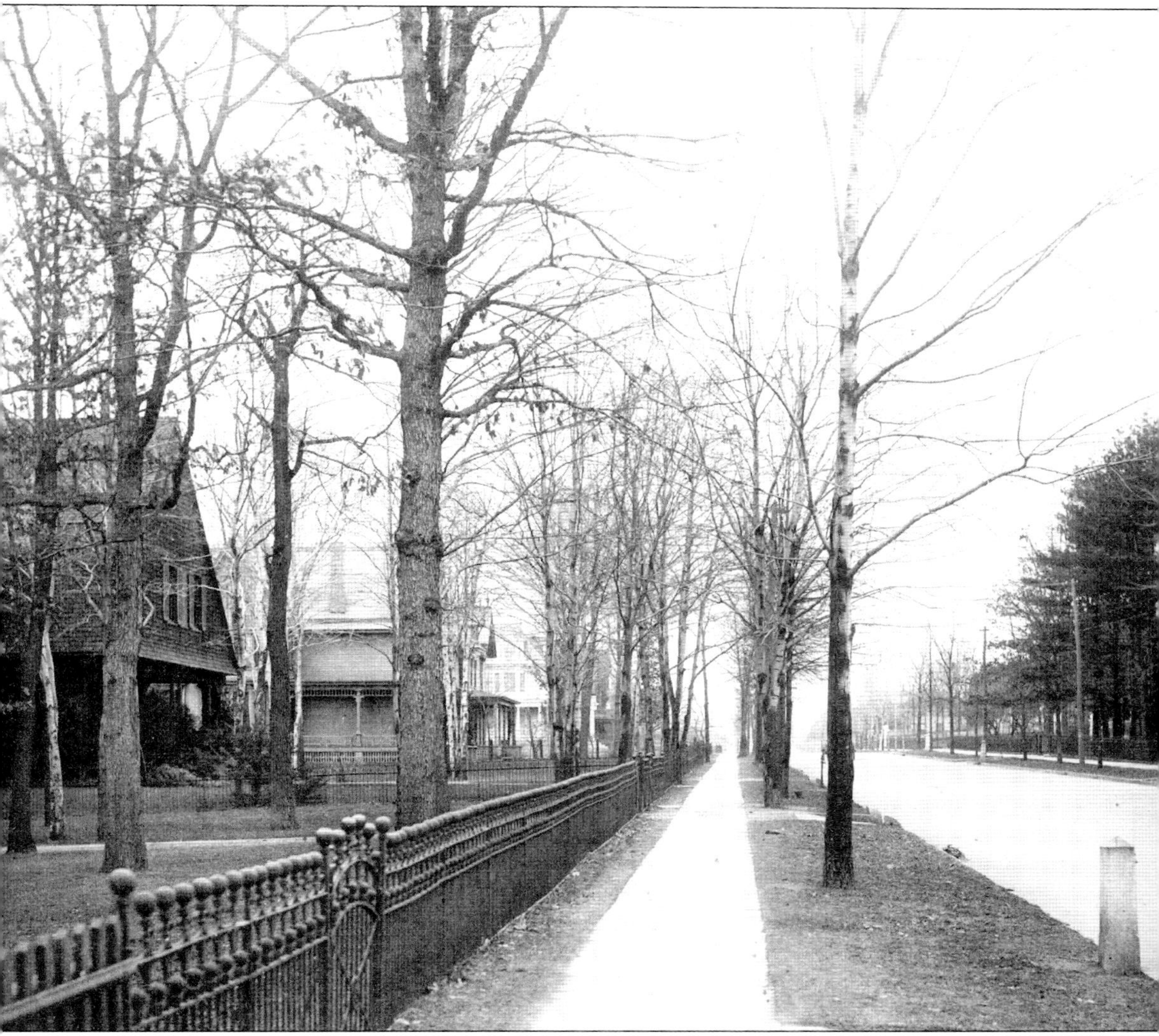

WASHINGTON AVENUE, c. 1897. This view is of North Washington Avenue from Green Ridge Street. Among the residents who lived here in 1897 were James Rittenhouse, Edgar H. Shurtleff, C.P. Davidson, E.B. Sturges, Col. George Sanderson, Charles H. Lindsey, James W. Garney, and F.L. Hitchcock. (Courtesy of the Lackawanna Historical Society.)

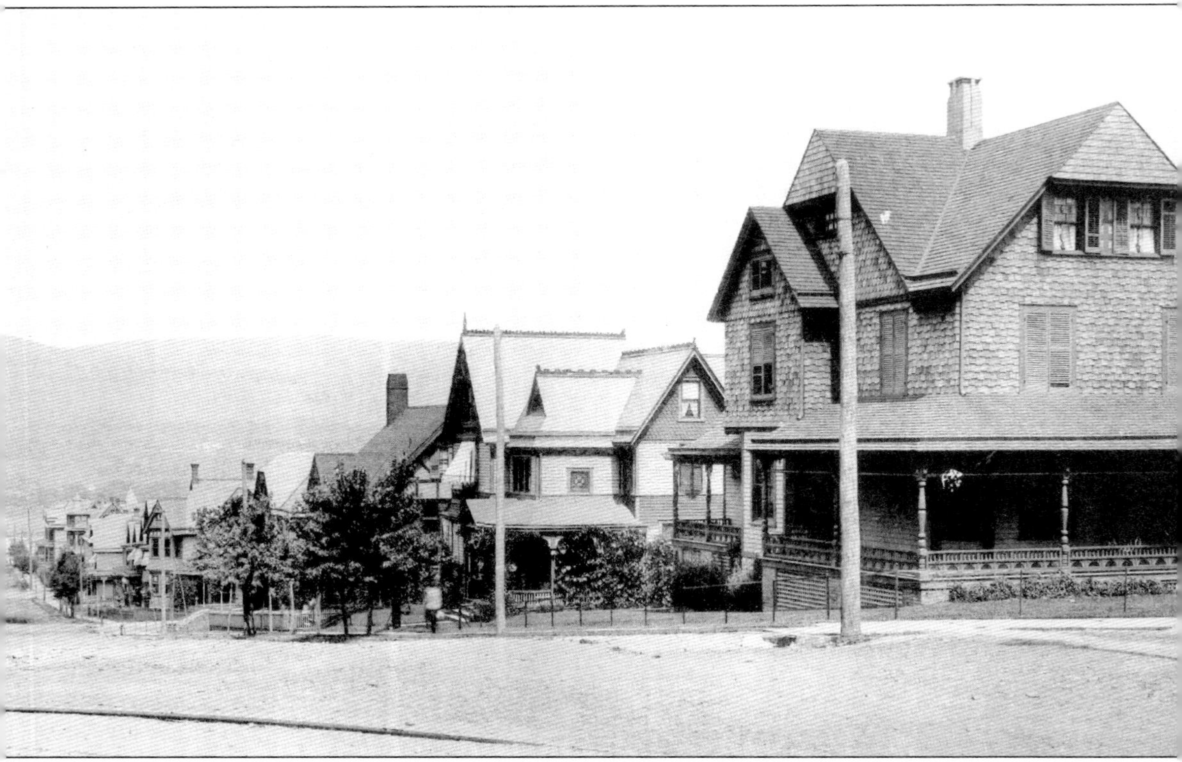

WALKING ALONG WASHINGTON AVENUE. Here is another view of the beautiful homes along North Washington Avenue. Green Ridge was officially developed by the Sanderson-Robb Improvement Company, a limited partnership created by George Sanderson. On June 11, 1881, the partnership was officially dissolved when George Sanderson received Green Ridge from the liquidating trustees, and Green Ridge was plotted in the Lackawanna County Book of Deeds. (Courtesy of the Lackawanna Historical Society.)

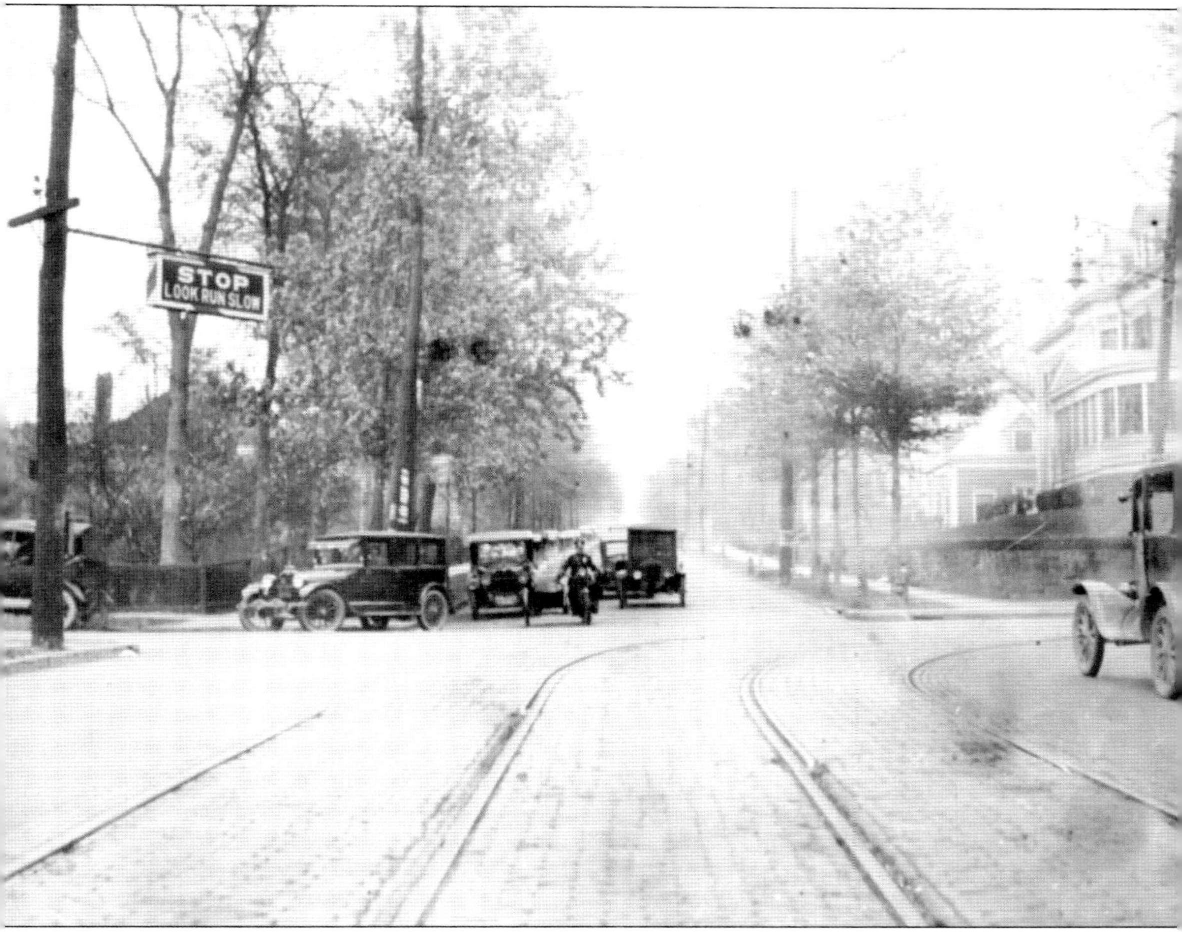

"Stop, Look, Run Slow." This is a view of Green Ridge Street and North Washington Avenue in 1924. Today, it is a heavily traveled intersection with Marywood University and St. Joseph's Center only a few blocks away. (Courtesy of the Lackawanna Historical Society.)

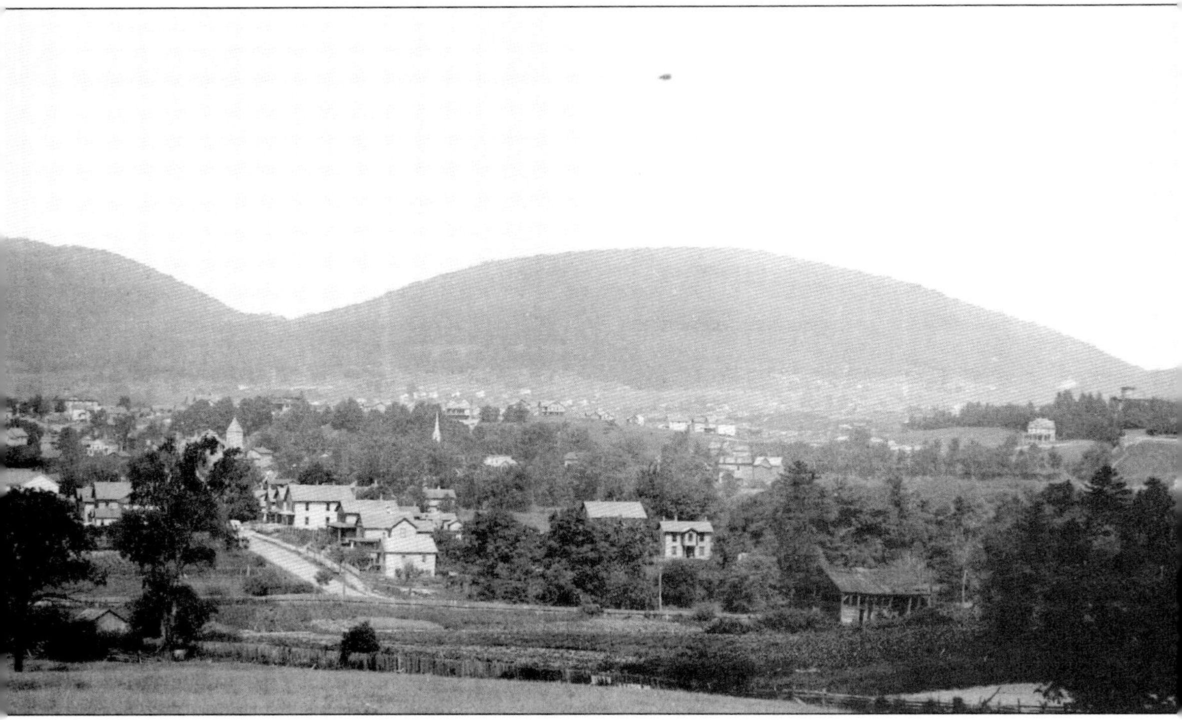

VIEW OF GREEN RIDGE. The landscape of Green Ridge is a breathtaking sight. It is hard to believe that this tranquil suburb of Scranton was once nothing more than a wilderness. (Courtesy of the Lackawanna Historical Society.)

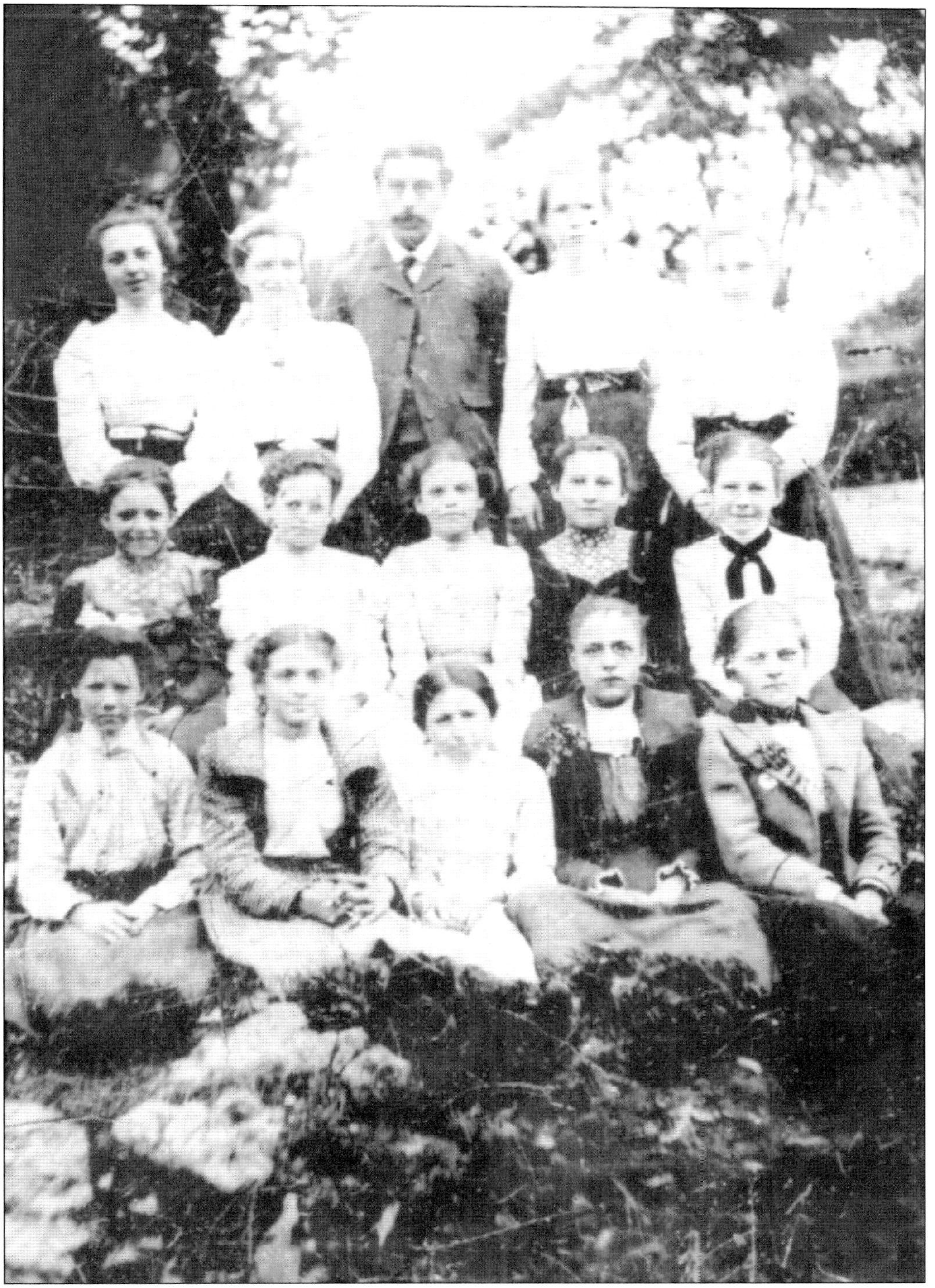

SCRANTON'S 13TH MAYOR. Mayor J. Benjamin Dimmick (in the middle of the third row) is seen here with possibly some of his future constituents. Dimmick was known for his courteous manner and eloquent way of speaking (Courtesy of Robert J. Walker.)

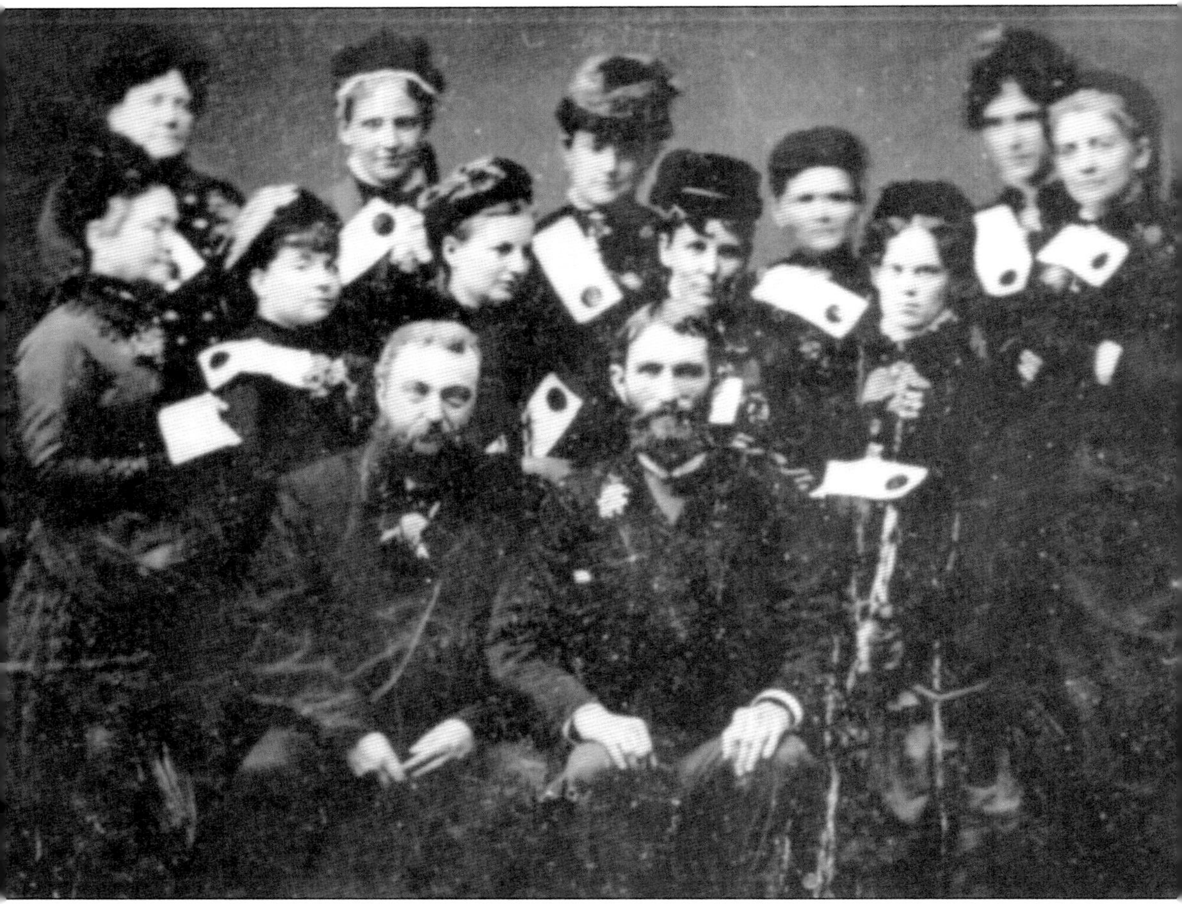

Neighbors in Early History. J. Benjamin Dimmick (right) and Edward Dimmick (left) are seated; others in the photograph are unidentified. (Courtesy of Robert J. Walker.)

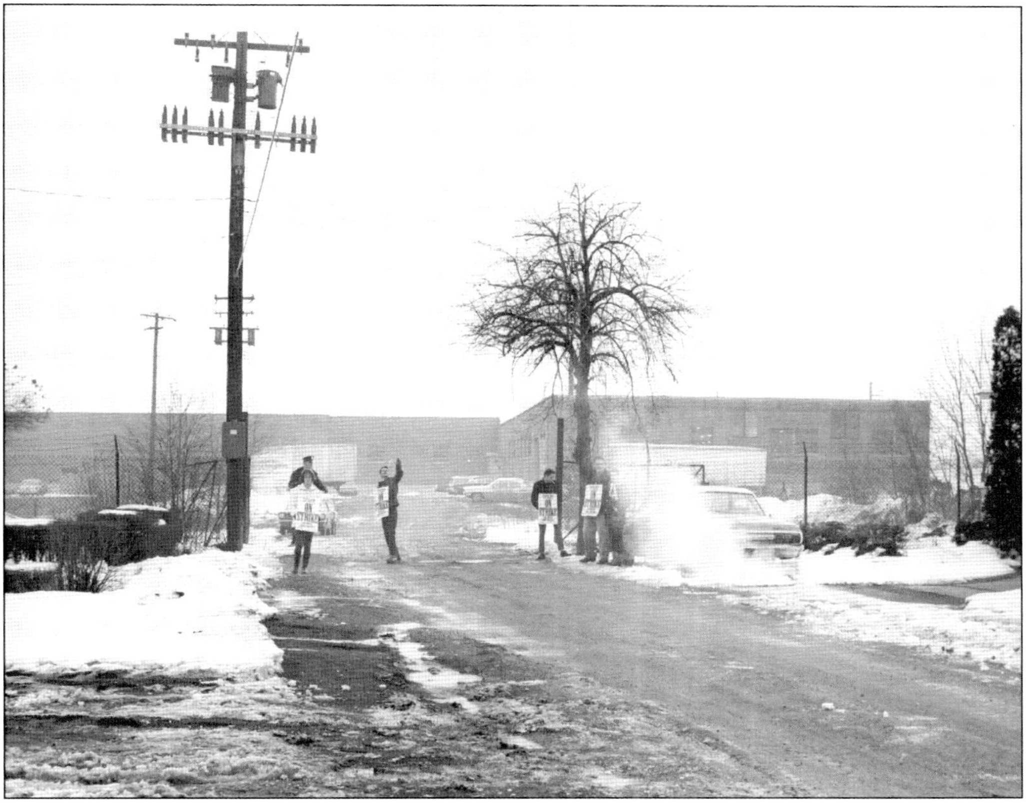

SCRANTON WIPING CLOTH. This labor strike occurred in the late 1950s or early 1960s. Workers picketed while the watchful eye of the law looked on. The factory was located on Rosanna Avenue and still stands today under the new name of Pennsylvania Clothing Recyclers, Inc. Accounts of the strike are very limited, and its outcome is unknown. (Both, courtesy of Jesse Hinkley.)

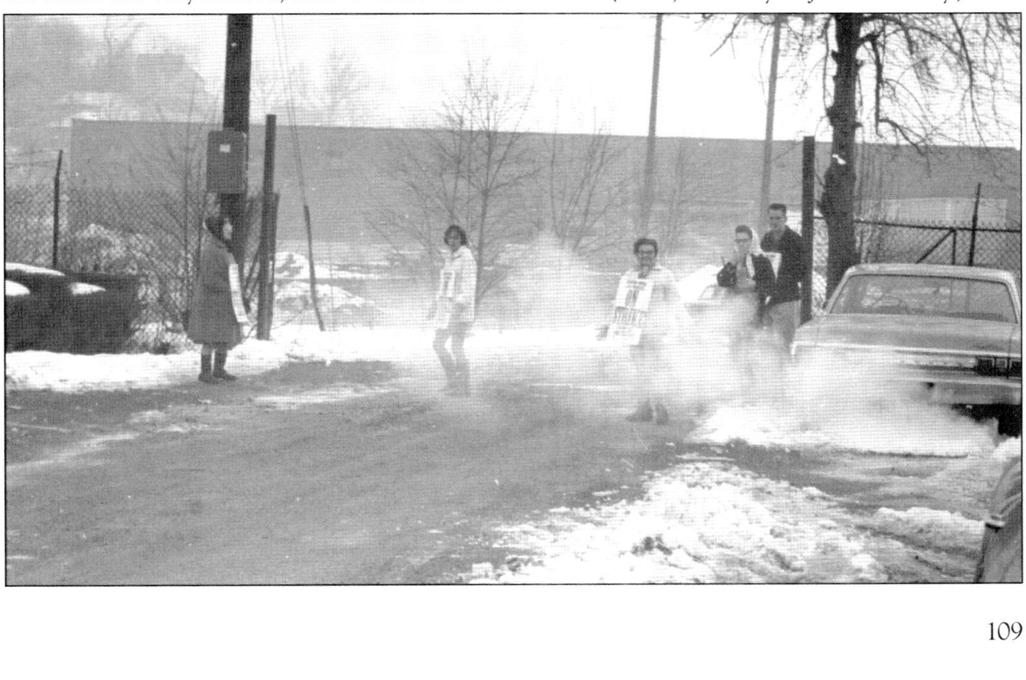

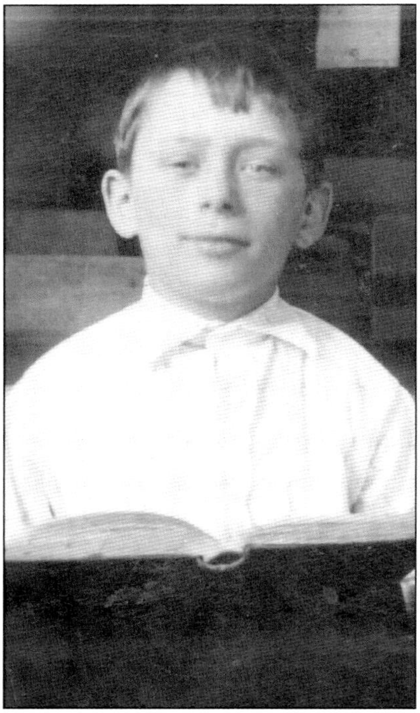

Harold H. Yarns. Harold H. Yarns was the son of Charles L. Yarns and Annie Jones. The family lived in the plot section of Green Ridge. Harold is seen here at his fourth-grade school desk. (Courtesy of Christine Yarns Schaefer.)

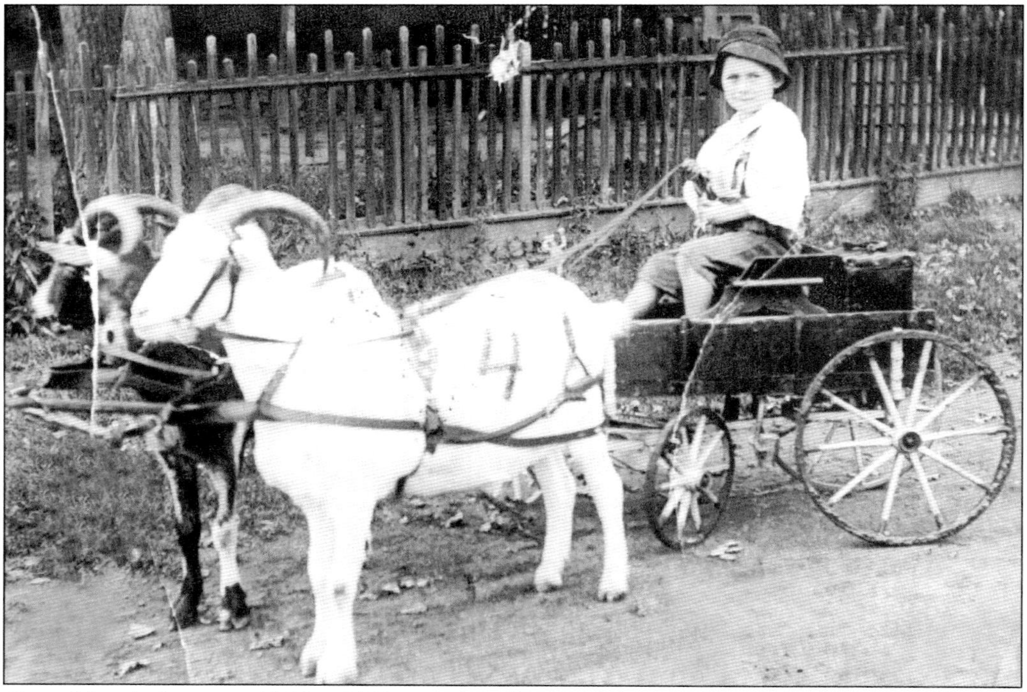

Goat No. 4. Six-year-old Harold Yarns takes charge of the reins of his goat-drawn carriage. It is possible Harold raced the goats at the Gentleman's Driving Park, which was located around Race and Dean Streets. The track was elliptical and famous for its horse and later bicycle races. (Courtesy of Christine Yarns Schaefer.)

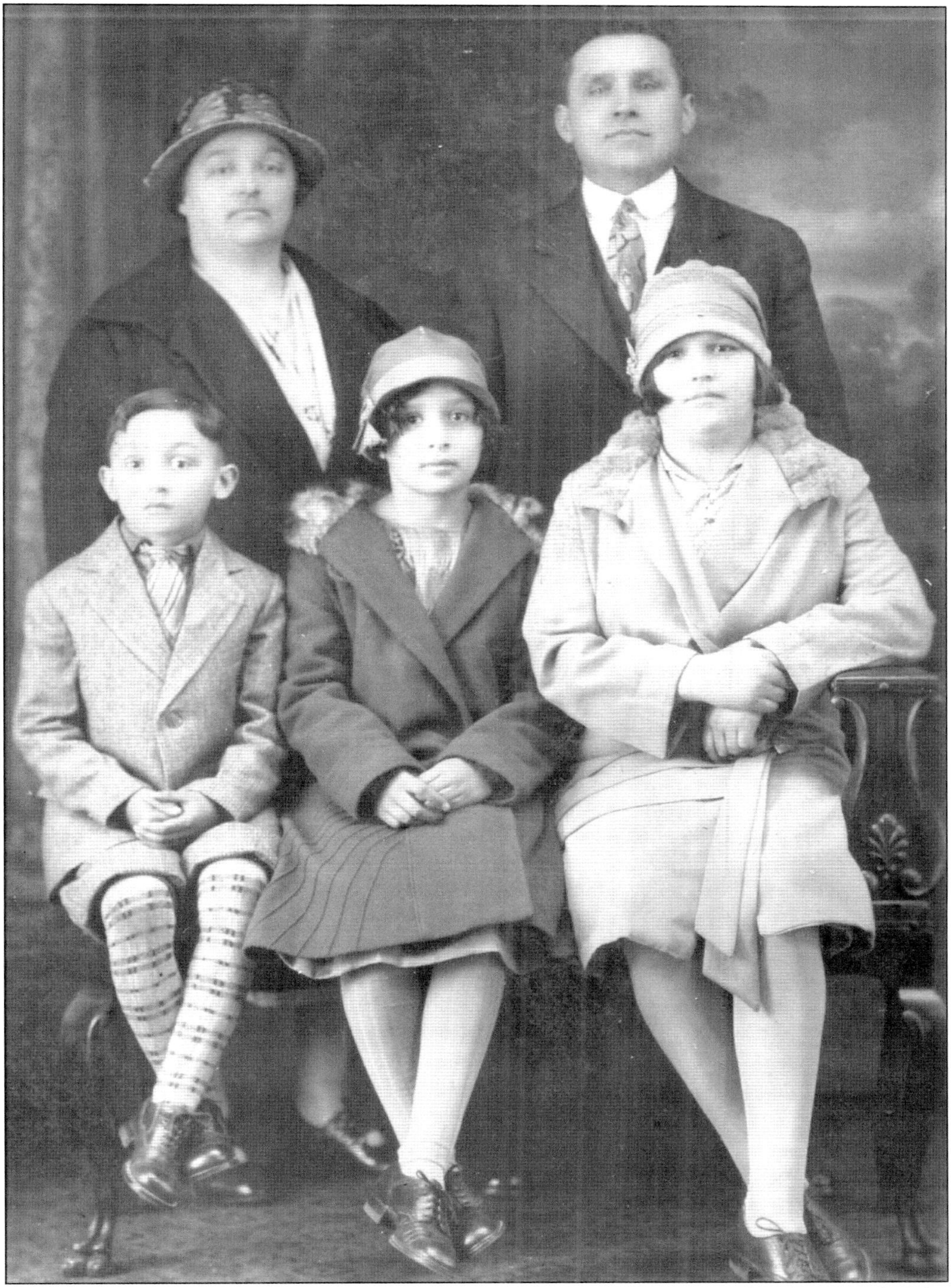

The Slish Family. Stephen Slish (top right), born in Austria-Hungary, owned and operated Slish's Grocery Store on Marion Street until his death in 1969. Slish was stricken ill and died in the grocery store while he was working. His wife Mary (top left) and three children, from left to right, William, Martha, and Margaret, are also in the picture. (Courtesy of Christine Yarns Schaefer.)

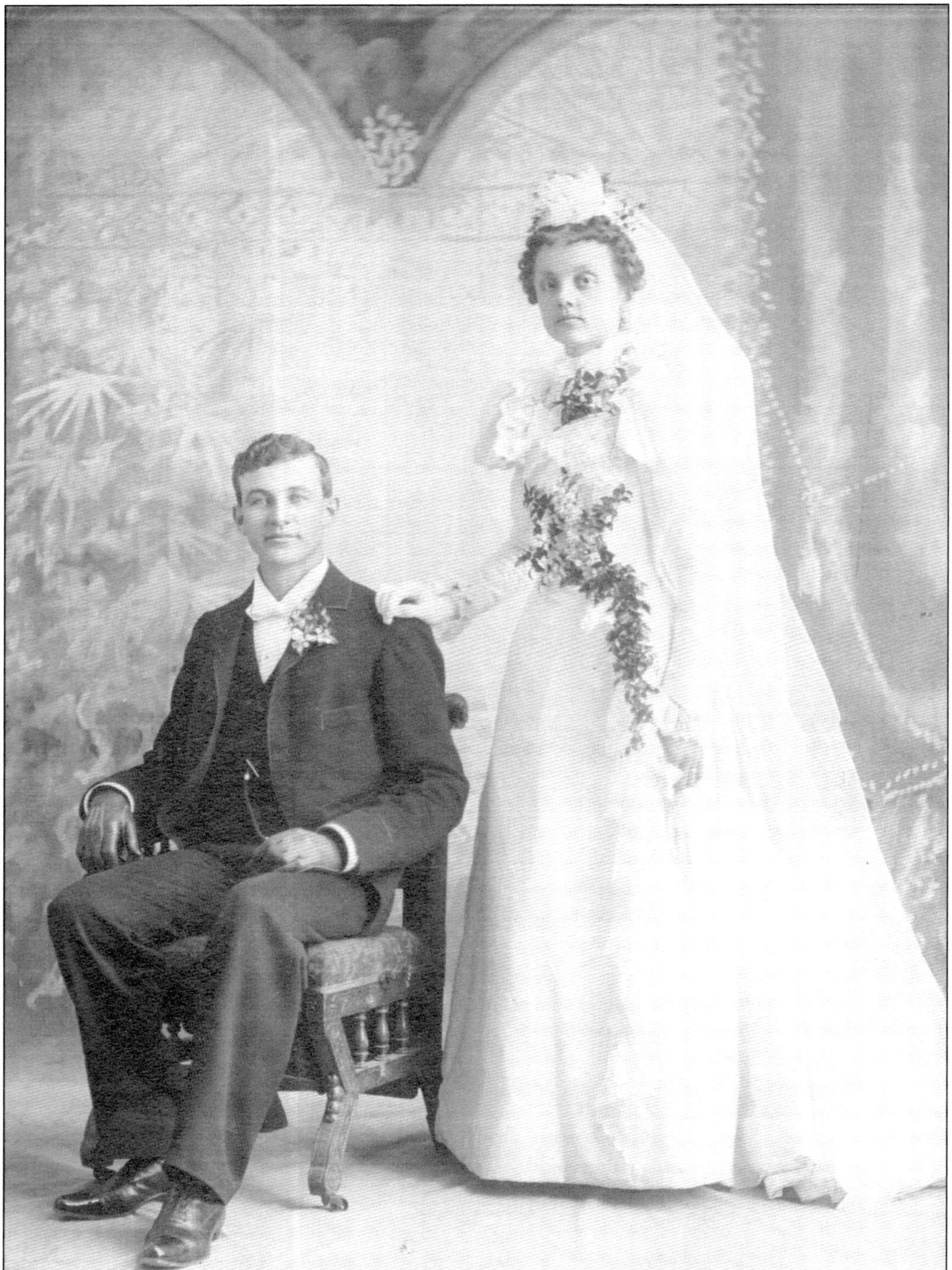

Jurisch-Cokely Wedding. Edith May Jurisch was wed to Bertrand Cokely in 1895 at Asbury Methodist Episcopal Church. They resided on Monsey Avenue and had one child, who they named Helen. Edith was a member of the Daughters of the American Revolution, Scranton City Chapter. (Courtesy of Christine Yarns Schaefer.)

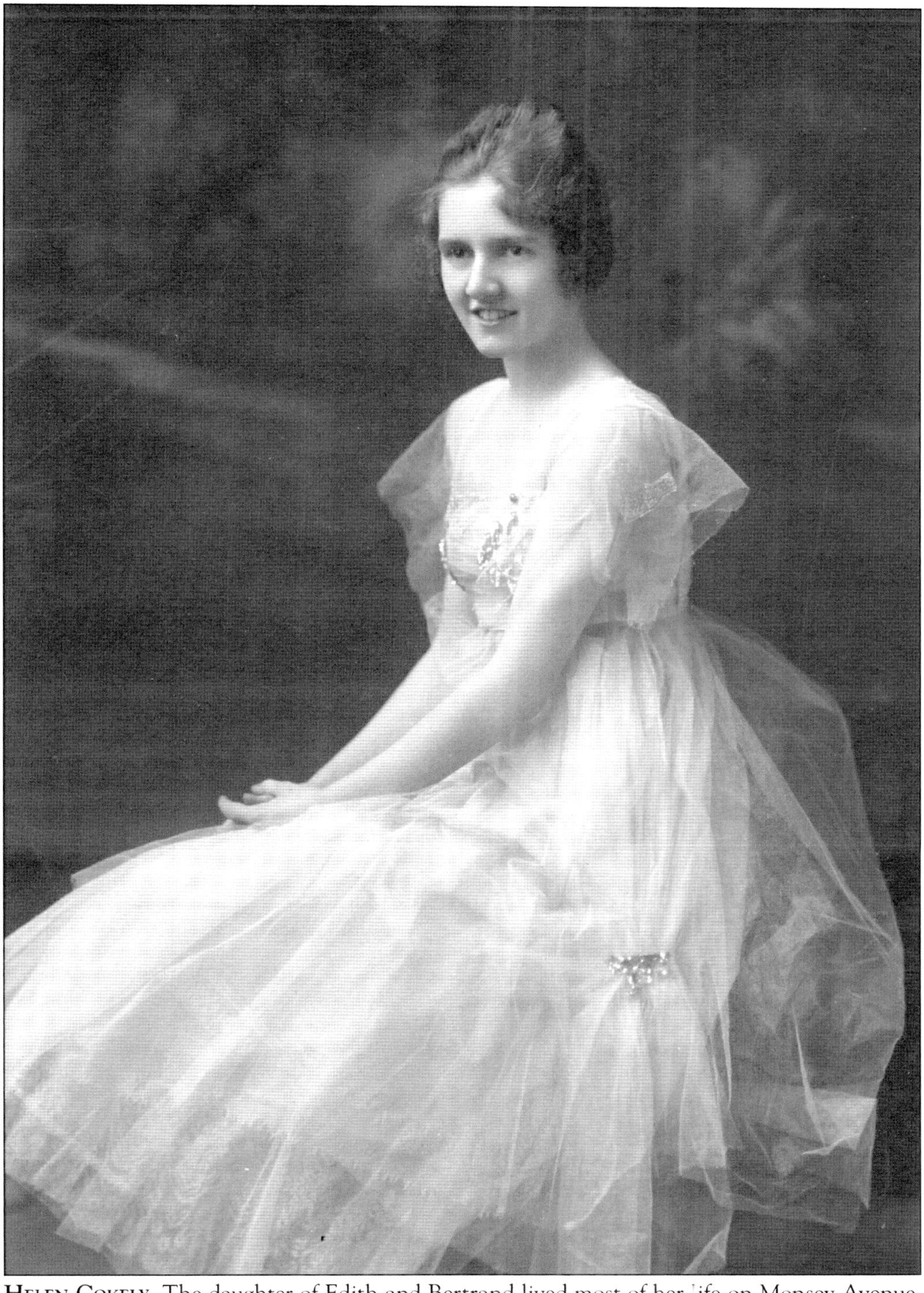

HELEN COKELY. The daughter of Edith and Bertrand lived most of her life on Monsey Avenue. She was educated in local schools and was a member of the Asbury Methodist Episcopal Church. Helen lived to be 92 years old. (Courtesy of Christine Yarns Schaefer.)

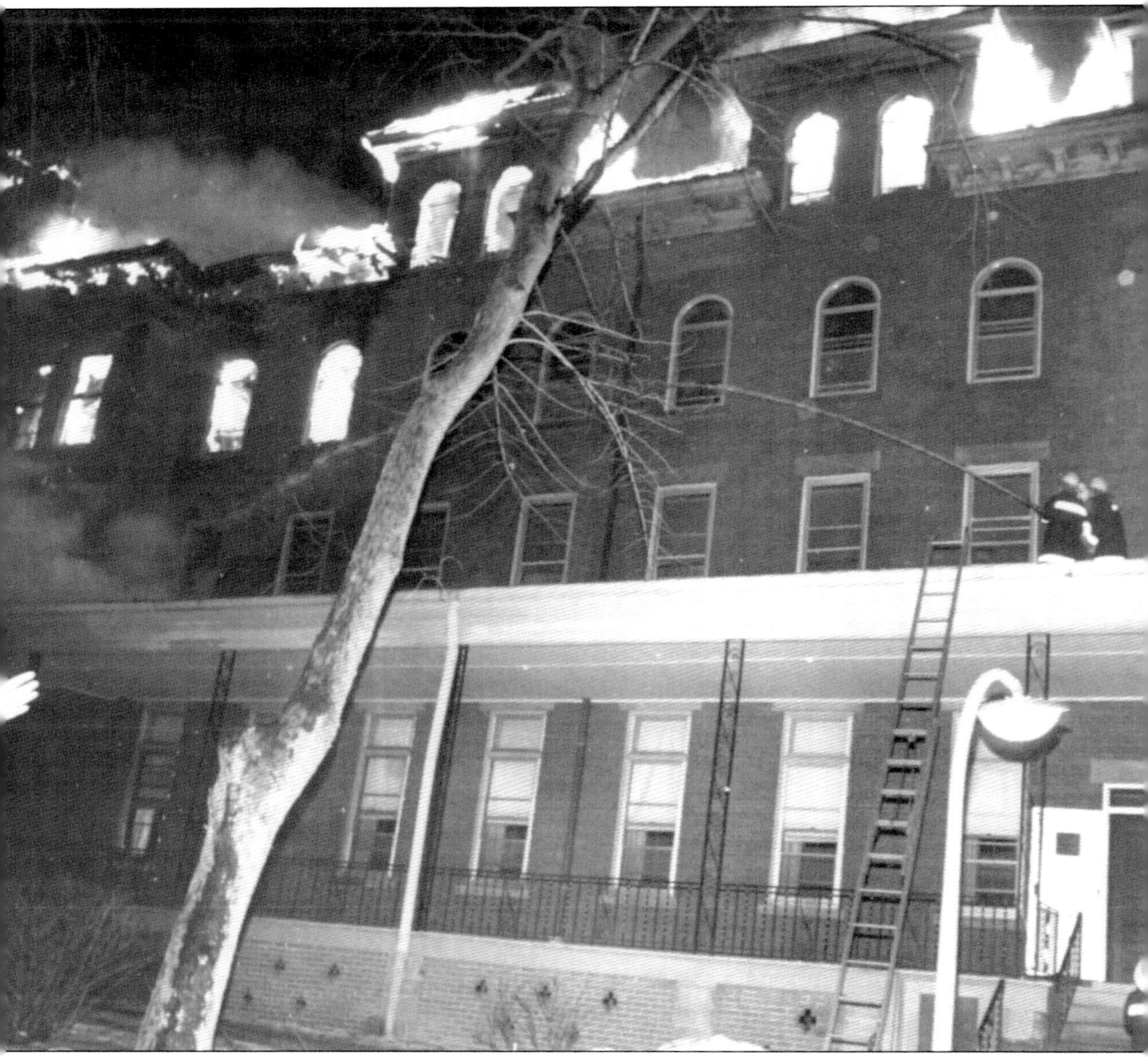

Fire at Marywood. This is another image that captures the intensity of the electrical fire that destroyed the original motherhouse on the Marywood campus in 1971. Marywood College was formally opened in September 1915. (Courtesy of Jim Sullivan, Marywood Archives.)

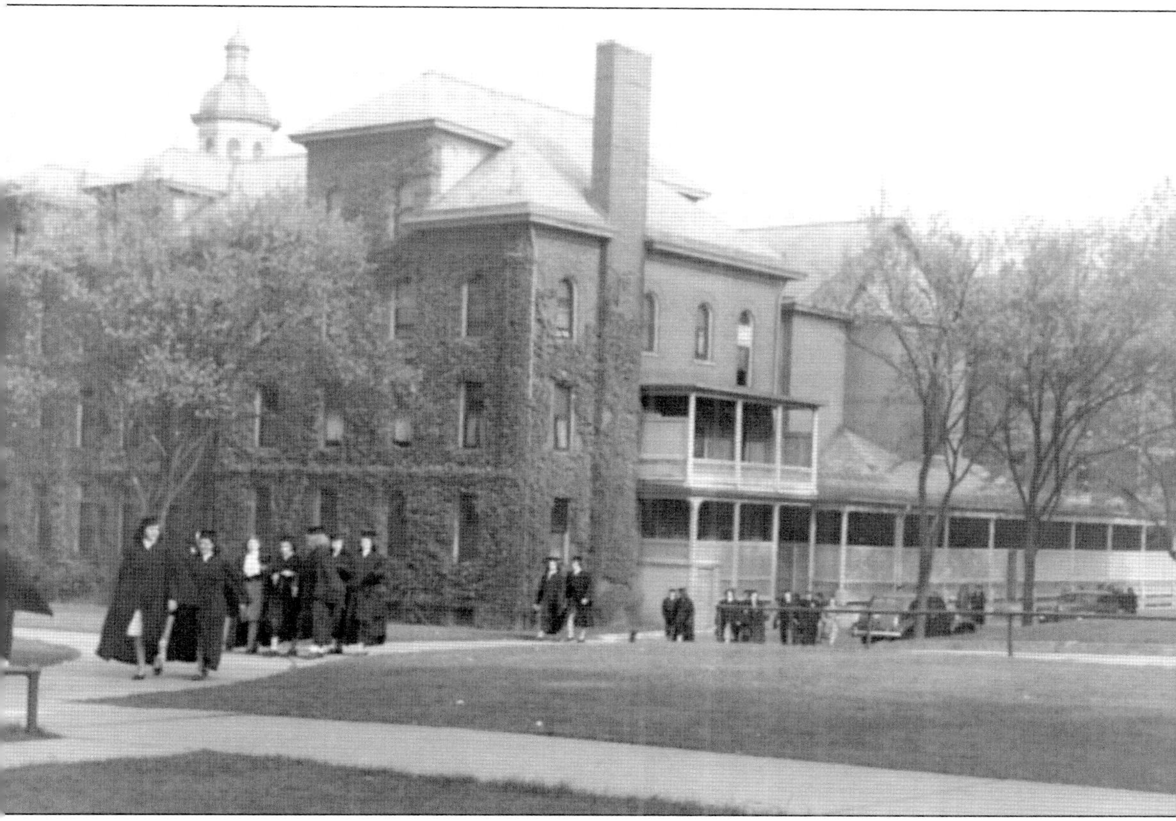

BEFORE THE FIRE. In the rear of the motherhouse, students in caps and gowns are on their way to graduation ceremonies. (Courtesy of Jim Sullivan, Marywood Archives.)

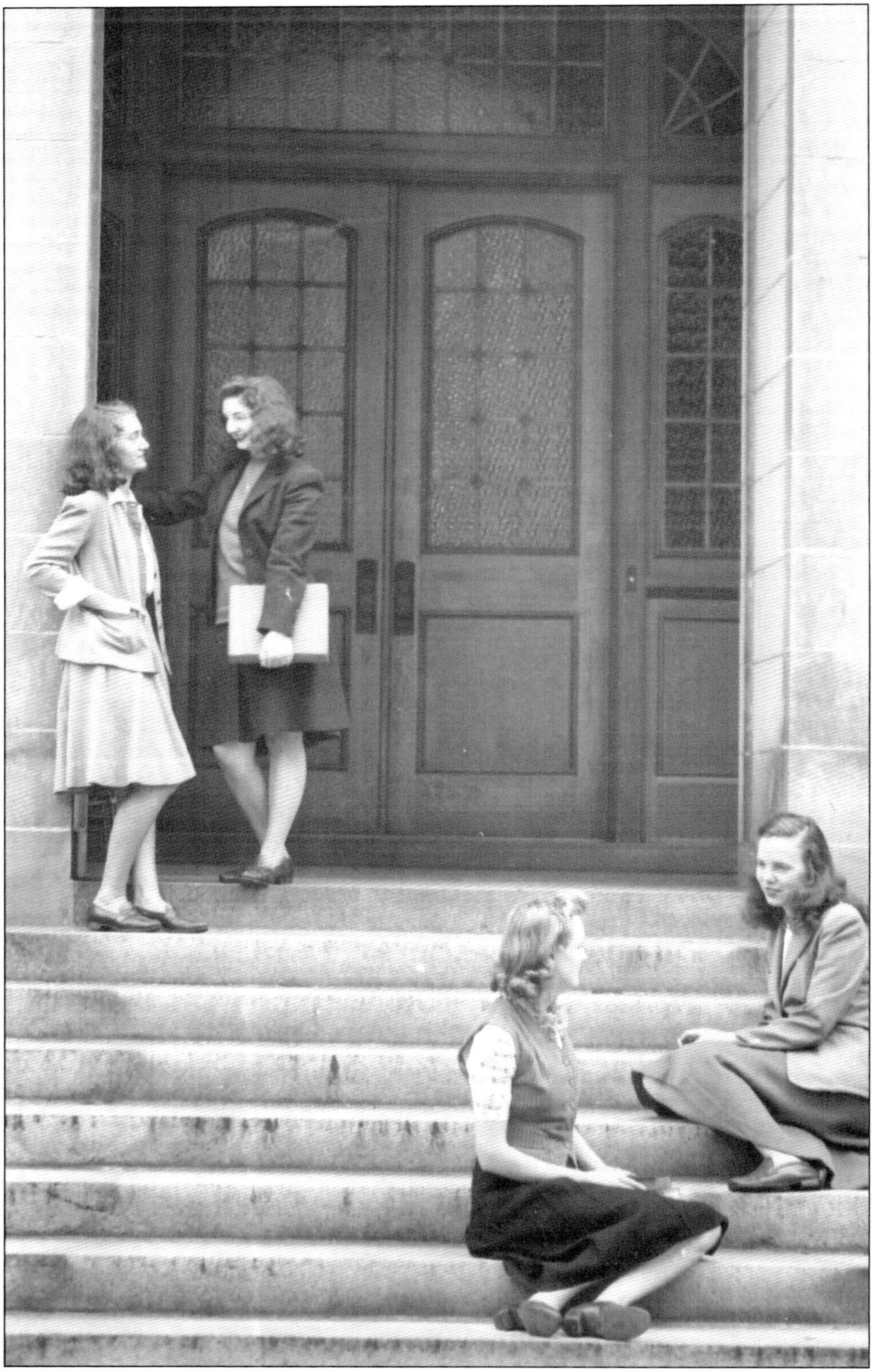

DOOR TO MOTHERHOUSE, C. 1948. Ann Pezanowski (standing next to the door holding a folder) and unidentified friends are seen here having a gabfest on the steps of the motherhouse. (Courtesy of Jim Sullivan, Marywood Archives.)

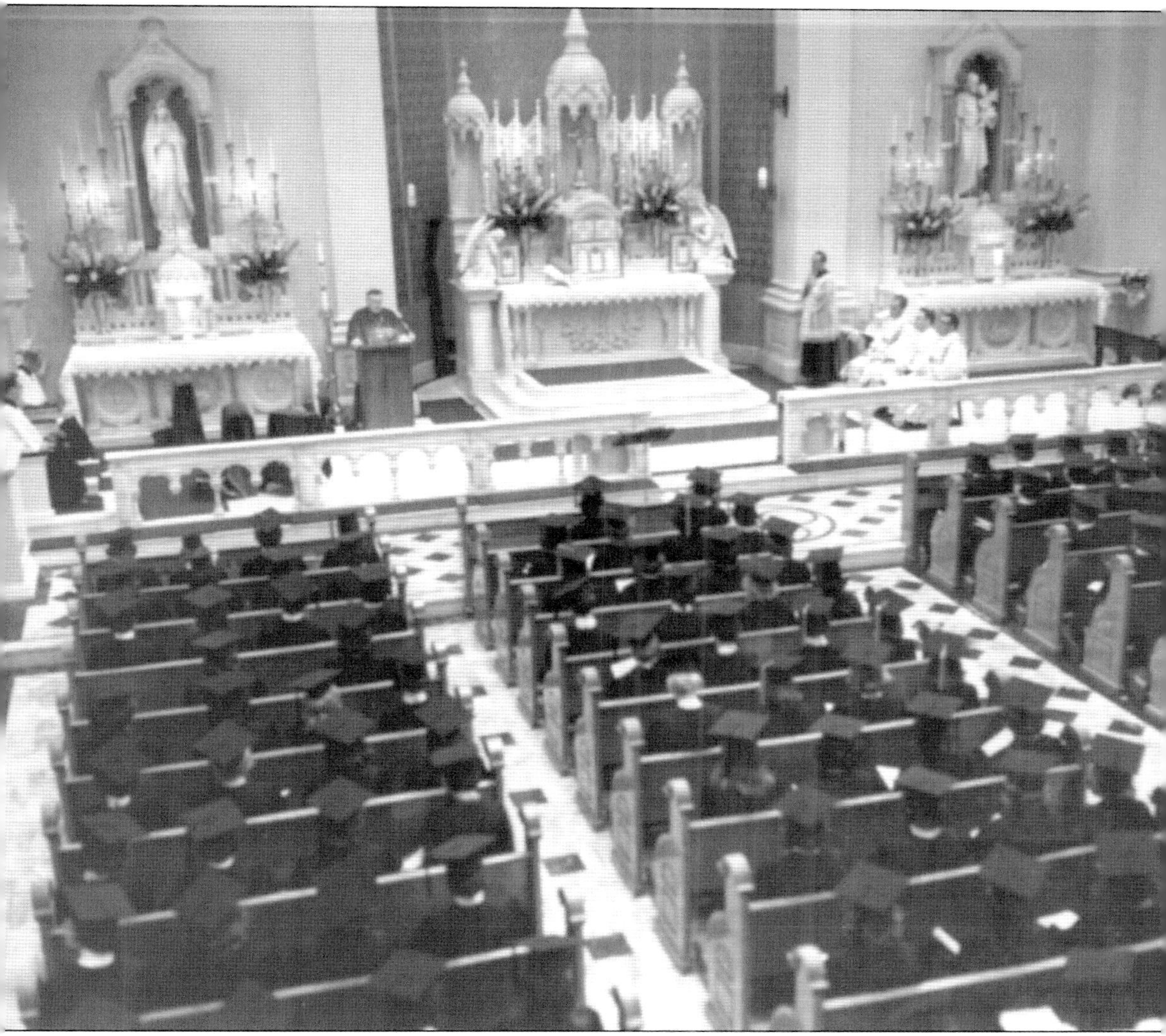

MISSION DAY, C. 1965. Mission Day was an annual event conducted by Marywood College that brought busloads of students from many of the high schools staffed by sisters to the campus. It was held in the spring. Usually, several sisters and lay faculty accompanied the students, and the entire day was dedicated to talks on the missions, touring the Marywood campus, and patronizing various booths that were set up. It was actually a "fair" atmosphere. Student enjoyed meeting others from out-of-town high schools, and games were played together, as well. Food was available for purchase. The income from the registration fee for schools and from the various booths was sent to the missions. There is no doubt that the Marywood Mission Society distributed these funds. Students and faculty came from New York, Delaware, and other points. (Courtesy of the Archives of the Sisters, Servants of the Immaculate Heart of Mary, Scranton, Pennsylvania.)

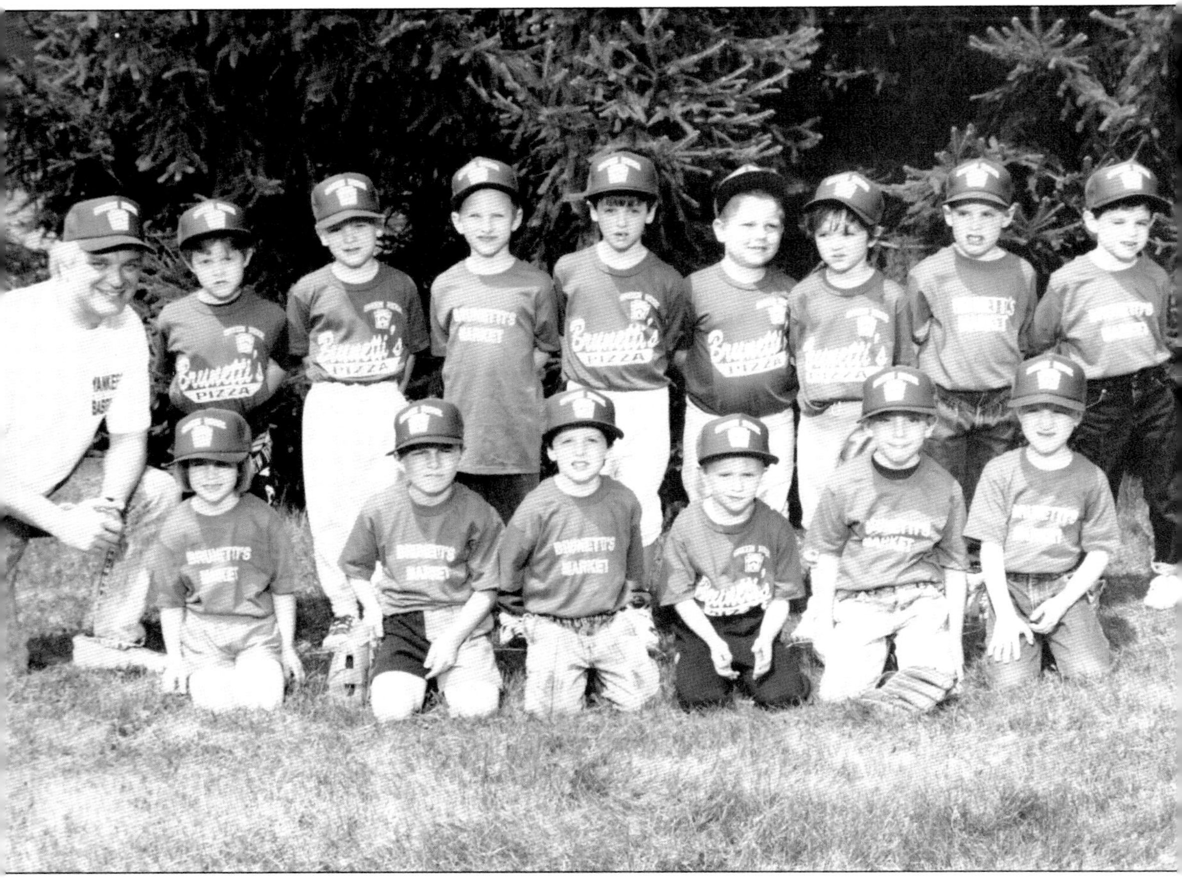

GREEN RIDGE LITTLE LEAGUE. Brunetti's Pizza gives a lot back to the community of Green Ridge, including sponsoring this group of Little League baseball players. (Courtesy of the Brunetti family.)

Nine

POLITICAL ROAD

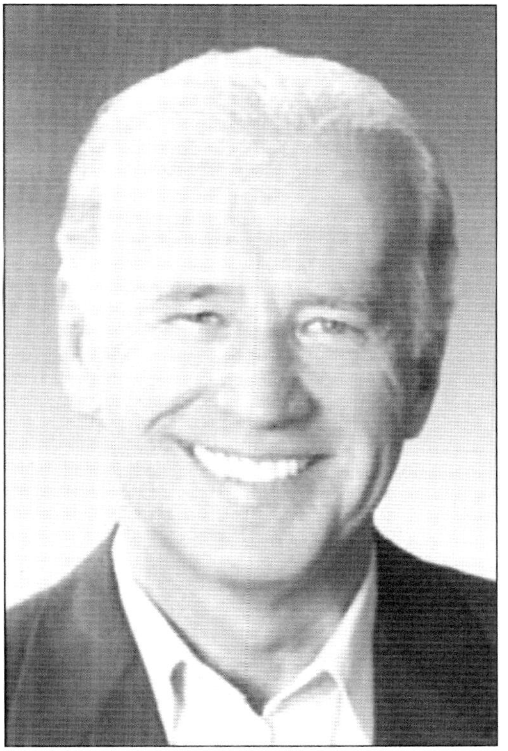

VICE PRES. JOSEPH BIDEN. Joseph Biden, the son of Joseph Robinette Biden Sr. and Catherine Eugenia Finnegan, was born in Green Ridge on November 20, 1942. He lived there until he was 10 years old, after which his family moved to Delaware. Biden became the vice president of the United States in 2008. (Courtesy of the author.)

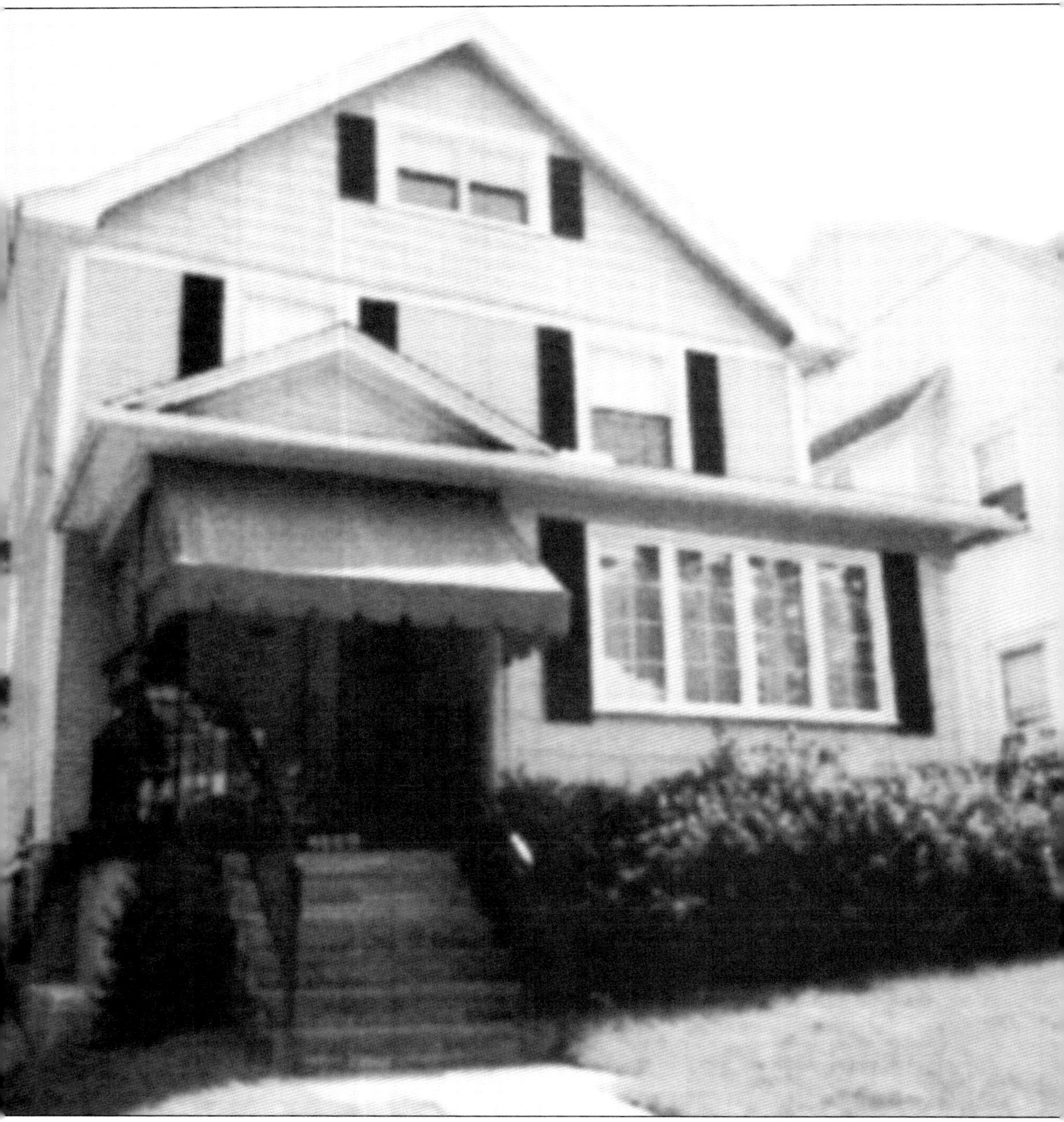

Biden's Childhood Home. For a decade, the vice president ate, slept, and played at the residence on North Washington Avenue. Biden admits he used to hang around Hank's Hoagies on Woodlawn Street as a kid. Hank's is still in operation and is as popular with the kids as ever. Today, the Kearns family resides at the vice president's former address. (Courtesy of the author.)

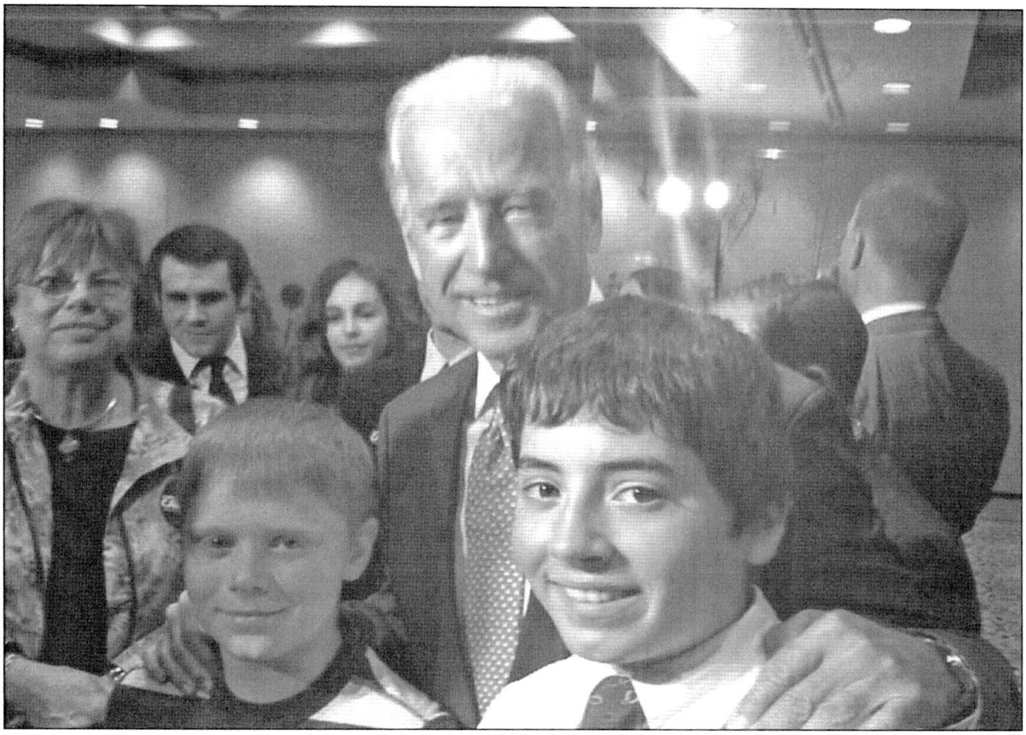

Biden's Visits to Scranton. The vice president has come back to his old stomping grounds several times since taking office. In 2011 he returned to visit flood victims and survey the damage caused by Hurricane Irene; shown below second from the right is local artist Constance Denchy. (Both, courtesy of Constance Denchy.)

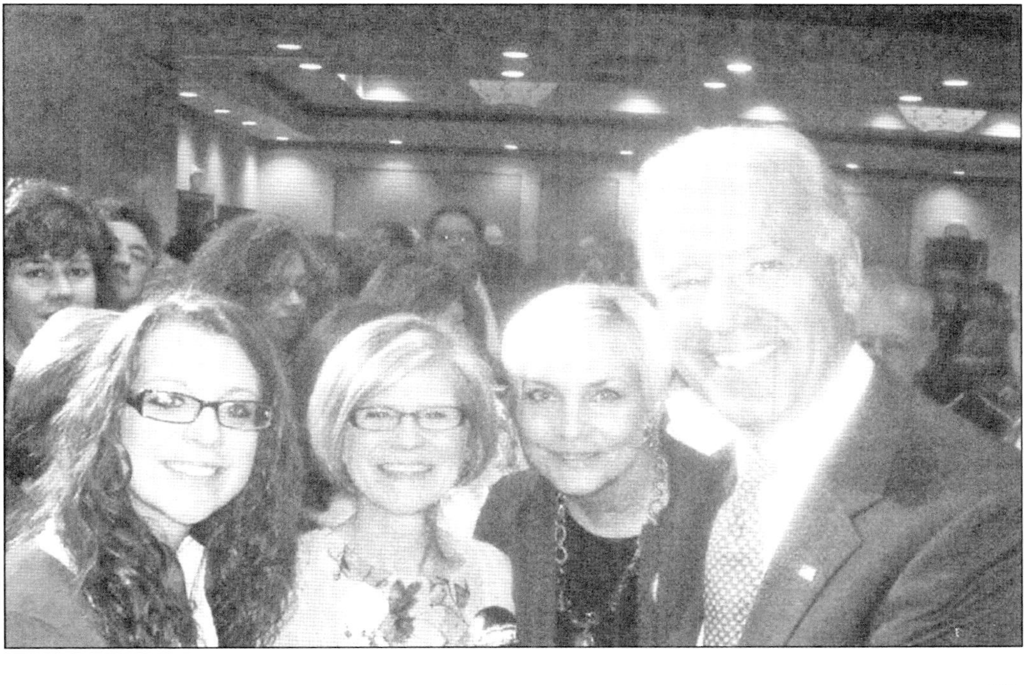

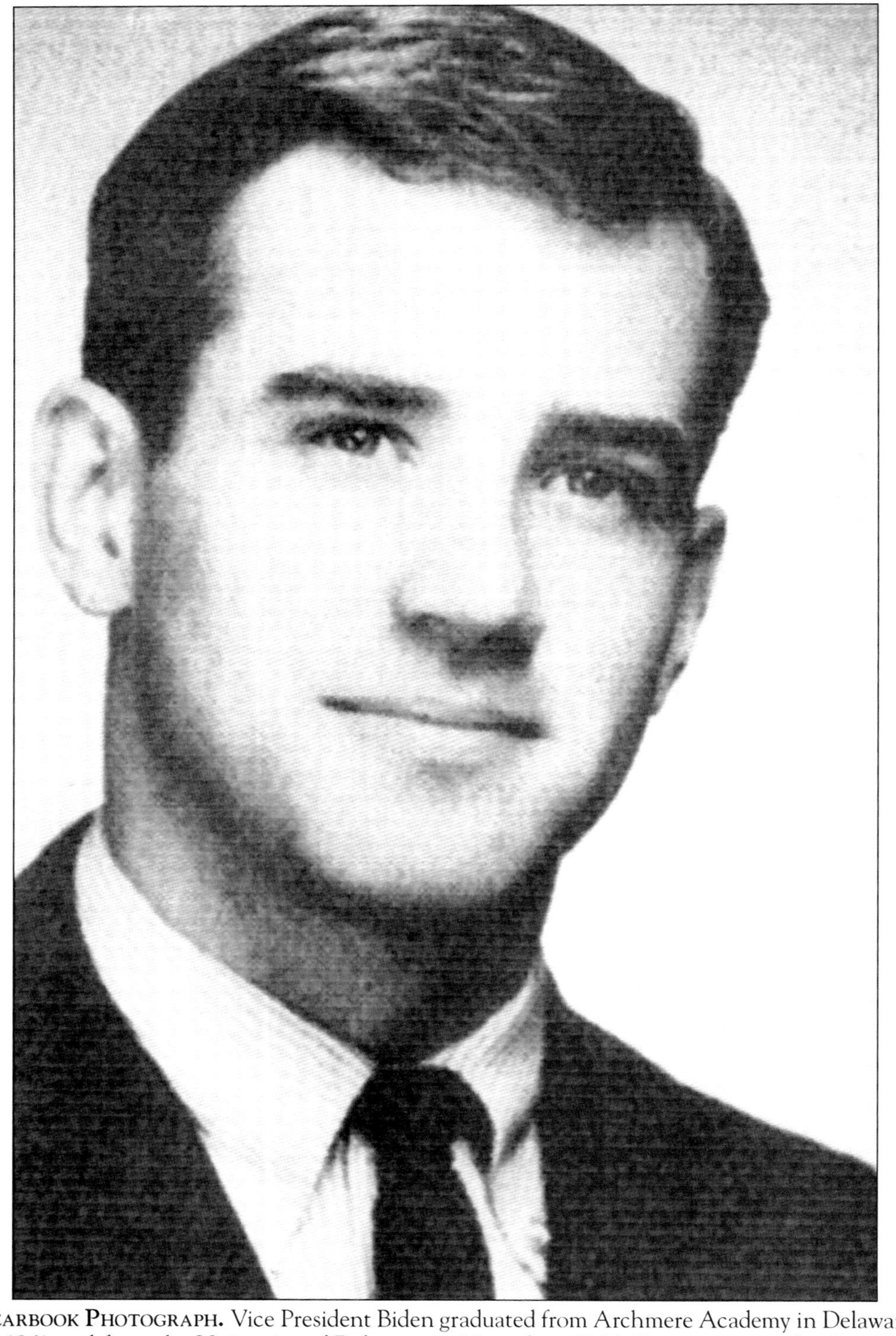

YEARBOOK PHOTOGRAPH. Vice President Biden graduated from Archmere Academy in Delaware in 1961 and from the University of Delaware in Newark in 1965. He went on to the Syracuse University College of Law and was admitted to the bar in 1969. (Courtesy of the author.)

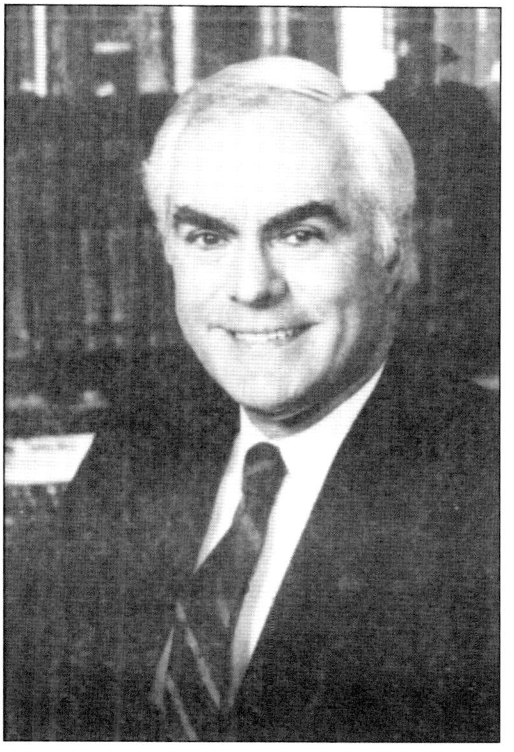

Robert P. Casey Sr. The 42nd governor of Pennsylvania was in office from January 20, 1987, to January 17, 1995. Casey was born in Jackson Heights, Queens, New York. His family was originally from the Green Ridge section of Scranton. They moved to New York for a period of time and returned to the city in 1931. (Courtesy of the author.)

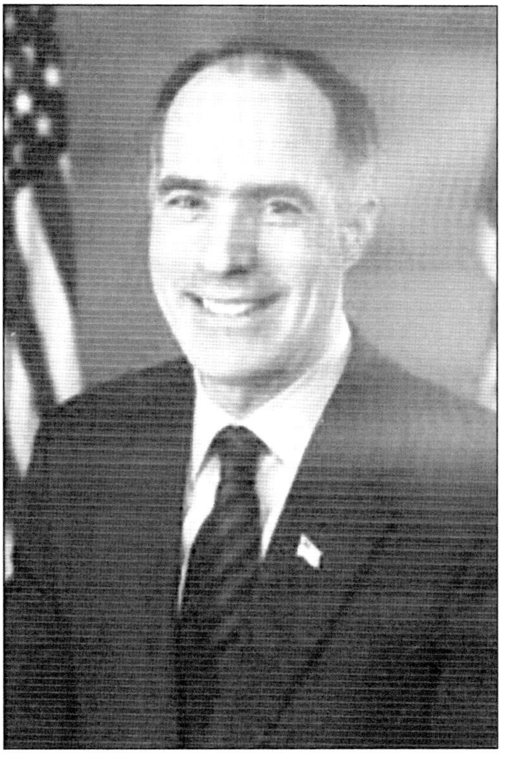

Robert P. Casey Jr. He is the son of former Pennsylvania governor Robert P. Casey Sr. Following in his father's political footsteps, Casey entered the US Senate in 2007. Born and raised in Green Ridge, he entered the practice of law in Scranton in 1988. Throughout his political career, Casey has been inspired by the legacy of his father and his father's principle that "all public service is trust, given in faith, and accepted in honor." (Courtesy of the author.)

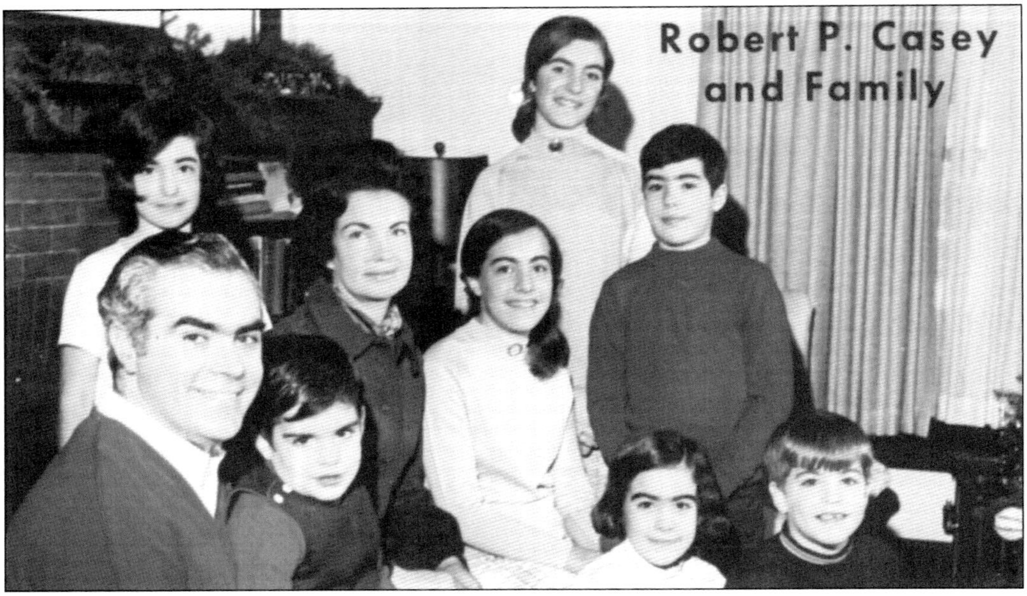

The Casey Family. As a candidate for governor of Pennsylvania, Casey brought to this office his legislative experience as a state senator. His goal was to revitalize Pennsylvania as a place of opportunity for families. His campaign slogan was "Go with Youth—Go with Casey." (Both, courtesy of Mark Boock.)

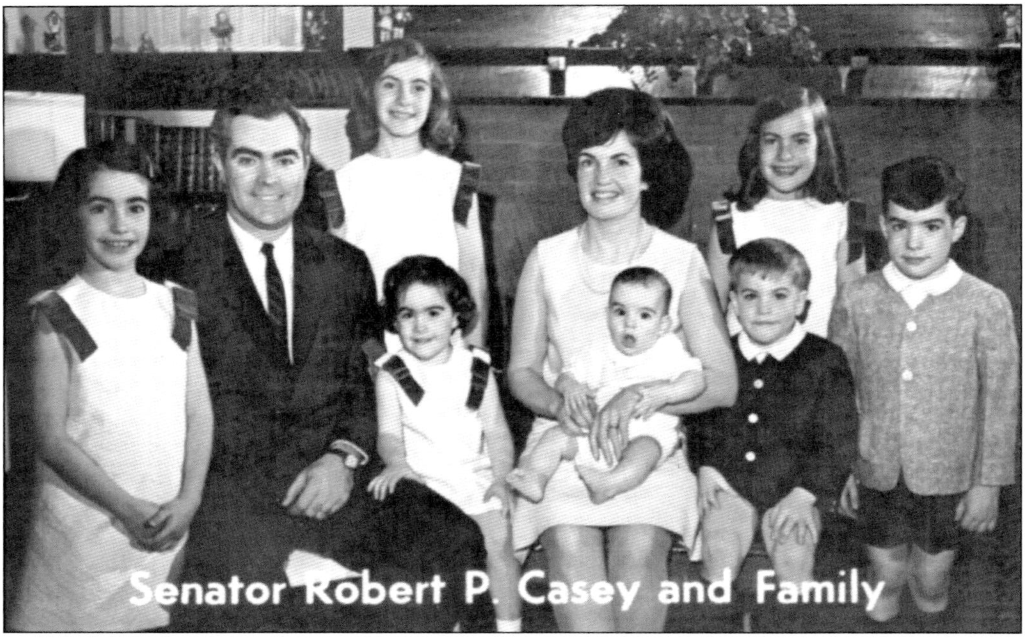

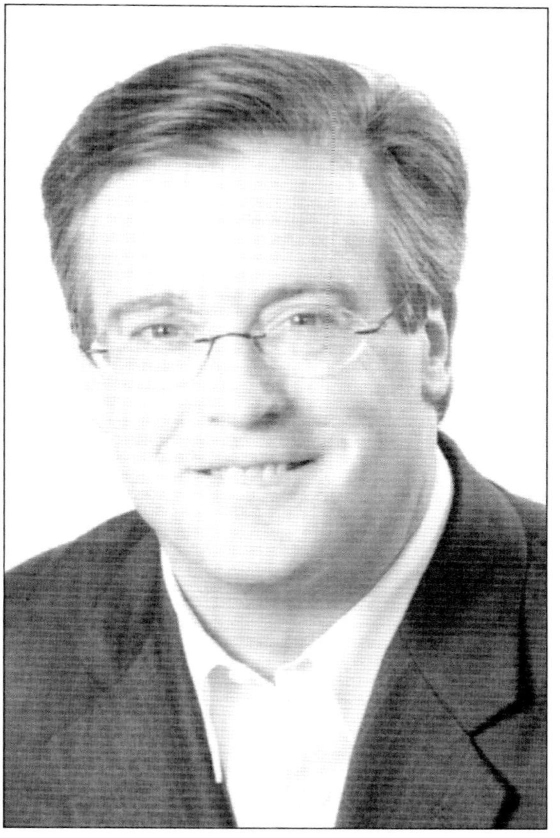

CHRISTOPHER DOHERTY. The current mayor of Scranton is pictured at right. He has brought about many positive changes to the city, such as neighborhood revitalization, since taking office in 2002. In 1997, he ran for city council, was elected, and served one term. Three years later, he threw his hat into the political ring, and for the first time in over 50 years, a member of the city council became mayor. A lifetime resident of Green Ridge, Doherty and his lovely wife, Donna, and their six children live in one of the historical mansions on North Washington Avenue, shown below. (Both, courtesy of the author.)

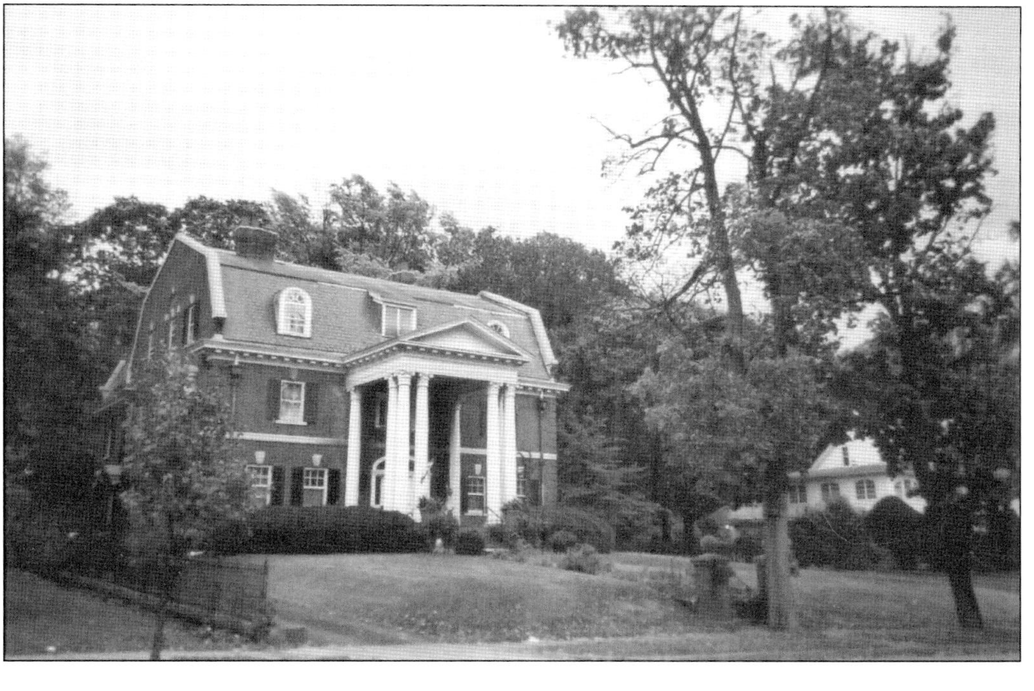

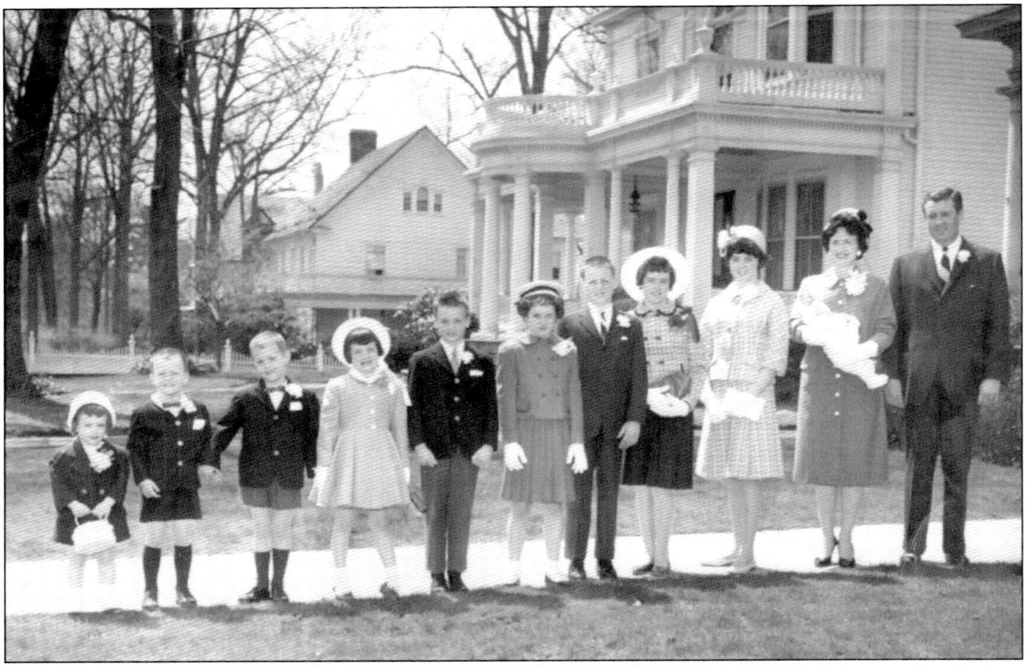

FAMILY PORTRAIT. Mayor Chris Doherty (second from the left) is one of 11 children. His father, James Doherty, served four terms as a city councilman (first on the right); their family home is on the 1700 block of North Washington Avenue. (Courtesy of Virginia McGregor.)

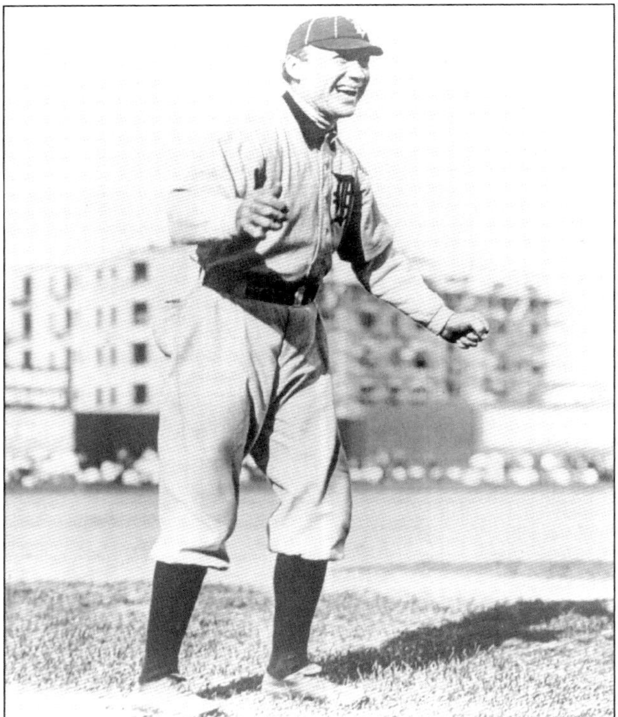

HUGH JENNINGS. Born April 2, 1869, Jennings was the great-grandfather of Scranton mayor Christopher Doherty. He played for the Louisville Colonels (1891–1893), Baltimore Orioles (1893–1899), Brooklyn Superbas (1899–1900, 1903), Philadelphia Phillies (1901–1902), and Detroit Tigers (1907, 1909, 1912, 1918). His career began as a shortstop before transitioning to manager. Jennings's distinctive "ee-yah!" yell from the coaching box was his trademark. He died on February 1, 1928, in Scranton and was elected to the Baseball Hall of Fame in 1945. (Courtesy of the author.)

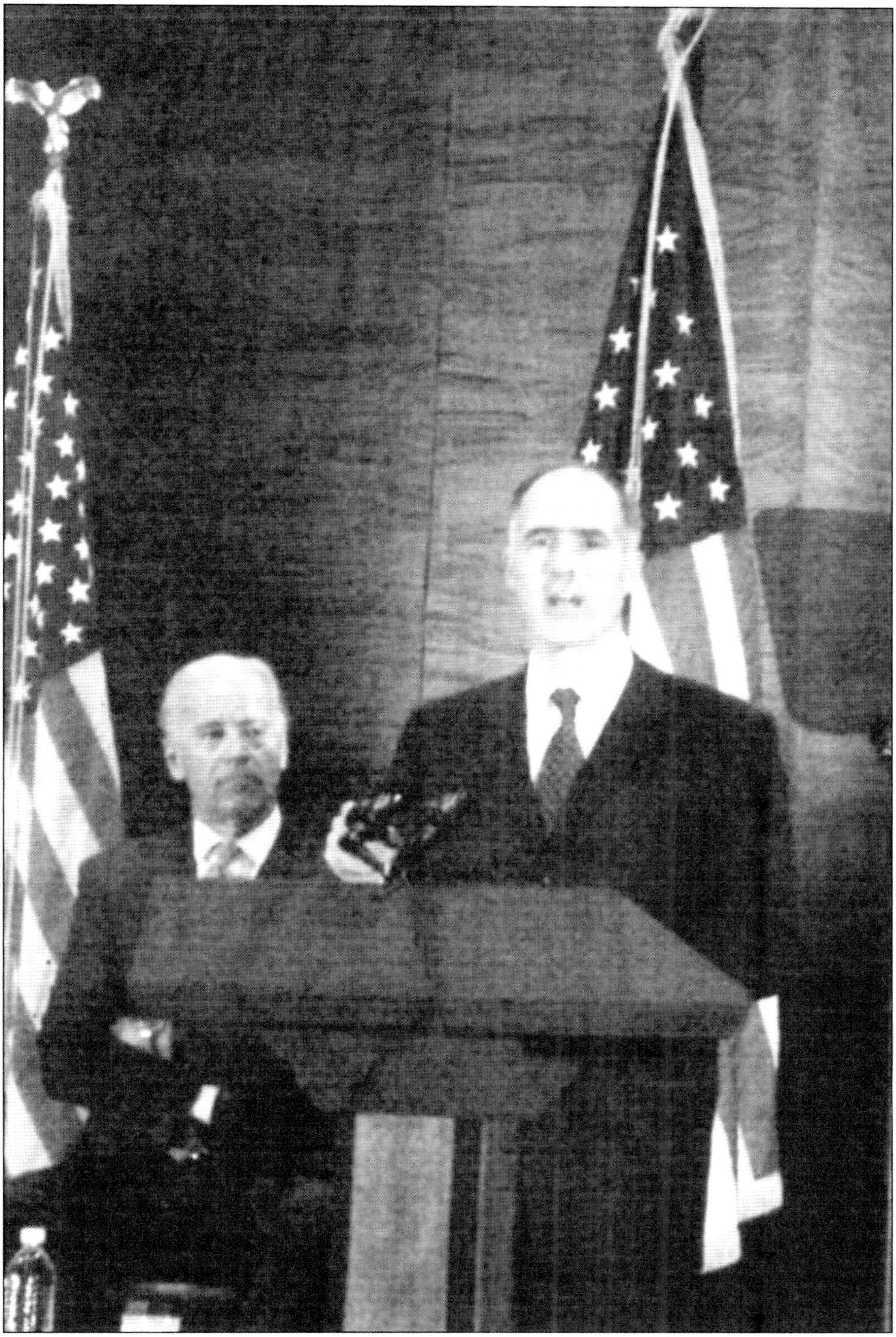

Political Aspirations. Pictured are Vice President Biden and Senator Casey during one of Biden's visits to Green Ridge. Once upon a time, a future vice president, governor, senator, and a mayor all lived within blocks of each other on North Washington Avenue. (Courtesy of the author.)